GOD THE ARTIST

GOD THE ARTIST

American Novelists in a Post-Realist Age

Jan Gorak

UNIVERSITY OF ILLINOIS PRESS
Urbana and Chicago

This book is printed on acid-free paper.

Library of Congress Cataloging-in-Publication Data

Gorak, Jan, 1952–
    God the artist : American novelists in a post-realist
age.

    Bibliography: p.
    Includes index.
    1. American fiction—20th century—History and
criticism.   2. God in literature.   3. Artists in literature.
4. Creation (Literary, artistic, etc.)   5. West, Nathanael,
1903–1940—Criticism and interpretation.   6. Hawkes, John,
1925–   —Criticism and interpretation.   7. Barth, John—
Criticism and interpretation.   I. Title.
PS374.G63G67   1987   813'.5'09   86-11318
ISBN 0-252-01341-7 (alk. paper)

In an age of naturalism the aesthetic hunger obtains many satis-
factions, though they may be furtive ones, from images that
echo the old official systems which the revolution has run out of
business, and so the age is still living on the remaining works
of a capital which it has stopped from further productive
employment.

—John Crowe Ransom
"Yeats and His Symbols"

There is now a widespread idea that nostalgic feelings about the
past are inherently vicious. One ought apparently to live in a
continuous present, a minute-to-minute cancellation of memory,
and if one thinks of the past at all it should merely be in order to
thank God that we are so much better than we used to be.

—George Orwell
Adelphi, 1948

Acknowledgments

An earlier form of portions of chapters one and six appeared in *English Studies in Africa*.

I should also like to thank the following for their material assistance with the book: Jill Botha; Irene Gorak; Charles Harris; Gordon Hartford; Peter Manning; Philip Stevick; and Ann Lowry Weir.

Contents

Introduction

In 1931, Edmund Wilson published *Axel's Castle*, his pioneering study of modern literature. Wilson ended his first chapter with a judgment that even thirty years later, Frank Kermode was to reiterate. "The literary history of our time," Wilson argued, "is to a great extent that of the development of Symbolism and of its fusion or conflict with Naturalism."[1] For Kermode, Wilson's judgment was a *donnée* for any future historian of modern literature.[2]

In the last few years, "the literary history of our time" has undergone sweeping changes. But two of the most potent images of the modern artist that we possess still square with Wilson's judgment. The first is Kermode's "romantic image," an image examined most thoroughly in the book of that name. Put briefly, Kermode's artist is in possession of an image "as a radiant truth out of space and time." Special election carries special griefs, since the artist is cursed by a "necessary isolation or estrangement."[3] This artist does not share his concerns with any large popular audience but is apt, rather, to become the property of a zealous band of exegetes and camp followers. Randall Jarrell, whose essay "The Obscurity of the Poet" appeared at about the same time as Kermode's *Romantic Image*, has dramatized the comic consequences of the symbolist dogma: "When I last read poems in New York City, a lady who, except for bangs, a magenta jersey blouse, and the expression of Palamède de Charlus, was indistinguishable from any other New Yorker, exclaimed to me about a poet whom the years have fattened for the slaughter: 'He read like a young god.' . . . This lady was less interested in those wonderful things poems than in those other things, poets."[4]

Jarrell's witty anecdote is a parable about the fate of the image maker in a commercial society. In practice, symbolist theory has almost farcical consequences: artists who snub their audiences are adored by them; an art supposedly hostile to interpretation ("out of space and time") recruits whole factories of interpreters. Poets and poems—"wonderful things"—become part of the stock-in-trade of a society that sees art as yet another luxury commodity.

The last point brings us to the next archetype for artistic activity. Jerome Christensen has spoken of the "daunting itinerary that awaits the post-Enlightenment man of letters,"[5] and it is to this image, the poet as a man of letters, that I now turn. This idea questions the primacy of the artist's subjectivity, stressing instead the priority of language and the power that institutional constraints exert over subjective consciousness. Denis Donoghue, no great admirer of such theories, has nonetheless provided a very useful account of their procedures. These critics, he says, "insist that as soon as a speaker uses words, he puts himself in their power; he says only what the structure of that particular language allows him to say . . . social structures dislodge the subject from the center of the circle of experience and present it rather as the function of the collective life of society."[6]

What Donoghue outlines is, in effect, a shift from symbolism to naturalism. Where symbolism is the art of privileged subjectivity, recent criticism has stressed the naturalistic power of institutions and language systems to reduce the artist from magus to minion, a printer's devil lost in the machine of language. And of course, Samuel Taylor Coleridge, "poor Coleridge" to his contemporaries and a test case for criticism ever since, typifies such a shift. The Coleridge of *Romantic Image* was the Coleridge of the *sum*, the imagination's sacred power. The Coleridge of Jerome Christensen's *Coleridge's Blessed Machine of Language* is all too literally a man of letters, his imagination doomed to materialize (dreadful word, this, for an image maker) as "an eternal wanderer on the face of the page."[7] This artisan in the sweatshop of language is a long way from the patron saint of *Romantic Image*, who, for all his domestic martyrdoms, did establish canonically the sacredness of the imagination, and, for all his alienation, did institutionalize the authority of the image.

What this new naturalism implies for our view of the artist has been best expressed by Frederic Jameson, who remarked that "in modern times . . . all creative and original speech flows from privation rather than from plenitude: its redoubled energies, far from tapping archaic or undiscovered sources of energy, are proportionate to the massive and well-nigh impenetrable obstacles which aesthetic production must overcome in the age of reification."[8] The most thriving outlets in the current age of reification are the ever-swelling warehouses of critical theory, none of them particularly well stocked with joy. Do modern writers really feel as oppressed as Jameson says they ought? These two dominant images of the modern artist—the symbolist image maker and the naturalist language mechanic—form two parts that do not quite add up to a satisfactory whole. The first secures the artist's sovereignty only to condemn him to the kingdom of his solitary imagination; the second releases him into the world only to vaporize artist and imagination into a void. Kermode's visionary martyr and Jameson's Chaplinesque clown cancel each other out. Contemporary criticism has indeed fallen into the very trap Wilson warned against: "In attempting to write literary history, one must guard against giving the impression that movements and counter-movements necessarily follow one another in a punctual and well-generalled fashion. . . . What really happens, of course, is that one set of methods is not completely superseded by another; but that, on the contrary, it thrives in its teeth."[9] Recent literary history has hardly been "punctual and well-generalled," nor has it taken account of the tendency of movements to merge and mingle, and of opposing poles to attract.

We need a model of the artist's activity, therefore, that will accommodate both the symbolic and naturalistic poles of the artist's imagination. And that model ought to tally, surely, with the way artists themselves have thought and felt about their work. One such model, entertained by artists from Petrarch to Joyce, turns on the godly maker or *deus artifex*. When Joseph Conrad says that "a creator must be indifferent; because directly the 'Fiat!' has been issued from his lips there are creatures made in his image that'll try to drag him down from his eminence";[10] when Gustave Flaubert informs Louise Colet that "art, like the God of the Jews, feasts on holocausts";[11] when John Hawkes praises John Barth because "he has not once but *twice* reinvented the world . . . pierc[ing] our most deplorable pretensions— public and private";[12] when Norman Mailer interrogates himself about "how God exists"[13] and then translates his bafflement into a paradigm for narrative form; when John Barth says that "the novelist's trade, like God's, is manufacturing universes,"[14] we recognize the presence of an idea as old as literature itself, an idea that makes the artist a kind of god and his work a kind of world.

But what kind of god? What kind of world? For many modern authors the idea of the *deus artifex* has become a battleground, forcing them to confront some overwhelming questions about imagination and reality, the nature of artistic illusion, and the status of fiction and fiction making. Does an artist-god rule over his creation like an absolute monarch, as Joseph Conrad proposes? Or does he use his omnipotence to imitate the shape of our inner compulsions, as John Hawkes insinuates? Is his task merely one of multiplying fictional worlds, as John Barth seems to imply, or must he, as Norman Mailer argues, organize them into some significant disorder? Each of these authors sounds embattled; in a world where, as Ronald Sukenick's *The*

Death of the Novel and Other Stories has affirmed, "reality doesn't exist, time doesn't exist, personality doesn't exist," it may well be that the artist-deity himself is only a disposable fiction.[15] Sukenick's words may point to the apotheosis of the godly maker. They may equally point to his demise, his necessary immersion in the onward tide of fiction.

In answer to these problems, this book advances three propositions. My first proposition is that the ubiquity of the *topos* among recent authors—its presence among writers as different as Günter Grass and Italo Calvino, John Hawkes and Gabriel García Márquez—reflects a radical weakening in its force. In Sukenick's sense, of course, an artist is like God because he "is forced to start from scratch." But so too is everybody else, according to Sukenick's Pyrrhonist premises. As Carl Becker recognized late in his career, when everyman becomes a historian the special crafts of the historian wither away.[16] Many postwar assertions of the artist's godly powers have the same effect: they expand the area of artistic activity only to narrow pitifully its operative force. It may well be that the postwar period is for the godly maker what dusk was for the Owl of Minerva—a space to flourish before expiring altogether.

My second proposition emerges directly from the first. For many contemporary authors, I would argue, the *deus artifex topos* has become a purely linguistic affair. The worlds created by postwar godly makers are like planets in a solar system that live for a day and then disappear. Postwar godly makers delight in the collision of fictions that creates their ever-multiplying worlds. But they do not try to organize these worlds into a significant pattern; they are not even willing to occupy them for very long. Books like Stanley Elkin's *George Mills* or Robert Coover's *Pricksongs and Descants* lean on only one half of the *deus artifex topos*: they fudge the confrontation between form and matter, imagination and reality that sustained more traditional godly makers—Shakespeare in *The Tempest* and Melville in *Moby-Dick*, for instance—turning the *topos* into a series of virtuoso performances given by a tricky magician. The reverse image of this all-encompassing fictionality is the skeptical symbolism of William Gass's *In the Heart of the Heart of the Country* or Susan Sontag's *The Benefactor*, where the artist-god retreats progressively further into his own fictions, in which he cannot believe, however much he is compelled by them.

My third proposition is a plea for realism. I shall argue that these symbolic and naturalistic cul-de-sacs can only be negotiated through a remobilization of the traditional mimetic energies of the *topos*, the energies Melville acknowledged when he promised to "write such things as the Great Publisher of Mankind ordained ages before he published 'The World,'" adding—and in our present situation the emphasis is a bracing one—"This planet, I mean—not the Literary Globe." [17] This sense of a world outside literature, resistant to the fabrications of language, has been important for novelists from Fielding to Dickens, from Diderot to Mann. It ought, I shall argue, to be important again.

My book, in other words, contains both a history and a prescription. It traces some of the major transformations of an idea with a seemingly endless pedigree (if its center lies in Plato, its circumference extends through Sontag, Elkin, Coover, and Grass to the icy infinity of Gabriel García Márquez's *One Hundred Years of Solitude*); and it shows how these transformations illuminate the special characteristics of a literature that has been aptly described as "without qualities" and "against itself." [18] To look at the *deus artifex topos* is not only to see how postmodern writing has reached the impasse Warner Berthoff and Gerald Graff have defined, but also to see where its liberating possibilities might lie. Where the symbolist sees the real as dead matter, and the fiction maker sees it as a basis for tall stories, the mimetic *deus artifex* shapes it into a moving, expanding image of a shared human world. To take on such a task involves the author in a battle with all kinds of illusion, not least those created by art itself. Ever since Sir Philip Sidney praised the poet's power to bring forth a golden world, godly makers have come to cherish their own illusions more than the world itself and have been correspondingly eager to deny the engagement of art with mere reality. With the arrival of romanticism, imagination laid claim to a new, enlarged authority, and the nature of the world beyond words became increasingly the object of a verbal sovereignty.

The *deus artifex topos* is one that modern criticism has largely overlooked. Edward Said, for example, has argued that modern literature proceeds from a completely secular set of assumptions, which began when "Renan first reduced texts from divine intervention in the world's business to objects of historical materiality." The result, argues Said, is the displacement of the authority of God by the authority of the interpreter. "In dispensing with divine authority Renan put philological power in its place. What comes to replace divine authority is the textual authority of the philological critic." [19] Frank Kermode's most recent criticism has intensified this secularization of critical language. In *The Genesis of Secrecy* and *The Art of Telling*, Kermode turns his wit and erudition to the construction of what he calls a "secret" paradigm, which is then imposed "across" the official assumptions of the books.[20] The Jesus who appears in *The Genesis of Secrecy*, perpetually misunderstood by the "dullness" of his disciples (the word is Kermode's), becomes another version of the romantic image maker, inevitably frustrated by, and isolated from, his uncomprehending audience. It is unlikely that either of these critics would take kindly to the idea of the artist as a deity, since Said denies the importance of religious assumptions in modern literature, while Kermode annihilates their authority in the genesis of narrative.

We might expect Harold Bloom, who tells us in his *Kaballah and Criticism* that "all religion is apotropaic litany against the dangers of nature, and so is all poetry an apotropaic litany, warding off, defending against death. From our perspective, religion is spilled poetry," to devote more attention to the *deus artifex*.[21] But Bloom's highly influential accounts of literary history present poets as titans, competitors, and overreachers; the generational battle ousts the idea of continuous literary creation. Like so many modern critics, Bloom can understand change—preferably catastrophic change—better than continuity. The idea of the artist as a god who creates a common world that accretes in meaning rather than explodes into apocalypse would appear to depend upon a set of assumptions about imitation, narrative, and authority that current critical discourse is occupied in demolishing.

The historical premises on which my own criticism is based dictate an early investigation of the background—both social and aesthetic—to the *deus artifex topos*. Accordingly, Chapter 1 analyzes its main transformations from Plato to Camus. The special difficulties encountered by the godly maker in the age of reification I explore in some detail in Chapters 2 and 3, through an analysis of the worlds—fictional and social—of Nathanael West, the first modern American *deus artifex* to experience these conditions at first hand. Chapter 4 examines the crisis of the godly maker in the postwar world—the postmodern transformations of the *topos* that endanger its continued life. The rest of the book discusses the success with which John Hawkes and John Barth have revived the mimetic potential of the *topos*, the former through an intensification of its satiric force, the latter through an expansion of its comic resources.

In sum, this book challenges the two irreconcilable ideas of the artist that have emerged in some influential modern criticism. The first idea—of the artist as symbolist, maker of images—sees him as omnipotent in mind, careless of matter, oblivious of his audience; the second—the naturalist in his various transformations—is so crushed by power structures and language systems, the wonder is he manages to write at all. The first presents the artist triumphant in his solitary vision; the second makes him a counter in the larger game of language, a dummy hand at bridge, as Frank Kermode has recently put it.[22] Neither model registers the peculiar mixture of hesitance and flamboyance, uncertainty and aggression that characterizes the voice of the modern artist. Only the idea of the artist as a godly maker suggests the paradoxes and uncertainties of the modern writer, a mythologist trapped in a secular world, a high priest caught in the blessed machine of language.

CHAPTER ONE

Deus Artifex: Transformation of a *Topos*

The time has come to say that the novelist is not God.
—Jean-Paul Sartre
"Francois Mauriac and Freedom"

I.

Two major authorities provide the traditional accounts of the artist's activity as a godly maker. Interestingly enough, they point in opposite directions. There is no reconciling, as Arthur Lovejoy pointed out, the Christian view of a God detached and absolute, a creator *ex nihilo*, and the classical view of an artificer informing matter with reason.[1] But, as Lovejoy added, if there is no reconciling them, there is no separating them either, and most creative artists have tried to exploit the tension between a God whose every wink is either providential or apocalyptic, and one who shapes matter into form with precision and patience.

The Christian story, as narrated in the opening chapters of Genesis, demonstrates the absolute sovereignty of God. Creator of a world through the authority of language ("God said, 'Let there be light,' and there was light . . . He called the light day, and the darkness night"), the Christian deity is an artist whose Word is law.[2] As Robert Davidson writes, "The entire conflict theme has disappeared. The God of the Genesis creation story is not one of the forces of nature, not even the supreme fertility god or Nature with a capital N. He stands over against the world as its sovereign creator, the source of everything in it, but not identifiable with it. He is wholly other, the transcendent God."[3] Davidson adds that behind the word *making* used to describe the Christian God's artistry stands the idea of "the absolute and effortless sovereignty of the God who brings the ordered universe out of primeval chaos" (15). Art seems too benign a word for this kind of creating, just as artist seems too gentle a word for this kind of maker. Such a view of God rests his authority in his visionary powers; as an artist, he is sublime in his projects, spectacular in his action. He is remote, distinct from his creation, and always ready—as an examination of Genesis shows—to reevaluate its status according to his own just design.

Against this view of the sublime *deus artifex*, we can juxtapose Plato's equally influential account of the Demiurge. In *Timaeus* Plato shows us an artist who proceeds not so much by a deity's omnipotence as by an artificer's patience. His eternal adversaries are necessity and chaos. These, as F. M. Cornford describes, he must somehow organize "like the given materials which the human craftsman must use as best he can, though their properties may not be wholly suitable to his purpose."[4] He neither creates *ex nihilo* nor reduces his creation to nothing; his design is provisional rather than providential, restrained by "materials which he does not create, and whose inherent nature sets a limit to his desire for perfection in his work." His authority operates like Auden's novelist who can

> . . . among the Just
> Be just, among the Filthy filthy too,
> And in his own weak person, if he can,
> Dully put up with all the wrongs of Man.[5]

Both the Christian and Platonic perspectives are necessary, I shall argue, if the *topos* is to achieve its full vitality. Without the first, the godly maker deteriorates into a kind of universal amanuensis, a spectral Mr. Casaubon; without the second, his creation becomes a series of catastrophes. The Christian sense of vision and the classical respect for matter are both necessary if the *topos* is to sustain a work of art that will make sense for artist and audience alike.

II.

So deeply rooted in our ideas about art and creation is the idea of the artist as a godly maker that Ernst Curtius has included it in his catalog of rhetorical *topoi*, the treasure house of commonplaces that he saw as sustaining Western literature until the approach of romanticism. Curtius has shown that these *topoi* exist at the crossroads of culture, a fact that surely accounts for their longevity. At the same time as they "address themselves to the hearer's mind and heart," they trace themes "suitable for development at the author's pleasure."[6] The complementarity of these *topoi*, their capacity for merging aesthetic impulse and social situation, more than compensates for the risk they run of stagnating. While Curtius acknowledges that they may become "clichés, as they spread to all spheres of life," he insists also on their capacity to open "store-houses or trains of thought." The idea of the *deus artifex* has certainly opened many of these: Curtius's own plentiful examples, which stretch from Plato's *Timaeus* through Chalcidius, Boethius, and the *Patrilogia*, can be supplemented by the even larger area covered by Ernst Kris and Otto Kurz, who pursue the *topos* into the Renaissance, where the idea sustains Albrecht Dürer, Leon Battista Alberti, Fra Angelico, and Nicholas of Cusa, as well as a host of other artists and theoreticians.[7]

Neither of these books, however, investigates the survival of the *topos* into modern times. Indeed, Curtius thought that the vitality of the *topos* depended on "the acceptance, transformation, and development of the Greek idea by Christianity."[8] In view of this omission, the rest of this book must estimate whether the idea of the godly maker can survive the challenge of modern secular assumptions about art and about reality. In the remainder of this chapter, I will examine some of the main transformations the *topos* has undergone during this crucial early modern period. Whether the godly maker has any life left in the late twentieth-century's postmodern, postindustrial culture will be the subject of the rest of this book.

III.

It is worth remembering Jacob Burckhardt's lyrical description of the Renaissance as a period that combined possibilities we now see as contradictory.

> In the Middle Ages both sides of human consciousness—that which faces the outside world and that which is turned towards man's inner life—lay dreaming only half-awake, as if they were covered by a common veil, a veil woven of faith, delusion, and childish dependence. Seen across the veil, reality and history appeared in the strangest colours, while man was only aware of himself in universal categories such as race, nation, party, guild and family. It was in Italy that this veil was first blown away and that there awoke an objective attitude towards the state and towards all the things of the world while, on the other side, subjectivity emerged with full force so that man became a true individual mind and recognized himself as such.[9]

Although Burckhardt's picture of the Renaissance has been complicated by his successors, his recognition of the imaginative, cultural, and social possibilities it embodied is still valid today. And in the con-

text he presents, it is not at all surprising that many Renaissance artists revived the idea of the godly maker in their own work.

One of the boldest of these revivals can be found in Petrarch's
Coronation Oration. Alvin Kernan has argued that "modern literature
may be said to have begun" [10] with this work, in which Petrarch regards the poet as God's chief beneficiary, and God himself as *Magister
artis ingenique largitor.* [11] What is perhaps most impressive, however, is
not Petrarch's modernity, but his capacity to consolidate and affirm his
relationship with the classical past at the same time that he demonstrates his affiliation with the Christian present. As Petrarch's "sweet
longing urges [him] upward over the lonely slopes of Parnassus" toward a Christ-like exile, it is significant that he receives his first push
from a quotation from Virgil. His exalted quest is nourished by poetic
tradition, a tradition ensuring that his climb will not become mere
lonely self-devouring. "This difficulty and this eagerness," he says of
his climb, "are closely related, and are dependent each upon the
other" (301).

It is in this spirit that Petrarch begins his meditation at the point
of ascent. It is important to note that his sense of poetry begins with
the motion toward achievement, not the achieved elevation. Similarly,
the oration itself turns on a few repeated quotations, fixed points
around which the axis of the poet's whole world moves. The effect is to
establish some crucial oppositions from which poetic energies can
draw nourishment. Petrarch's originality is buttressed by his learning,
while his learning is not the dead letter of the pedant but the live
tissue of specific invention, woven into the texture of his oration like
living voices that can be called upon whenever their help seems necessary along the way.

Petrarch's *Familiar Letters* carry on a similar conversation with the
past. Acknowledging Virgil's mastery in one letter, Petrarch nevertheless criticizes a young writer whom he suggests is so much in love
with Virgil's charms that he inserts bits of the master into his own
work. Bits of Virgil: for the copyist, Virgil becomes *disjecta membra*
rather than part of the living tissue of a whole work. Petrarch continues: "A proper imitator should take care that what he works resembles the original without reproducing it. The resemblance should
not be that of a portrait to the sitter—in that case the closer the likeness is the better—but it should be the resemblance of a son to his
father. Therein is often a great divergence in particular features,
but . . . as soon as we see a son, he recalls the father to us." [12] Petrarch
recognizes that an art reeking too much of artifice will produce
nothing more than still life. Just as an individual family member is the

distinct outcome of a complex marriage of biological and social forces, so Petrarch's artist embodies a continuous interplay between novelty and stability, growth and change.

For Petrarch, literary invention takes place along a spectrum of possibility, one that includes "a basis of similarity" among "many dissimilarities." This is why, in a passage bristling with a sense of the family resemblances among the craftsman's creations, he describes the patient, meditative craftsmanship and subtle interaction between observation and inspiration that his idea of literary criticism entails.

> Similarity should be planted so deep it can only be extracted by quiet meditation. The quality should be felt rather than defined. Thus we may use another man's conception and the color of his style, but not use his words. In the first case the resemblance is hidden deep; in the second, it is glaring. The first procedure makes poets, the second makes apes. This is the substance of Seneca's counsel, and Horace's before him, that we should write as the bees make sweetness not storing up the flowers, but turning them into honey, thus making one thing of many various ones, but different and better. (199)

When Renaissance aestheticians take up the idea of a *deus artifex*, they draw nourishment from Petrarch's view of creation as a hive of delightful industry. For Giambattista Guarini and Torquato Tasso, for instance, an *artifex* becomes a *deus* insofar as he mimes a world, a bustling hive of packed variety. Polydore Vergil argues that poetic regularity imitates the regularity of the world that God created: "The begynner of meter was God, whych proporcioned the world, with all the contente of the same, with a certain order, as it were a meter."[13] Guarini, likewise, sees human art as a reflection of God's finest creation, the art that produced the world and mankind. "Beginning with the creation of the world, does it not appear that when the divine workman produced it . . . he produced it in conformity with the divine idea that had been in his breast from all eternity . . . this condition is the sign of a nature that does not perish. . . . in forming man as a little world, the divine voice of the divine artist indicated that he was pleased with the work of imitation, saying: Let us make man in our image, after our own likeness."[14] On a vertical plane, Guarini's cosmos sweeps from the artificer-god through the universe formed in accordance with the idea of a "nature that does not perish"; man, the intermediary of all this, partakes of God's intellect and the world's variety. The effect is to establish a binding set of correspondences and congruences that act as paradigm and guarantee for any subsequent artifice undertaken by man.

In Torquato Tasso's *Discourses on the Heroic Poem,* the basis of the poet's authority is also clearly identified. Just as God created a various reality, so the poet must create an imaginative world of similar variety, if indeed he is to be called divine. In the poet's world, Tasso suggests, one may look out upon "armies assembling, here of battles on land or sea, here of conquests of cities, skirmishes and duels, here of jousts, here descriptions of hunger and thirst, here tempests, fires, prodigies, there of celestial and infernal councils, there seditions, there discord, wanderings, adventures, enchantments, deeds of cruelty, daring, courtesy, generosity, there the fortunes of love, now happy, now sad, now joyous, now pitiful" (501). The precedent for poetic variety is the heterogeneity of the universe; the happy combinations of the one reduplicate the felicitous blendings of the other. "The art of composing a poem resembles the plan of the universe, which is composed of contraries, as that of music is. For if it were not multiple it would not be a whole or a plan, as Plotinus says" (501). Tasso's respect for multiplicity allows him to pay similar respect to poetic invention, which also bends fact into striking resemblances. The test of skill for the artist must be the kind of world he projects. Ideally, his world satisfies an audience because "its ordered and interrelated parts will not only be clearer and more distinct, but will afford more novelty and wonder." Audience and universe underpin the projects of the artist, whose intuition produces a synthesis that resembles the cosmic comedy of God's creation.

Such happy balances are difficult to sustain. Tasso's "idea" had conformed to nature; an opposing tendency in Renaissance aesthetics was for the idea to oust nature. Cristofero Landino's tantalizing definition of poetry reveals such tendencies, hedged by a tricky evasiveness. "The Greeks say 'poet' from the verb piin [*sic*], which is half-way between 'creating' which is peculiar to God, when out of nothing he brings forth anything into being, and 'making,' which applies to men when they compose with matter and form in any art. It is for this reason that, although the feigning of the poet is not entirely out of nothing, it nevertheless departs from making and comes very near to creating. And God is the supreme poet, and the world is His poem." [15] Landino's description reveals a point of stress in the Renaissance synthesis. As godly makers, Renaissance artists managed to fuse the intensity of the Christian vision with the plastic power of the classical. Landino's equivocal "half-way between. . . . comes very near to," however, begins to blur the relationship between art and nature; his daring elevation of the poet's creation is not strictly reconcilable with the perfunctory pieties he appends to his risky speculations.

As the poet comes more and more to resemble God, so the intensity of his inner life comes to achieve an emphasis that shrivels nature. Here, for instance, is Albrecht Dürer's account of the artist: "The great art of painting has been in great esteem with the powerful kings many hundred years ago, for they made the outstanding artists rich and honored them, considering such talent to be a creative thing like unto God. For a good painter is inwardly full of figures, and if it were possible that he live forever, he would have from the inner ideas, of which Plato writes, always something new to pour out in his works." [16]

There is a personal undertow to Dürer's intimations of immortality that we do not catch in Guarini or Tasso. Dürer's artist dwarfs the mightiest contexts (the ancient palaces that artists once occupied). He outlasts rank and station by virtue of his permanent capacity to bring forth inward treasure. A similar impulse toward inner artifice fires Sir Philip Sidney's eloquent description of the way poetry's golden world shames nature: "The poet, disdaining to be tied to any such subjection, lifted up with the vigour of his own invention, doth grow in effect another nature, in making things either better than nature bringeth forth, or, quite anew, forms such as never were in nature, as the Heroes, DemiGods, Cyclops, Chimeras, Furies, and such like: so as he goeth hand in hand with nature, not enclosed within the narrow warrant of her gifts, but freely ranging within the zodiac of his own wit." [17]

Though Sidney describes a partnership between art and nature, he implies something quite different. Nature is confined, "enclosed within . . . narrow warrant"; invention soars, its aim "to draw us to as high a perfection as our degenerate souls, made worse by their clayey lodgings, can be capable of." Where Guarini saw the flesh as incarnating the word, Sidney sees it as imprisoning it. The body is to the soul as nature is to art; the vision of the godly maker is beginning to burst the frame that had previously provided him with his shaping form.

IV.

The most substantial account of the lines of continuity between Renaissance and Augustan aesthetics is Martin Battestin's *The Providence of Wit*, which argues that for eighteenth-century writers, "the metaphysical notions which had nourished Renaissance aesthetics and given meaning to the metaphors of poetry were sophisticated, but they did not change fundamentally." [18] We would expect, therefore, the Augustan godly maker to differ only marginally from his Renaissance predecessor, and to function as a cornerstone in the overarching cosmic syntax that the century would consolidate as its chief cultural inheritance.

But the evidence of this syntax that Battestin marshals is sometimes less than compelling. In the masterpieces of eighteenth-century godly creation—works like *A Tale of a Tub*, *Macflecknoe*, and *The Dunciad*—and where the idea is invoked in discursive or expository prose—as in Fielding or Cudworth—the purpose is more frequently to score a debating point than to celebrate a lasting conviction. My own view is that, for the most part, the eighteenth-century godly maker is a thoroughly secular phenomenon, a yardstick by which to chart the activities of the Grub-street world of literary manufacturing, or, at the very best, a rod to measure the distance between God and man. John Upton's *Critical Observations on Shakespeare*, for example, presents us with a godly maker who weaves mysteries and composes plots too teasing for human comprehension: "And were it not a degree of prophanation, I might here mention the great Designer, who has flung some things into such shades, that 'tis no wonder so much gloominess and melancholy is raised in rude and undisciplined minds, the sublime Maker, who has set this universe before us as a book; yet what superficial readers are we in this volume of nature? Here I am certain we must become good men, before we become good critics, and the first step to wisdom is humility."[19]

Upton's artist-deity is concealed among ruins and gloom. Since the evidence for his design is so scattered, the unschooled mind can meet it only with despair; such sublime and complex mysteries require sustained human attention. Unlike the Renaissance commentators who thought that God's creation required only a celebrant to complete it, late seventeenth- and eighteenth-century essayists see the world as in perpetual need of an editor, an annotator who can collate and present the material so as to convince us of an authoritative reading. For this reason, the period sees the growth of what Maximilian Novak has called "reasonable mythologies," attempts to justify the ways of God without actually showing him in operation. Novak reports that "the Boyle lecturers, whose job it was to prove that God created and governed the universe, would deliberately avoid references to the Bible in working out their model theodicies. God's existence was shifted to the heavens where he acted as the overseer of a predominantly self-regulating system."[20]

One of the most famous "reasonable mythologies" was proposed by Thomas Burnet, whose *The Sacred Theory of the Earth* invested the commonplace of the godly maker with a new empirical rigor. For Burnet no longer saw evidence of a regular design in the world as it was ordinarily experienced: "What a rude Lump our World is that we are so apt to dote upon." [21] Where Guarini had seen the variety of nature as guarantee of the operation of a divine author, Burnet sees only a chaos that evidences a divine intention gone askew. "We have," he tells his royal dedicatee, "the broken Materials of that first World, and walk upon its Ruines. . . . this unshapen Earth we now inhabit, is the Form it was found in when the Waters had retir'd." Inhabiting a chaos, Burnet chooses to become a godly maker himself, creating a system that will describe "the Changes and Revolutions of Nature [that] are to come, and see through all succeeding Ages." This, he recognizes, will "require a steddy and attentive Eye, and a retreat from the noise of the World; especially so to connect the parts, and present them all under one view, that we may see, as in a Mirrour, the several faces of Nature, from First to Last, throughout all the Circle of Successions" (13).

Although Burnet designed his system to reinforce the authority of revealed religion, it actually functions quite differently. First, the work of the author of nature becomes a matter for private research rather than public display. To discover its truth, he tells us, "will require a steddy and attentive Eye, and a retreat from the noise of the World." Moreover, the evidence is not such as to yield total coherence: the parts need to be connected, since they point not to one overarching design but rather to "several faces of nature" perceived through a "circle of successions." The order Burnet describes needs an individual mind to construct it and hold it together; it does not give of itself the universal texture of resemblances and differences celebrated by Francesco Petrarch.

Ralph Cudworth, likewise, insists that the succession of events that nature offers cannot be immediately comprehensible to untrained minds. Cudworth's solution, however, is rather different from Burnet's. Where Burnet encourages his reader to construct meanings, Cudworth advises him to consume them. In each case, however, it is the individual mind, as producer or consumer of its own drama, that the author focuses upon, not the interanimating varieties of Petrarch or Guarini.

> But they who, because judgment is not presently executed upon the ungodly, blame the management of things as faulty, and Providence as defective, are like such spectators of a dramatick poem, as when wicked and injurious persons are brought upon the stage, for a while staggering and triumphing, impatiently cry out against the dramatist, and presently condemn the plot; whereas,

if they would but expect the winding up of things, and stay till the last close, they should see them come off with shame and sufficient punishment. The evolution of the world, as Plotinus calls it is . . . a truer poem. . . . God Almighty is that skilful dramatist who always connecteth into good coherent sense, and will at last make it appear, that a thread of exact justice did run through all, and that rewards and punishments are measured out in geometrical proportion.[22]

Cudworth's account of divine performance is interesting on several counts. First, unlike Guarini or Polydore Vergil, he does not dramatize creation as a *theatrum mundi* with men playing a starring role; his human beings are consumers of a *pièce bien faite,* not participants in a mystery cycle. Moreover, his divine artifice is ongoing and unending, not an existential fiat that releases men into the free play of individual will. And when Cudworth adds that men would find satisfaction "if they would but expect the winding up of things and stay till the last close," he clearly argues from a counsel of perfection, since human beings, by virtue of their very mortality, can do no such thing. The rhythm of divine artifice is no longer timed to the human pulse; when Cudworth suggests that providential justice works "in geometrical proportion," he invokes a measurement that takes least stock of human contingency. The secularization of the *topos* becomes a prelude to its mechanization, and the *deus artifex* turns into a *dieu caché,* a motor in a finely calibrated mechanism that testifies only to the ingenuity of its erector.

The secularization and mechanization of the *topos* also affects its literary transformations. Defoe's novels are full of references to providence; yet they figure only as allusions rippling over the surface. Barbara Hardy has suggested that providence in *Robinson Crusoe* functions "not as a convenient *deus ex machina* . . . but as an informing principle."[23] But this remark does not account for the principle by which Defoe's providence works; the signals Crusoe transmits to us of its workings are fragmentary, a matter of "secret hints" and "strange concurrences."[24] If Guarini's God was an artist, Defoe's is a cryptographer, producing signs that Crusoe must translate for himself into evidence of a design: the tides that bring him tobacco and a Bible, or the mysterious footprint that he discovers on the seashore. Similarly, the providence that elevates Smollett's Roderick Random and Peregrine Pickle from imprisonment to prosperity is skittish, the evidence for it asserted across the plot rather than within it. As godly makers, Smollett and Defoe are as furtive and willful as their characters. The universal masquerade of Moll Flanders's life enables her to justify the

ways of providence and self-reliance in turn and suggests the power
of the human mind to sanction the activities it wishes to pursue rather
than the ordered progression of a godly maker. These novels continue
to invoke, however remotely and obliquely, the authority of a shaping
deity; the actions they describe, however, testify to the emergence of a
thoroughly secular world.

Fielding's *Tom Jones* has been seen as the last masterpiece of
Christian humanism, its form and structure embodying "the moral
drama of the individual life enacted within a frame of cosmic and social Order."[25] Yet Fielding's most audacious reference to the godly
maker aspires to no such universality, insisting rather on the novelist's
authority to demarcate his own autonomous area of operation and
control. And that area Fielding closes off from the attentions of in-
truding critics, whom he warns

> not too hastily to condemn any of the Incidents in this our His-
> tory, as impertinent and foreign to our main Design, because thou
> dost not immediately conceive in what Manner such Incident may
> conduce to that Design. This Work may, indeed, be considered as
> a great Creation of our own; and for a little Reptile of a Critic to
> presume to find Fault with any of its Parts, without knowing the
> Manner in which the Whole is connected, and before he comes to
> the final Catastrophe, is a most presumptuous Absurdity. The Al-
> lusion and Metaphor we have here made use of, we must ac-
> knowledge to be infinitely too great for our Occasion, but there is,
> indeed, no other, which is at all adequate to express the Differ-
> ence between an Author of the first Rate, and a Critic of the
> lowest.[26]

Fielding's thrust is polemical, not cosmic, and his reference to
the *topos* as an "allusion and metaphor" shows his awareness of its
self-conscious fictionality. His godly artificer operates in a context of
secular activity, not divine design; the religious side of the *topos* fades
into the background as the writer borrows its authority to boost his
own stock in a local skirmish with critics, the foulest creation of a new
system of literary production.

Secularization—in bookmaking, in intellectual life, in the social
and political realms too—deprives the *topos* of anything but a comic
force. The narrator in Swift's *A Tale of a Tub* insists perhaps over-
emphatically on his own prerogative to be persuasive to anyone other
than himself. When he claims "an absolute Authority, in Right, as the
freshest Modern, which gives me a Despotick Power over all Authors
before me," the reader cannot assent as easily as he can to Petrarch.[27]
For where the earlier author tests his modernity against the frame of a

universal design, Swift's modern narrator can offer only the conditions of the marketplace in support of his priority. And when he hints that like the God of Genesis, he speaks in riddles and latent profundities so that "where I am not understood, it shall be concluded, that something very useful and profound is coucht underneath: And again, that whatever word or Sentence is Printed in a different Character, shall be judged to contain something extraordinary either of Wit or Sublime" (28), we realize how the eternal correspondences of Renaissance Platonism have become confused with the mechanical accidents of typography. The result, a discourse that systematically mistakes obscurity for profundity, is flatulent rather than inspired.

When the narrator makes the inevitable gestures toward the argument from design, it is with just the kind of harebrained ingenuity that shows how far from commonplace the idea has become for Augustan authors: "Proceed to the particular Works of the Creation, you will find how curious Journey-man Nature hath been, to trim up the vegetable Beaux: Observe how sparkish a Perewig adorns the Head of a Beech, and what a fine Doublet of white Satin is worn by the Birch. To conclude from all, what is Man himself but a Micro-Coat, or rather a compleat Suit of Cloaths with all its Trimmings?" (47).

Swift's playful and systematic substitution of social trivia for eternal correspondences points to an important truth. The world is now too old, and men are now too proud for anyone to take very seriously the idea of a godly maker or of a man who forms a little world, the apogee of God's creation. Without some injection of the larger vision that had supplied the *topos* with much of its imaginative energy, the idea of the godly maker shrinks into a toy for the learned in their impregnable castles of wit.

V.

For eighteenth-century authors, the *deus artifex topos* functioned within a system of "reasonable mythologies," attempts to cope with a new secular world by the construction of self-contained fictions. Fielding and Swift exploited the comic incongruity of the *topos*, demonstrating its sheer inapplicability to the market forces they saw as becoming dominant in the world of letters. In these conditions, where sales were more important than vision, divine inspiration turned into quackery and the godly maker became a brash and prolix mountebank. Their romantic successors were unable to content themselves with such comic half-measures, for they were convinced, as the young Samuel Taylor Coleridge assured Thomas Poole, that "all Truth is a species of Revelation." Accordingly, where Swift and Pope mock the solitary enthusiast, Coleridge and his contemporaries apotheosize him. The visionary, Coleridge continued, "is sticking up little *i by itself, i* against the whole alphabet. But one *word* with *meaning* in it is worth the whole alphabet together."[28] Romantic aesthetics is founded in the conviction that any serious artist, by virtue of his superior vision and sacred imagination, can become a self-elected deity, and that the authority of the imagining consciousness is sovereign and absolute. Coleridge's "little i," then, is on the threshold of transmutation into the sovereign and all-powerful "I AM" of *Biographia Literaria*. "The PRIMARY IMAGINATION I hold to be the living Power and prime Agent of all human Perception, and as a repetition in the finite mind of the eternal act of creation in the infinite I AM."[29] But the arbitrary, sudden nature of Coleridge's coup points to the precariousness of the authority to which the romantic godly maker lays claim.

Characteristically, the romantic godly maker grounds the authority for his superior perception in the quality of his inner vision. The program for this apotheosis of the sovereign consciousness was first mapped out by Friedrich Schlegel, who stood the godly artist idea on its head. In Schlegel's eyes, God is refashioned in the image of an artist, an inversion of the Renaissance idea whereby the artist became a man working in the image of God. Schlegel's godly maker is not so much a human shape as an inspired mood, whose "divine breath of irony . . . surveys everything" and becomes "elevated above the poet's art, virtue and genius."[30]

The shift from commonplace to privileged perspective can be regarded as the beginning of modern art, an art founded on the basis of a gap between "lived" and "observed" reality. As Ortega y Gasset has pointed out, "For the modern artist, aesthetic pleasure derives from . . . a triumph over human matter."[31] Schlegel's godly maker takes pleasure in creating an art untouched by human hand. The distance between this maker and the maker of Guarini amounts almost to a difference in kind. Where Renaissance artists saw matter as fulfilling its potential through the mediation of a godly maker, Schlegel's artist-gods are creators *ex nihilo*. Where Renaissance artists saw their art as guaranteed by natural and theological processes, Schlegel can only see the perpetually shifting boundaries that constitute his *universal-poesie*. The vision that underlies his strangely unbalanced view of literary creation is advanced in his "Talk on Mythology," where the ingenious Ludovico remarks to his peers that "you yourselves have written poetry and while doing so you must often have felt the absence of a firm basis for your activity, a matrix, a sky, a living atmosphere" (81).

Schlegel's is a professional's criticism, written for professionals who fear the increasing redundancy of their skills. His aggressively worded hymns to the interior have at their heart a doubt about poetry's capacity to work on the exterior. The authority of the godly artist must be reborn from a world withered of any external supports or props. When the ancients sang, whole tribes listened; Schlegel's muse composes in a vacuum.

His solution to this problem is to absorb the universe into his imagination. "The new mythology must be forged from the deepest depths of the spirit" (82). The modern poet, as Schlegel sees him, is a god simply because he occupies a world so unaccommodating to art: "the modern poet must create all these things from within himself . . . each part separately." All art, asserts Schlegel, has its own beginning, emerging "like a new creation out of nothing" (82). Guarini's artist was a god of plenitude, but Schlegel's is a god of vacancy; where the old mythology had hoped to marry form and matter, "directly joining and imitating what was most immediate and vital in the sensuous world" (81–82), the new can achieve its totality only through the transformation of nature into art, an art eventually expanding to become a choric poem, the "infinite poem concealing the seeds of all other poems." Schlegel's new mythology aspires to the old's totality: "One block of material is only explained and clarified in the light of another. It is not possible to understand one part by itself, that is, it is foolish to consider it only in isolation" (107). But the totality is purely artificial.

For Schlegel, autogeny begets mythology. Simply because poetry lacks reference outside itself, criticism must tunnel inward. Schlegel sees the critic as a connoisseur rather than a moralist; his task is to probe inward to discover true knowledge through "a desire to understand, to fathom as much as possible the history of the poet's mind" (106–7). Schlegel himself accomplishes this masterfully, but it is a nimble reader who, while in pursuit of Schlegel's pursuit of an aphorism, can be sure that he is not pursuing the ghost of a meaning rather than a real one. Very often it is clear that Schlegel's business is not the common pursuit of true judgment but rather the perfection of a prismatic unfathomability that will sparkle and obscure simultaneously. "An aphorism," he tells us, "ought to be entirely isolated from the surrounding world and complete in itself like a hedgehog" (143). A reader of Schlegel's aphorisms is probably ready to concede anything after a few dozen of them, but can also be left feeling unnerved. Like the reader of a cartoon strip supplied with only the captions, he is left to guess at the authority and identity of the unseen oracle who produces epigrams so effortlessly. Schlegel is on the brink of art as pure image, outside space and time and vehicle for an epiphanic, self-contained wisdom. But such a drastic foreshortening cannot be maintained in the face of actual creative practice.

This program works well enough for criticism, but can it possibly be put into a creative work? Coleridge's *Kubla Khan* shows how tricky Schlegel's scheme can become. Coleridge can justly be called a godly maker in spite of himself, his imagination a puzzling and impermanent possession. A prefatorial note to *Kubla Khan* provides, in best Schlegelian fashion, a reflection on the poem's genesis. Coleridge's slumbering external senses give way to the imperial self of the mind, in keeping with Schlegel's program for a "new mythology." In sleep, he writes, "all the images rose up before him as *things* with a parallel production of the corresponding expressions."[32] Locked into a purely private world, Coleridge's imagination becomes a thing of pure power. But the arrival of a courier from the public world—"a person on business from Porlock"—is all that is needed to shatter the palace of art. "All . . . passed away like the images on the surface of a stream into which a stone had been cast, but, alas! without the after-restoration of the latter" (296). Renaissance artists strived to integrate many levels; for Schlegel and Coleridge, the artist became godly in his intense domination of one region, the interior and imaginary. Coleridge's storehouses of thought are betrayed by the quotidian, not complemented by it, as the "phantom world—so fair" splinters into "a thousand circles," each misshaping the other.

In the world of *Kubla Khan*, plurality is almost a guarantee of formlessness. The arrival of the person from Porlock reduces the emperor-god to the artist-editor, laboring "to finish himself what had originally, as it were, been given to him" (297). Coleridge's "distinct recollections" are severed irrecoverably from the world around him. He constantly apologizes for the unfinished condition of his "fragment," which is a poor relation of Schlegel's own. If the *Athenaeum Fragments* are distilled wisdom, granitelike in their self-sufficiency, Coleridge's *Kubla Khan* is an apologetic renovation of a more glorious original. Where Schlegel affects a disdain for his audience, teasing them with riddles, Coleridge is embarrassed by his, apologizing almost interminably at the paradise he has lost. What unites both writers is a sense of the separate realms of poetry and action, their shared desertion of a common storehouse from which poetic activity could gain strength.

Whether as Schlegel's absent master or Coleridge's blundering Dogberry, the tendency of the romantic godly maker is to occupy a chimeric private world. What characterizes this stage of the development of the *topos* is the distance between the artist's consciousness and the real world, the world of persons on business from Porlock. M. H. Abrams has remarked that "as Baudelaire's pure work of art takes on some of the attributes of a self-sufficient Deity, so Baudelaire's 'dandy' assimilates to the figure of the social aristocrat the qualities of the Christian saint who emulates God by substituting the detachment from life of the *vita contemplativa* for the engagement with life of the *vita activa.*"[33] The Baudelaire who creates his diminished "artificial paradises"; the Baudelaire whose rallying call therein had been "Perhaps I did dine poorly, yet I am a God";[34] the Baudelaire who tells us with the sober precision of an ecclesiastical historian, "I was not far wrong when I compared dandyism to a kind of religion" (before going on to compare it to the old monastic orders) is perhaps the limiting instance of the artist's power to create a world of pure artifice.[35]

At the beginning of "Any where out of the world," Baudelaire's narrator sees life as perpetual confinement in a hospital, with art as the sole discharge. But if life is a hospital, then art is a prison in which the cells shrink with every separate world that the artist creates. Even though he scours the universe, he can find only "lands constituted in the likeness of Death."[36] The artist's imagination can move only from sickness to moribundity.

Baudelaire's solution to this predicament is dramatized in "The Evil Glazier," which exposes the clash between the symbolic imagination of the godly narrator and the impoverished reality of urban Paris. Baudelaire's narrator occupies a sixth-floor eyrie, from which he catches sight of an itinerant street vendor. Beckoning the merchant up to his apartment, the narrator is suddenly possessed by hatred of the commonplace reality reflected in his wares: "What! you have no colored glass? Rose, blue, magical glass, worthy of Paradise!" (12). Because the godly maker occupies an entrepreneurial market rather than a paradise, his sole recourse is to offer violence on reality: "I pushed him quickly down the stairs, where he stumbled, grumbling." Such violence provides access to the ecstasies of a sublime vision. "Intoxicated with my folly," the narrator concludes, "I cried furiously 'Life is beautiful!'" But this kind of sublimity does violence to words as well as to objects and people; when the narrator goes on to describe his act of felonious assault as a declaration of war; when he says that the glazier's "itinerant fortune gave off the sound of a crystal palace shattered by lightning" (12), it becomes clear that the world of everyday reality and the world of the artist's consciousness have separated completely. Even the "evil" referred to in the title, which slides imperceptibly from the narrator to his adversary, evidences the godly artist's

declaration of hostility toward the objective world. It is clear from
Paris Spleen as a whole that the deification of the artist has led to the
dehumanization of art; Baudelaire's godly artists are raw and unpredictable deities, who make lightning raids on the quotidian in order to
replenish their icy palaces of art.

VI.

In the work of Coleridge and Baudelaire, the distance between
artistic consciousness and quotidian reality enlarges to a frightening
degree, transforming the artist-deity into a legislator or even a victimizer in the process. And the most unrepentant of these godly legis-
lators are the great realistic novelists, whose power over the worlds
they create they may indeed be called "omniscient." As W. J. Harvey
has remarked, the realistic novelist's relationship with his characters
"is not human but god-like."[37] In the same way, Steven Marcus has
described Dickens in *Martin Chuzzlewit* as a "disciplined, magisterial
sensibility, acting as a kind of deity, freely creating and controlling the
experience he imposes on his readers."[38] Henry James was convinced
that the creator of *The Human Comedy* could be understood only as a
deity "gilded thick, with so much gold-plated and burnished and
bright, in the manner of towering idols."[39] Marthe Robert has similarly described Balzac's desire to "play for the public the one role of
omniscient, omnipotent, divine creator that can correspond to his immense thirst for domination."[40] A similar combination of panoramic
extensiveness and interior compulsion appears to underprop the fiction of Tolstoy or Dostoevsky.

But what of the authors for whom the *topos* is an explicit creed?
In these cases, it is the harsh justice of the nineteenth-century godly
maker that immediately captures our attention. We notice it first of all
at the level of plot, where the nineteenth-century godly maker becomes a legislator rather than an informing agent. His characters thus
become his counters, to be moved according to his chief design. What
E. M. Forster has said of Thomas Hardy, one of the most representative nineteenth-century godly makers—"The fate above us, not the
fate working through us—that is what is eminent and memorable"—
can be applied to all these writers.[41]

Boris Pasternak saw causality as the center of nineteenth-century
realism, telling Ralph Matlaw that "in the nineteenth century masters
. . . if you take away the characters and characterization, the imagery,
the description, and so on, you still have left *causality*, the concept
that an action has a consequence."[42] The godly vision of the realistic

novelist makes his word law in the world of his novels; Pasternak's choice for the supreme embodiment of this principle was Gustave Flaubert, the man who decreed that "the artist in his work must be like God in his creation . . . everywhere felt but never seen."[43] This comment is often regarded as Flaubert's attempt at a scientist's objectivity, but the course of his career suggests that his real concern was to assume a deity's authority. When he asks for the capacity to "set down the facts as the Good Lord sees them from on high," he is not simply petitioning for the capacity to record the facts, but for the ultimate strengthening of his will to do so. Why he should have to steel himself for this becomes clear from his cynical rider: "From the point of view of a divine joke."[44] Flaubert's god's-eye view of reality sees only an inevitable process of deterioration; his merciless sense of causality always colors what he discovers. Hs own books, he knows, will never have the encyclopedic verve of the works he likes best. He tells Louise Colet that "people like us were born a little too soon; twenty-five years from now, the points of intersection of all these quests will provide superb subjects for a master . . . we may once again have books like the *Satyricon* and the *Golden Ass*, but bubbling over with intellect as those bubble over with sensuality."[45] His own urge for an encyclopedic fiction becomes, however, a literal encyclopedia: *The Dictionary of Received Ideas*.

In another revealing phrase, Flaubert says that "art, like the God of the Jews, feeds on holocausts." Whenever Flaubert attempts a panoramic scene, he impales his characters with a Jehovah-like ferocity. The famous Yonville show episode in *Madame Bovary* reveals a society at odds with itself, a society where materialism and romanticism have become mutually contaminating. What Flaubert presents is a series of fractured totalities, moments of a collective action that are revealed as meaningless bourgeois window dressing. Everything goes its separate way in this chapter: Homais tries to coin a proverb, but Madame Le François will not accept the currency; the land itself becomes the subject for every kind of cliché—military, technological, scientific, commercial—even Rodolphe's transcendental banalities. The dismal roll call of names, objects, and materials, each followed by its price tag (it is interesting to note that pigs are more valuable than farmhands) leaves us with no doubt that persons from Porlock have control of the things of the earth. But Flaubert retains his aesthetic control, which he wields with a sacrificial fury; in the center of this crowded panorama can be glimpsed the author himself, creator of *Salammbô*, wallowing in two female sacrifices: Emma Bovary sacrificed to Rodolphe Boulanger's small-town lust and Catherine Leroux sacrificed to Yon-

ville's rural idiocy. Rodolphe Boulanger's cynical "There are two moral-
ities" and Monsieur Lieuvain's pious banalities dissolve in the all-
enveloping amorality of their victimizing godly maker.

The logical culmination of Flaubert's twin goals of anatomy and
sacrifice comes in his last novel, *Bouvard and Pécuchet*. Now Flaubert
will write as a god—angry enough to consume his worlds in an
apocalypse. He tells Ernest Feydeau he would like to drown the human race in his vomit. But Flaubert had reckoned, on this occasion,
without his other gift, the parodic energy that propels the description
of the Yonville show. In his last book, parody deflects even Flaubert's
relentless purpose, so that his projected apocalypse becomes the
damp squib inventoried in the plan he made for an ending to the
book: "They have no more interest in life"; and "A good idea cher-
ished secretly by each of them. They hide it from one another. From
time to time they smile when it occurs to them, then at last communicate it simultaneously: To copy as in the old days." [46]

Flaubert begins by mocking his own precocious ennui. The author, who had become a connoisseur of boredom by thirteen years of
age, now creates two bourgeois inflicted with ennui. Bouvard and Pécuchet, by dint of sheer native ineptitude, have achieved in several
slow strokes what Flaubert, in a lifetime devoted to art, could not. His
own apocalypse has been preempted by theirs: "Everything has come
to pieces in their hands" (347). The self-mockery continues, as Flaubert's search for the mot juste is ironically echoed in his characters'
search for a "good idea," fated, one suspects, for the inevitable transformation into an *idée reçue*. And their last action as, quite alone, they
begin "to copy as in the old days," parodies the enterprise of the realistic novelist. Flaubert ends his career wallowing in the sacrifice of his
own art; the inexorable logic of realistic fiction reaches its bizarre
fulfillment in this excoriating self-parody.

Flaubert's impulses toward self-parody and malign victimization
are both important features of the later fiction of Mark Twain and Herman Melville. *The Mysterious Stranger* and *Pierre, or the Ambiguities*
both reveal the peculiar withering of the metaphoric life of the *topos*
that perhaps reaches its climax in Thomas Hardy's famous: "The President of the Immortals . . . had ended his sport with Tess." [47] In these
books, the godly maker is a literal presence in the narrative, applying
peculiar tricks and wrinkles to his plot to ensure that all will go badly.
In the same way, Rudyard Kipling's *The Light That Failed* repeatedly
affirms that art is a special grace, bestowed and withdrawn by a god
whose motives cannot be fathomed. All these writers show a literal-
mindedness in the handling of the idea that gives their novels a cage-

like structure. The *deus artifex topos* becomes a contraption the novelist uses to keep his characters trapped.

Melville's case is particularly instructive. His early fiction, as Warner Berthoff has shown, derives its special energy from its determination to discover "the universe."[48] *Moby-Dick*, en route from Nantucket to New Guinea, conducts a quest that is as literal as it is internal; *White-Jacket*, with its brief of rendering "the world in a man of war," again shows Melville's desire to imitate a collective reality. These books are written by a man who thinks that an artist in the nineteenth century can still penetrate the formidable accretions of literary association and convention in order to open an original intercourse with his world.

Paradoxically, however, this combination of inner compulsion and external expansiveness failed Melville as he continued to write. In *Pierre,* a narrator spasmodically wise but increasingly incoherent tells us that "the world is forever babbling of originality; but there never yet was an original man, in the sense intended by the world; the first man himself—who according to the Rabbins was also the first author—not being an original; the only original author being God."[49] In his earlier fiction, Melville had playfully referred to God as his competitor; he now appears as the limiting constraint of artistic invention, the guarantor of its insignificance and its severance from human perceptions. What remains in *Pierre* is a nihilist fable, a series of bottomless boxes that the narrator manipulates like an increasingly desperate magician. As "far as any geologist has yet gone down into the world," he tells us, "it is found to consist of nothing . . . but superinduced superficies" (323); the godly maker has constructed an ingenious abyss.

The result is a kind of metaphysical scrimmage between narrator and protagonist. Pierre, a true child of his time, is bent on transcendence; however, his narrator knows already that "with every accession of the personal divine to him, some great land-slide of the general surrounding divineness slips from him" (345). Like a glowworm in a universal darkness, Pierre becomes exceptionally isolated; the destiny of this would-be redeemer is to become, as Clive Bush has noted, a forerunner of West's Miss Lonelyhearts.[50] The narrator's voice becomes correspondingly more hectoring, as Pierre becomes increasingly obsessed by a variety of heroic ideals—spiritual, military, historical, and even artistic. But the narrator, who knows the outcome of Pierre's quests even before he has undertaken them, has already determined his fate. What was once a metaphor for order and connection is now a decree of limitation.

Twain's fascination with the godly maker is a long-standing one. As early as 1867, he was quoting for *Alta California* readers from the Apocryphal New Testament. "Jesus and other boys play together and make clay figures of animals. Jesus causes them to walk; also clay birds which he causes to fly, and eat and drink. The children's parents are alarmed and take Jesus for a sorcerer."[51] Apparent even in this quotation is the godly maker's distance from adult sympathies, his corresponding proximity to the freedom of the child, and an implicit profligacy in his artistry.

In 1897, when Twain began the series of manuscripts eventually to emerge (through the creative diligence of his literary executor) as *The Mysterious Stranger*, he began to strengthen these aspects of the godly maker's character. In the earliest of these manuscripts, Twain's godly maker is called Philip Traum or young Satan, a name that underscores for us the gap between divine intentions and human perceptions. Twain's maker, like the Jesus of Apocrypha, works in clay: "He made a toy squirrel out of clay and it ran up a tree and sat on a limb overhead and barked down at us. Then he made a dog that was not much larger than a mouse, and it treed the squirrel and danced about the tree, excited and barking, and was alive as any dog could be" (47). As Twain's narrative continues, however, Satan's virtuoso skills begin to reveal a chilling lack of sympathy: "He told of the daily life in heaven, he had seen the damned writhing in the red waves of hell, and he made us see all these things, and it was as if we were on the spot and looking at them with our own eyes. And we *felt* them, too, but there was no sign that they were anything to him, beyond being mere entertainments" (50).

"He made us see": Twain's Satan has the gifts of the fiction writer as well as the artificer in the plastic arts. All that is lacking is the least tincture of human sympathy. The vision of the damned is to him something that "he was as bland about . . . as if it had been so many imitation rats in an artificial fire." Satan can see the human only in terms of artifice, from a dangerously elevated perspective that is disillusioning for the artificer and disastrous for his creation. Artifice itself now becomes synonymous with victimization. It would appear that the presiding deity behind our nineteenth-century version of the *topos* is Hardy's President of the Immortals or the God of Kierkegaard's *Fear and Trembling*: unfathomable and even foreign to all human perspectives, these artificer-deities have reduced the idea of deity to its lowest element of human sacrifice.

VII.

Twentieth-century revisions of the *deus artifex topos* are—at least until 1945—of two main kinds. First of all, there is the strong sense exhibited in Conrad's *The Secret Agent*, Kubin's *The Other Side*, and Orwell's *1984* that the world constructed by the godly maker is essentially unfit for human habitation. These books expose the political consequences of a world created by a sovereign maker. On the other hand, the twentieth century has also witnessed in books like Joyce's *Ulysses*, Mann's *Dr. Faustus*, and Camus's *The Fall* a series of sustained attempts to return the *topos* to the matrix of shared experience and history.

Ian Watt's biography of *Conrad in the Nineteenth Century* leaves no excuse for ignorance about that author's debt to the period. In the same way, the description Conrad offered John Galsworthy of the nature of artistic creation is almost an abstract of the ideas we have traced through Flaubert, Baudelaire, Melville, and Twain. Like them, Conrad sees the artist-god as a man in possession of an idea, and willing to sacrifice his whole creation to the successful realization of the idea of his own godliness that possesses him. What intrigues Conrad, like Flaubert and Melville, is his godly power to bend his characters to the sway of this governing principle. But like these authors too, Conrad must gradually acknowledge the pockets of resistance that plot, character, and event make against the construction of his palace of art: "In a book you should love the idea and be scrupulously faithful to your conception of life. There lives the honour of the writer, not in the fidelity to his personages. As against your people you must preserve an attitude of perfect indifference. . . . A creator must be indifferent; because directly the 'Fiat!' has issued from his lips, there are creatures made in his image that'll try to drag him down from his eminence."[52] The creation of Marlow represents Conrad's attempt to exploit creatively the tensions he here describes to Galsworthy. Marlow explains and annotates the creator's idea in contexts that either threaten to dissolve that idea in a generalized nothingness (as in *Heart of Darkness*) or to show it fenced in by the pressures of circumstance (as in *Lord Jim*). But what happens when the author's godly idea is unmediated by a narrator who is both inside and outside the action he describes?

The answer comes in a book that reveals the conflict in its purest form, that troublingly "simple tale," *The Secret Agent*. Here, as his earliest reviewers recognized, Conrad created a London in the image of the Inferno. But Conrad's ironies are more unruly even than his city, spilling over constantly from religion to art so as to drag down both from any trace of eminence. The book is heaped with parodies of art: the idiotic Stevie's circles are "the symbolism of a mad art attempting the inconceivable";[53] Mr. Verloc's shop contains "photographs of more or less undressed dancing girls" (13); even Mr. Vladimir's conversation belongs to the drawing room comedy rather than the political intrigue. His wit, we learn, "consisted in discovering droll connections between incongruous ideas" (25). Similarly, the god's-eye view is repeatedly revealed as dehumanizing; from Conrad's elevated perspective, Mr. Verloc becomes "a rock—a soft kind of rock" (21), while Michaelis's elbow looks "more like a bend in a dummy's limb" (43). By the end of the book the sacred mission of the artist has fused with the political absurdity of the characters. "Apostle" Michaelis diets on carrots and milk, an activity described as "angelic" (243), while at one point the revolutionaries as a group enact only an "impenetrable mystery" (246), a blot that stains the purity of art and faith alike. Conrad's "simple tale," like Christ's simple parables, secretes a holy scorn that corruscates its creator's own stated premises. In the world Conrad realizes in this novel, the presiding deity is someone all too faithful to a "conception of life." But Conrad's plot-hatching Professor, "terrible in the simplicity of his idea calling madness and despair to the regeneration of the world" (249), is a menacing figure whose ruling obsession is not to make but to destroy.

Conrad's view of the destructive potential of the solitary godly maker is pursued further in Kubin's *The Other Side* and Orwell's *1984*. Kubin's Claus Patera creates a "Dream Kingdom" on the Asian Steppes whose "whole economic life was 'symbolic.'"[54] In this world, "to impose an illusion on one's opponent . . . was the trick," and consequently, one "became steadily more enmeshed in [one's] own fantasies and those of others" (58). Enticed into the kingdom by his desire of riches through art, the narrator initially feels confident of a "strong hand" behind its apparent chaos. "Behind even the most incomprehensible circumstances one detected its secret mastery. . . . An immense Justice, reaching even into hidden places . . . brought all events back into balance" (58). Yet, once again, the course of the narrative betrays the aesthetic order asserted at its beginning. When an insurgent American forces Patera to declare war on his creation, the Dream Kingdom becomes an all too literal shambles, while its inhabitants fall "helpless victims to dreams in which they were given the command to destroy themselves" (213). Rescued from this saturnalia by a regiment of Europeans, the narrator comes to realize that the god of his dreams "possessed only a partial dominion" (235), that his very existence as a god depended on the power of the personalities ranged against him.

Kubin's narrator enters Patera's Dream Kingdom out of aesthetic curiosity, only to discover a social and political disaster. In *1984*, Winston Smith, trapped in the social and political disaster of Oceania, seeks an aesthetic release. Oceania has expelled art and God. Instead of art, there is the never-ending panel beating by which Julia's Fiction Department pumps out a supply of pornographic prole feed, while God himself has been replaced by Big Brother, whose omnipresence acts as the capstone for the architecture of social control.

Winston's activities in the Ministry of Truth involve him in Oceania's sinister parody of the creative process, the fabrication of history that the Ministry practices daily. "All history was a palimpsest, scraped clean and reinscribed exactly as often as was necessary. . . . Most of the material that you were dealing with had no connection with anything in the real world, not even the kind of connection that is contained in a direct lie."[55] These are the conditions that inspire the search of Winston and Julia for their own personal history, "a secret world in which you could live as you chose." But where Julia thinks that sex creates "a world of its own which was outside the Party's control" (109), Winston hopes to gain access to such a world through memory, even though he realizes that of all possible releases from history, memory is the least reliable. The old man whom Winston meets in a pub has a memory that "was nothing but a rubbish heap of details. . . . the few scattered survivors from the ancient world were incapable of comparing one age with another" (77–78). Winston himself, who can remember only half a nursery rhyme, suffers from the same affliction. If organized totalitarian escape from history presupposes a disconnection from the real, so too do the sensual rebellion and the frantic reconstructions of the irresolute single soul. In the world of Orwell's *1984*, as in Kubin's kingdom, public and private dreams of godly recreation stand and fall together.

In Conrad, Kubin, and Orwell, the nineteenth-century elevation of the godly maker finds its political critique. But at the same time, another important group of twentieth-century novelists was attempting to reinvest in the *topos* some of its earlier imaginative energy, and it is to these novelists—Joyce, Mann, Camus—that T. S. Eliot's review essay on "*Ulysses*, Order, and Myth" provides the authoritative guide. Defending Joyce's book against the charge that it libelled humanity, Eliot argued that its "continuous parallel between contemporaneity and antiquity" gave "a way of controlling, of ordering, of giving a shape and a significance to the immense panorama of futility and anarchy which is contemporary history."[56]

Joyce's work had long shown a fascination with the idea of the artist as a godly maker. In *A Portrait of the Artist as a Young Man*, Stephen Dedalus offered his definition (closely cut in the cloth of Gustave Flaubert) of an "artist, like the God of creation" who "remains within or behind or beyond or above his handiwork, invisible, refined out of existence, indifferent, paring his fingernails."[57] Yoking this comment to Lynch's sardonic response—"trying to refine them also out of existence"—Joyce presents both the nature of Stephen's predicament and the solution to it. Stephen's imagined artist-deity is too impalpable; he needs the broader perspectives of comedy or myth if he is to become capable of taking on a human shape.

When Stephen next thinks of a godly maker, his attention turns to Thoth, the god of writing. Somehow, the deity will not stay up on the pedestal Stephen has erected for him. "He smiled as he thought of the god's image for it made him think of a bottle-nosed judge in a wig, putting commas into a document which he held at arm's length, and he knew that he would not have remembered the god's name but that it was like an Irish oath" (209). Stephen can only recall the author's sacred role through the intercession of the profane; it is an oath that brings his writer-god back to life.

The same thrust toward the reconciliation of opposites motivates Stephen's parable of art in *Ulysses*. His two main adversaries, the Quaker librarian of the National Library and A. E. Russell, propose views of art that from their opposing extremes meet in a shared sense of literature as closet solipsism. For the librarian, there is no more to art than biography; for Russell, art begins and ends in ideas. Stephen's Shakespeare parable attempts to fuse both in a view of art that combines biography (his Shakespeare heaves a butcher's axe in his native Stratford) and vision (in *Hamlet*, Stephen argues that "through the ghost of the unquiet father the image of the living son looks forth" [249]). The art that will be written today will be the product of generations (Stephen offers his thanks to Drummond of Hawthornden, among others). Accordingly, the most lasting image of the artist will see him as a maker, a deity who weaves and unweaves his material: "As we, or mother Dana, weave and unweave our bodies," Stephen said, "from day to day, their molecules shuttled to and fro, so does the artist weave and unweave his image."[58]

Paradoxically, however, Stephen's new vision leads to his own elimination as the novel's godly maker. Joyce's new sense of the artist as reaching down the enormous vistas of time and memory begins the

movement that culminates in *Finnegans Wake.* In the "Ithaca" chapter
of *Ulysses,* Joyce enlarges his perspective to the point where Bloom
and Stephen shrink, and art becomes subsidiary to a large unending
pattern of natural process. Joyce's voice modulates from the catechizer
to the scientist, as his prose becomes small and dry, accumulating evidence of a universal forlornness. "At Stephen's suggestion, at Bloom's
instigation both, first Stephen, then Bloom, in penumbra urinated,
their sides contiguous, their organs of micturition reciprocally rendered invisible by manual circumposition, their gazes, first Bloom's,
then Stephen's, elevated to the projected luminous and semiluminous
shadow" (825). The closing experiments with language, which couple
Bloom with an assortment of magical mariners, from Sinbad the Sailor
down to Xinbad the Phthailer (871), ultimately dissolve what they began by celebrating. Although Joyce is no artist-god as solitary destroyer, his later experiments do tend to bury his heroes under the
language of the tribe.

Like Joyce's *Ulysses,* Thomas Mann's *Dr. Faustus* casts the godly
artist as a protagonist in a larger fiction. Mann's Adrian Leverkühn
sells his soul to the devil in order to achieve a godlike mastery of his
art. In *Genesis of a Novel,* Mann's account of the period in which he
wrote the work, he remarked that the idea presented itself to him as "a
radically serious menacing subject around which the lightning of
grave sacrifice seemed to flash."[59] The idea of the artist sacrificed to
his art was not a new one to Mann; *Death in Venice* and *Tonio Kröger*
both include this theme. What startled Mann was the way an idea that
had come to him in youth could be rediscovered in old age, granting
him an almost tentacular grasp of the subject. Now he plunged into
mythology, folklore, musicology; the backdrop to the artist's sacrifice
was no longer solid burgherlike respectability, but the whole of German history since the Reformation.

But if Mann's search for the origins of Leverkühn's "dear purchase" of artistic superiority took him into Germany's mythical and
historical past, then current events forced him to confront his own
Germany's possession under the spell of the Third Reich.[60] However
different their motives, Mann could not ignore the similarity in rhetoric—sacrifice, power, godliness—that German artists shared with
their politicians. His novel accordingly shifted course, as he reported
in *Genesis of a Novel*: "A novel of music? Yes. But it was also conceived
as a criticism of culture and our era" (28). For this reason, Leverkühn's
Lutheran archaisms are juxtaposed against painfully contemporary
events; his mythical pact is forced against the grim political course of
Nazi Germany; music, the most abstract of the arts, is thrust against

the most particular of disciplines, the history whose very particu-
larity has always made it disturbing to the classical mind. Like Joyce,
Mann refuses to permit the godly artist to dictate the terms by which
we are to understand him; the structure of the novel forces him into
the context of a larger narrative, so that his actions can be weighed in
terms of their consequences and origins.

But Mann's work does not end here. If his novel fuses mythology
and history, it also records the growth of new social institutions that
will threaten the life of both. Serenus Zeitblom, Mann's gentle but
uncomprehending narrator, comments on the birth of a new type of
world, one that will have little use for Leverkühn's solitary mastery:
"No longer is 'the world' embodied in the figure of a shrouded tute-
lary goddess showering priceless symbolic gifts. In her place we have
the international business man and concert agent, naively persistent,
profuse of promises, rebuffed by no reserve, certainly superficial, yet
for all that to me even an engaging type." [61] The subtly parodic skein
that Mann weaves into the texture of his narrative is perhaps a recognition of the coming preeminence of marketers and consumers, men
for whom Leverkühn's godly eminence will seem ridiculously over-
emphatic. Both Mann and Joyce acknowledge the authority of the artist as a godly maker; but both burlesque the idea in order to suggest
the larger ramifications and consequences of a godly vision that extends beyond the view of a single consciousness.

In this light, Albert Camus's defiant experiment in *The Fall* assumes fresh audacity. Mann had speculated that a postwar artist
could depend on neither an audience nor a hearing. Camus's fate was
to watch himself transforming from prophet to pariah for an audience
that had earlier welcomed him as an original talent. And the reason
for Camus's rebuff was his godlike solitary grandeur, a natural grace
that seemed increasingly inapposite to the world that Jean-Paul Sartre
and the staff of *Temps Modernes* saw emerging after 1945. Sartre told
Camus that "you bring a portable altar with you. [You] only accept
those who look at you with bowed heads." [62] Sartre's protégé, Francis
Jeanson, had opened the whole controversy with a blunt essay in
Temps Modernes, a document that is one of the few recorded instances
of a postwar audience issuing a *non serviemus*. Jeanson told Camus
that he viewed history "from on high," through "an abstract subjectivity which did not live events but merely contemplated them. . . .
By adopting the objective tone of a chronicler, of one who is not in the
thick of things, you posed as an Olympian observer. Seen from this
lofty vantage point, the struggles of men could only seem vain, absurd." [63] Jeanson saw Camus as an artist in the tradition of the Flaubert

who had considered entitling *Bouvard and Pécuchet* "The Memoirs of Two Cockroaches." For Jeanson, Camus too reduced history to a sub-species of entomology. Remoteness from events breeds bad faith with an audience: Schlegelian irony seems unsuitable for the world of the concentration camps.

Camus's response in his last novel, *The Fall*, is best seen as his vindication of the wonders of the "lofty vantage point." His narrator, Jean-Baptiste Clamence, becomes Camus's unrepentant spokesman. "You understand what I mean when I spoke of aiming higher. I was only talking, it so happens, of those supreme summits, the only places I can really live. Yes, I have never felt comfortable except in lofty surroundings. Even in the details of daily life, I needed to feel *above.*" [64] From this passage a reader might expect a text of orthodox Schlegelianism. And Clamence's commentary on his own narrative— "I navigate skillfully manipulating distinctions and digressions" (102)—has indeed the familiar tone of self-conscious artifice used for its author's delight.

But in fact the novel swerves toward far different ends, as Camus's narrator daringly restores the earlier mimetic and ethical force of the *topos*. In his solitary arrogance, he tells us, he is made in the likeness of us all. For in a world as unsustaining of mythologies as our own, we have all become our own diminished deities. In such a world, Narcissus, not Zeus, is the presiding eminence. "The portrait I hold out to my contemporaries becomes a mirror" (102). But Clamence presses the recognition further; he wants us to cast off self-admiration for self-scrutiny: "We are in the soup together," he reminds us (103). Even his own eloquence is no more than "the lyricism of the prison cell" (91). Clamence's world is one where only one voice can be heard (his own), but that voice cannot rely on a captive audience: he even must annotate his own Christian name—Jean-Baptiste—for an audience unfamiliar with Scripture. Consequently, Clamence recognizes that his own authority lasts only as long as he speaks; when he *acts*, he returns to the phantasmagorical world of everyone else. In his closing speech, therefore, Clamence dissolves apocalyptic scorn into farcical wryness:

> I grow taller, très cher, I grow taller, I breathe freely, I am on the mountain, the plain stretches before my eyes. How intoxicating to feel like God the Father and to hand out definitive testimonials of bad character and habits. I sit enthroned among my bad angels at the summit of the Dutch heaven and I watch ascending towards me, as they issue from the fogs and the water, the multitude of the Last Judgment. They rise slowly; I already see the first of them

arriving. On his bewildered face, half hidden by a hand, I read
the melancholy of the common condition and the despair of not
being able to escape it. (104–5)

Clamence's highly self-conscious presentation of his Last Judgment, burlesqued and *en travestie*, reduces its authority to that of a
virtuoso performance. No longer, he tells us, can the godly artist victimize the world; instead, he must testify to a mutual victimization
and must therefore display "the melancholy of the common condition
and the despair of not being able to escape it." The wheel has come
full circle; the solitary victimizer has become the representative victim. But the world as we find it in the last pages of *The Fall* is an odd
place, more like Madame Tussaud's than any universe we inhabit.
Similarly, Clamence's scriptural references to Saint John the Baptist
and the Last Judgment have a sort of spectral life about them, as if a
whole world were on the wane. The *deus artifex topos* now testifies to
the disintegration of a world, rather than to its creation. Camus's
godly artist has reopened lines of communication with his audience,
only to demonstrate to them their shared incarceration in an imaginary prison cell. Like so many of the authors who resuscitate the *topos*
in the twentieth century, Camus uses it to explore social conditions
that provide the ultimate denial of its imaginative force. In the twentieth century, the very existence of the godly maker has to be hedged
with paradox and farce.

CHAPTER TWO

The Art of Significant Disorder: The Fiction of Nathanael West

And of what consequence are the evils and the lunatic hours
And the vats of vice in which the city ferments
If some day, from the fog and the veils,
Arises a new Christ, in a sculptured light,
Who lifts humanity toward himself
And baptizes it by the fire of new stars?
                    —Emile Verhaeren, "L'âme de la ville"

The world is an oyster that but waits for hands to open it. Bare
hands are best, but have you any money?
                    —Shagpoke Whipple in *A Cool Million*

I.

Nathanael West's ambitions reveal the fervor and the doubt of the godly maker in a commercial world. Like Emile Verhaeren, he hopes to redeem the secular city with the vision of a "new Christ" who "arises from the fog . . . lifts humanity toward himself and baptizes it by the fire of new stars." Like Shagpoke Whipple, he knows that any redeeming vision is likely to be the means toward fresh expropriation conducted by grasping hands. Accordingly, one of West's greatest fears—voiced repeatedly just before his death—was that his work had been at best only half successful. Very late in his career, he character-ized his fiction as a "peculiar half world which I attempted to create," a description that reveals his diffidence about his procedure and final achievement. West thought that his fiction was unclassifiable, so that he completed a book "only to find nowhere any just understanding of what the book is about—I mean in the sense of tradition, place in scheme, method, etc., etc."[1]

West need not have worried. Since his death the name West has come to mean whatever a commentator wants it to mean. This, at least, is the opinion of Maria Ujházy, who alleges that "critics, with great effort, have managed to purge West's novels of their vital con-tent, their critical realism, and have allegorized and interpreted them

into kinship with the critics' own outlook."[2] Like his own Lemuel
Pitkin, West has been dismantled and reconstituted according to
the ideological persuasions of his commentators. Hence we have the
Jungian West, the Freudian West, the Kierkegaardian West, and even
Ujházy's own critical-realist West.

Such critical strabysmus does West a double disservice, as this
and the next chapter will argue. First, the picture that emerges of West
is a grossly distorted one; instead of the living, breathing author we
have the child of no natural parents described very wittily by Warwick
Wadlington. "One influential critical portrait that has grown over the
years is an intriguing Daumier creation: West as an exotic plant on our
shores whose genus is really the Continental-Decadent-Existentialist
family of literature."[3] The objection to this portrait lies not so much in
the fact that it resembles no author yet sighted on sea or land—
though that is certainly an important objection—but that it totally
overlooks West's own uniqueness and ignores the conditions of the
"peculiar half world" West attempted to create.

The nature of this half world is particularly interesting. West's
drastically curtailed apprenticeship in Dada was followed by his prolonged eyewitness experience of the Great Depression at two of his
father's New York hotels. His period as a Hollywood scriptwriter
brought him into contact with a California that, as Edmund Wilson
acknowledged, has always been a center for American class conflicts.[4]
West's fiction consequently straddles categories that were increasingly
investigated separately by his contemporaries. One of his signal
achievements was to take the modernist cliché of the artist as hero,
where the artist becomes "the higher example of and the only escape
from the common predicament," and return him to the center of experience.[5] Max Schulz has pointed to the dual status of West's artists,
as modernists in aspiration, but illusion makers by profession; out of
that dualism West explored the limits and the potential of the artist as
a godly maker in a commercial world.[6]

This achievement has not yet been given its due critical acknowledgment. Ever since James Light published his pioneering critical biography (*Nathanael West: An Interpretative Study*), West's critics have
generally locked themselves inside their author's head.[7] Although
Light was an incisive critic, the Jungian thrust of his interpretation
had a disastrous effect on the course of West criticism. To watch
Light's insights harden into Freudian orthodoxies, and then expire
into Gnostic obscurity, one need only look at some of Light's successors. Stanley Hyman and Victor Comerchero, who prowl around
the edges of West's fiction in search of a stray neurosis, still report on

a recognizable author; but Harold Bloom, who finds in *Miss Lonely-hearts* "another displaced version of the Miltonic/Romantic crisis-poem" with progenitors in Wordsworth's *The Borderers* and Blake's *Milton*, clearly does not.[8]

But the most shameless—and the most brilliant—psychocritical reading of all belongs to W. H. Auden. Auden's famous essay "West's Disease" begins by pronouncing that West "is not, strictly speaking, a novelist; that is to say, he does not attempt an accurate description either of the social scene or of the subjective life of the mind." Confronted by the seemingly incontrovertible evidence that *Balso Snell* engages precisely with "the subjective life of the mind," Auden displays remarkable resourcefulness. The book, he argues, "adopted the dream convention, but neither the incidents nor the language are credible as a transcription of a real dream."[9] West's real gifts, Auden decides, belong not to fiction but to pathology; his fame rests on his authority in diagnosing the disease to which he gave his name. Just as he had rebuilt Dickens's Dingley Dell as the Garden of Eden, Auden refashions West's environment to suit the needs of his own parable.

Such criticism shrinks more than West's head; it shrinks the size of the fiction too. However, Leslie Fiedler's West promises much more. Fiedler sees West as a fictional innovator who becomes

> the inventor . . . of a peculiarly modern kind of book, whose claims on our credence are perfectly ambiguous. Reading his fiction, we do not know whether we are being presented with a nightmare endowed with the lineaments of reality, or with reality blurred to the uncertainty of a nightmare. In either case, he must be read as a comic novelist, and his anti-heroes understood as comic characters, still as much shlemiels as any imagined by Füchs, though they are presented as sacrificial victims, the only Christs possible in our skeptical world. In West, however, humor is expressed almost entirely in terms of the grotesque, which is to say, on the borderline between jest and horror; for violence is to him technique as well as subject matter.[10]

Although anyone writing on West owes much to Fiedler, some murmurs of dissent are nonetheless in order. First of all, we might question the basis for Fiedler's rigid generic constraints. If we do not know what kind of world West is writing about, if we are uncertain whether it is nightmare or reality, how can we be so sure that "he must be read as a comic novelist"? Fiedler's generic certainties conceal a kind of scholastic disdain for the world in which his author operates. There is something Brahminical about Fiedler's approach to West; this critic enrolls his author in the ranks of genius without making clear the field in which that genius operates. It is all very well to call West "the inventor of a peculiarly modern kind of book," but under what peculiarly modern conditions does West make his innovations?

We are no nearer to an answer to this question after reading Jonathan Raban's essay "A Surfeit of Commodities: The Novels of Nathanael West." [11] Raban's West becomes a commodity to be exploited by all the flotsam of postindustrial society: graduate students, assistant professors, the *PMLA* index, and a host of others not too numerous for Raban to mention. From a sense that West merely looked into his troubled psyche and wrote, we move to the sense that he observed the monuments of trash around him, collated them in verbal form, and then buried himself and his words in them. Such responses are two sides of a common coin that devalue West's role as an artist whose disorder was significant in a way that more perfectly realized works perhaps were not.

At the heart of West's work lies his recognition of the changed relationship between the artist and his society. West's four books show the American economy moving from mass production to the production of illusion. His artists, however, cling to their goal of creating a world, even though the world they wish to create remains only an ideal memory in the America of the Great Depression. By the time West began to publish, the economic prosperity of the 1920s had vanished, leaving only the massive cultural and spiritual disillusionment that Miss Lonelyhearts diagnoses in Delehanty's speakeasy. As he drinks, West's hero reflects that he is one who, like his colleagues, "had believed in literature, had believed in Beauty and in personal expression as an absolute end." And, like them, he believes no longer, and now shares their disgust: "When they lost this belief, they lost everything. Money and fame meant nothing to them. They were not worldly men" (83). The role that they all play now requires them to become "machines for making jokes" (84).

The transformation of the artist from visionary deity to machine for making jokes rounds one crucial arc of West's imagination; the increasing disenchantment of an audience starved by an abundance of illusion completes the circle. West's peculiar half world is one where he becomes progressively more aware of the diminution of his powers and the growing aggression of his audience. Because of this his work reveals acutely—and very early—the kinds of strain that the idea of the artist as a godly maker will encounter in the kind of society where illusion is ubiquitous but unsatisfying. West's own peculiar kind of joking derives from his knowledge that what is happening all around him is hardly funny at all.

II.

West's first novel, *The Dream Life of Balso Snell*, has generally been regarded as a nasty little squib, a juvenile *jeu d'esprit* that West somehow dragged out into his late twenties. Alan Ross, in his introduction to *The Complete Works of Nathanael West*, saw the book as "a sneer in the bathroom mirror at art," an assault that Randall Reid extended to an "attack on all art." [12] It has been usual to acknowledge that West's ambitions exceeded his capacities; Jay Martin, who tactfully suggested that the book grasped "only tentatively" the themes of West's later fiction, shows—for a man dealing with a minor author—exemplary caution here. [13] On the other hand, all the existing evidence shows that West took much trouble with his books—and *Balso Snell* appears to have been no exception. Jack Sanford told James Light that most of the book was known to him as early as 1924, when West entertained him with an early version in a college dormitory. [14] Moreover, from 1927 to 1930, West revised the manuscript repeatedly, even making a very late change of title from *The Journal of Balso Snell* to *The Dream Life of Balso Snell*. The extended genesis of the book, its multiple revisions over a seven-year period, its tonal incongruities, and its strange oscillations between intensity and farce all point less to a *jeu d'esprit* than to a book (and an author) genuinely confused about its own identity.

Some hint of this confusion becomes apparent in the book's opening pages. We are introduced to West's first godly maker, Balso Snell, a lyric poet who has created a whole race of imaginary men. But Balso does not glory in his creation; he shudders at the thought of his *Phoenix Excrementi* because they "eat themselves, digest themselves, and give birth to themselves by evacuating their bowels" (5). Balso's dream life has a disturbingly visceral quality; the inspired man merges, as in *A Tale of a Tub*, with the flatulent man. Balso's imaginary men are as much the limits of his invention as the outcome of it; his shudder acknowledges the unwelcome duality that afflicts his imagination, his dual commitment to vision and profit.

Balso's authority as a godly maker is limited by the aspirations of his creation. As Balso tours his own interiors, he confronts truths he would rather not acknowledge: the contradictory impulses behind his own goals; the belatedness of his own imaginative life (so much a rescrambling of his own reading, so little the result of any genuine invention); the small margin that separates artistic self-assertion from simple violence. In the face of all this, the lyric poet and godly maker takes on the form of George F. Babbitt. "Stop sniffing mortality. . . . Eat more meat" (13), he tells Maloney the Areopagite, as the philistine stares down the martyr. West uses the dream journey and burlesque forms to explore the contradictory impulses in his own aesthetic and moral makeup. His own sense of the moral purpose of art (something West was never to overlook) can only emerge in Balso's leaden clichés; his own highly literary form of religious conviction has its bizarre reflection in the creation of Maloney and Gilson, a pair of dime-store martyrs. The journey begins as a structural device but gradually discovers an ethical purpose: through the journey West can make one side of his imagination talk to another, so that the angst-ridden young man can confront the dishonest commodity broker.

Balso's first guide hails him as "an ambassador from that ingenious people, the inventors and perfectors of the automatic water closet," a salutation that rams together Henry James's superior consciousness and Thomas Crapper's superior technology. Perhaps warming to these interdisciplinary fusions, Balso's guide now blends Hellenic classicism and Poe's romanticism in a somewhat aborted tribute to Balso's dual heritage as a child of Europe and the Americas, "My people are the heirs of Greece and Rome. As your own poet has so well put it, 'The Grandeur that was Greece and the Glory that was Rome'" (6).

Balso's mixed origins beget a mixed art. The book continually darts between high aspirations and low consequences, so that it blends farce and high symbolism in a fashion that troubles even its protagonists. Balso cannot be sure whether he is voyageur or tourist; wherever he goes he finds commerce ousting culture, as the commercialization of art steadily deteriorates into the corruption of art. In the *anus mirabilis* everyman is an artist. "The wooden horse," Balso realizes, "was inhabited solely by writers in search of an audience." Balso's reaction to this shows the competitive chain response this situation sets off. "He hit Miss McGeeney a terrific blow in the gut." If another story had to be told, "he would tell it" (36–37). Stripped of his special privileges, the American godly maker becomes a competitor amid a system of self-enhancing fictions; his task is to assert his authority, something he must do through violence rather than vision.

All art in *Balso Snell* tends to soliloquy in design, victimization in method, and mass circulation in distribution. Because artists must attract attention to survive, their means must become correspondingly elaborate. Maloney's flea, Gilson's precocity, Miss McGeeney's collapsible box of biographies—these are tertiary industries rather than contributions to the world of letters. But they are, as George Mowry's

The Urban Nation shows us, an accurate reflection of American writing in the 1920s, which fed a public increasingly ravenous for life in the raw an endless diet of biography, or rehashed romanticism.[15] Gradually, West's book takes on the appearance of a novelization of "Tradition and the Individual Talent," with Balso hurled from specimen to specimen, each one a testimony to a half-digested art.

The artists in *Balso Snell* behave like spoiled suburban pets, biting the hands that uncomprehendingly feed them. Art is transformed into anxiety as Gilson is attacked by "a fear so large that I felt I could not contain it without rupturing my mind" (21); Beagle Darwin wants to wrap his predicament round him, until he can snuggle into it, "letting it cover me completely"; Balso himself retreats into his less complicated youth, which in turn dissolves into his career-conscious present. Such art is always closer to hysteria than inspiration, the product of artists who can only becalm themselves by removal to the margins of experience. The case of John Gilson, an Olympian whose top-floor Schlegelian eyrie shelters a man just as remote from human sympathies, is typical here. Gilson's art insulates him from his own mother, whose grief he can then work up as material: "My mother visited me today. She cried. It is she who is crazy. Order is the test of sanity. Her emotions and thoughts are disordered. Mine are arranged, valued, placed" (14).

From a sardonic recycling of the works of other hands, the book turns to a recycling of its own structural devices, as if to confess that so massive a consumption of culture as that conducted in this novel inevitably accelerates the exhaustion of all resources but its own. Balso's journey through the *anus mirabilis* is reworked as Beagle's to Paris; Gilson's tyranny over his mother becomes Beagle's over Janey Davenport; Gilson's introversion becomes Darwin's lyrical drama; Balso's earlier recognition of the basically hostile relationship between artists and audiences (21–22) is reshaped into Gilson's Wildean parable, which in turn has been filched from Chekhov: "It would be more profitable [writes Chekhov] for the farmer to raise rats for the granary than for the bourgeois to nourish the artist, who must always be occupied with undermining institutions. In case the audience should misunderstand and align itself on the side of the artist, the ceiling of the theatre will be made to open and cover the occupants with tons of loose excrement. After the deluge, if they so desire, the patrons of my art can gather in the customary charming groups and discuss the play" (30). No wonder Balso Snell shudders; his *Phoenix Excrementi* are always on the point of returning to their original material. The parable

that Beagle composes emphasizes once more the impotence of the artist; however heinous his devices, his patrons will "gather in the customary charming groups and discuss the play."

If art for a commercial audience becomes degraded art, what of
the artist? The soliloquies of Gilson and Beagle Darwin reveal the nature of the artist's inner world. Both these artists have become deliv-
erers of voids that are always threatening to consume them first, as
Gilson's narrative discloses: "My imagination is a wild beast that cries
always for freedom. I am continually tormented by the desire to indulge some strange thing, perceptible but indistinct, hidden in the
swamps of my mind. The hidden thing is always crying out to me
from its hiding-place 'Do as I tell you and you will find out my shape.
There, quick! what is that thing in your brain? Indulge my commands
and some day the great doors of your mind will swing open and allow
you to enter and handle to your complete satisfaction the vague shapes
and figures hidden there'" (16).

When the imagination takes on the shape of an emporium, its
doors swinging open to allow easy access, what is left for West's artists
but to take to trade themselves? Accordingly, the artists Balso encounters occupy themselves alternately with lofty aspirations and financial
transactions. Maloney the Areopagite blends his unearthly interests
with a desire to strike a hard bargain. He is, he tells Balso, occupied
with "the biography of Saint Puce. If you are interested, I will give you
a short précis of his life" (10). The summary, we have no doubt, will be
shrewdly marketed. Similarly, Miss McGeeney, "a middle aged woman
dressed in a mannish suit" (32), is conducting a number of projects,
including a literary biography and "a novel in the manner of Richard-
son." John Gilson, disturbingly precocious as well as murderous, becomes almost predatory when he hears of Balso's magazine: "Maybe
you run a magazine," he ponders. Would Balso perhaps buy his journal? "I need money" (23). The reason for his avarice is very revealing.
"I'm fed up with poetry and art. Yet what can I do? I need women and
because I can't buy or force them, I have to make poems for them. God
knows how tired I am of using the insanity of Van Gogh and the adventures of Gauguin as can-openers for the ambitious Count Six-
Times. And how sick I am of literary bitches. But they're the only kind
that'll have me. . . . Listen Balso, for a dollar I'll sell you a brief outline
of my position" (23–24).

Gilson's head is a crematorium for postromantic styles. He houses
jaded aestheticism, the embers of the decadence, the ashes of Nietz-
schean hyperbole, and a few stray live coals of Russian fiction. All of

this to seduce women he hates. Similarly, Beagle Darwin's script for Janey Davenport reveals a revulsion for the very audience his career so sedulously courts. In this way, the book reflects its extended period of composition. It is the work of a precocious ingenu who has also studied the market, a man already tired of artistic milieus even before he has gained a foothold in them. And it is also the work of a man who knows that a godly maker in a commercial society cannot expect to have too much control of his own creation.

III.

West's insight into the dwindling control of the godly maker over a mass audience is extended and modified in *Miss Lonelyhearts*. In this book, the godly maker's authority over his audience becomes the crucial issue. An important context for the novel is the diminishing power of religious values to maintain a purchase on American lives, a pattern that, during the course of the 1920s, became increasingly apparent. By degrees, religion was able to ensure its audience only by borrowing from the stock of business. Bruce Barton's corporate Christ, with his twelve hand-picked fellow executives, and Elbert Hubbard, for whom Moses became a self-appointed "ad-writer for Deity," are only the most outstanding examples of the drift toward a secularized religion.[16] One of the principal surrogates for religion is provided by Miss Lonelyhearts's main competitor, Willie Shrike, who, as *Post-Dispatch* editor, has staffed his newspaper with creatures made in his own image and likeness. In this way, Willie can supply the mass therapy that religion has always provided and become a deity in his own right.

It is important to note, however, that Shrike is not the book's only secularized artist-deity. Miss Lonelyhearts himself has substituted the God of the symbolist poets for the God of Israel, a substitution that means he no longer speaks the language of the masses he hopes to redeem. When he and Shrike compete for the mass audience whose grievances turn up on Miss Lonelyhearts's desk every day, each of them identically deprived and identically inarticulate, the advantage is decisively Shrike's, since Shrike is a master of eloquence while Miss Lonelyhearts is at best an ironic visionary. (It is as if Wallace Stevens were competing with Chuck Barris.) Miss Lonelyhearts employs a visionary language drained of religious content and conviction, so that his position is at least two removes from his audience's desires. If his symbolist predispositions are untranslatable to a mass audience, the language of his Baptist childhood and Puritan past is equally incomprehensible to a public nurtured on the visual delights of *Picture Post* and *Blonde Beauty*.

Like Balso Snell before him, Miss Lonelyhearts awakens to find himself in a world completely alien to his assumptions. Even his appearance belongs elsewhere: "Although his cheap clothes had too much style, he still looked like the son of a Baptist minister. A beard would become him, would accent his Old-Testament look. But even without a beard no one could fail to recognize the New England Puritan" (69). Since he belongs to a people that saw God's design as revealed in the landscape, Miss Lonelyhearts repeatedly examines his environment for signs of salvation. What he finds, however, are marks of urban woe or his own exhaustion. A Puritan-trained introspection leads him to question the purpose of his professional duties, so that instead of fulfilling his occupational role as a spiritual accountant, balancing his books on the right side of misery, he spends his time scrutinizing large blank cards or granite columns in an attempt to read God's design into the structure of urban life.

If nature imposed on Miss Lonelyhearts his godly mission, nurture encouraged him to convert this errand into art. His sources for inspiration are Dostoevsky, not the Bible; stained-glass windows, not Cotton Mather. What balks this city Puritan is not the inauthenticity of his desires (like Barth's Ebenezer Cooke, whom in many ways he resembles, Miss Lonelyhearts seems almost incorrigibly sincere); rather, the problem is that the sources of his spiritual inspiration seem too literary for the audience they are designed to convert. Miss Lonelyhearts's God, the God of Rimbaud and Dostoevsky, is far too recondite to meet the claims of the "sick of it all" and the "desperate" who write to him at the *Post-Dispatch*. His very vision is based on metaphor and symbol: when Broad-Shoulders corresponds with him, she ends her letter with a pathetically literal postscript: "Dear Miss Lonelyhearts, dont think I am broad shouldered but that is the way I feel about life and me I mean" (121). How can a visionary like Miss Lonelyhearts work with an audience for whom metaphor is incomprehensible?

Willie Shrike, feature editor of the *Post-Dispatch* and the book's second godly artist, shows how. Shrike is the forerunner of all those postwar nominalists who, like Barth's Burlingame or Elkin's God Almighty, see language as a means of self-promotion. Like Elkin's God in *The Living End*, Shrike uses human beings as counters in a game he conducts for his own delight. Like Henry Burlingame in *The Sot-Weed Factor*, Shrike has a ventriloquist's gift for parody and can range through chauvinism, art-cant, success story, and religious enthusiasm. Just as Balso's godly creation dissolved in the waste matter of the *anus mirabilis*, so Miss Lonelyhearts's godly mission withers in the face of Shrike's corrosive burlesque.

Shrike's most hysterical outbursts are carefully scripted bids to consolidate his own authority. Miss Farkis's pretentious reference to Aquinas is a cue unlikely enough to make Shrike's entrance all the more effective:

> "St. Thomas!" he shouted. "What do you take us for— stinking intellectuals? We're not fake Europeans. We were discussing Christ, the Miss Lonelyhearts of Miss Lonelyhearts. America has her own religions. If you need a synthesis, here is the kind of material to use." He took a clipping from his wallet and slapped it on the bar.
> ADDING MACHINE USED IN RITUAL OF WESTERN SECT . . . (73)

Shrike's mastery is based on his awareness that like mathematics the newspaper business has only a notional relationship with reality. It computes misery—it does not remedy it. It is no surprise that Shrike's speeches are littered throughout with references to Mussolini and the Renaissance princes. In a world where Miss Lonelyhearts's agony column makes daily testimony to the failure of the family, it is the newspaper men who control and mold public consciousness into an orderly shape. The period in which *Miss Lonelyhearts* was written was the age of the Hearsts and Luces, and Shrike has all the fervor of this era, but none of the faith.[17] On the subject of faith, he is uncompromisingly nihilistic. Some of his most abrasive scorn is directed at religion: "I am a great saint, I can walk on my own water. Haven't you heard of Shrike's Passion in the Luncheonette, or the Agony in the Soda Fountain?" (74). Shrike does himself an injustice: his own *Post-Dispatch* performs the miracle of changing misery into nonsense every day of the year.

West makes clear that Shrike's mastery of words is only part of the mastery he enjoys as editor. It is not enough for him that his constituency comes from the anonymous millions who read his paper while Miss Lonelyhearts's sole and uncomprehending audience is May and Peter Doyle. Shrike's artistry requires public acknowledgment just as surely as Miss Lonelyhearts's dream life shirks it. This is why Shrike persists in employing an apparently catatonic agony columnist; he hopes that the private griefs endured so openly by his employee will, by their absurd extremity, become public benefits for his organization. The aim of Shrike's party game "Everyman his own Miss Lonelyhearts" is to intensify his own control, to extend it over reality as well as over language. He wants to enact once and for all the impossibility of the Miss Lonelyhearts dream, to show once and for all that in the real world it can never succeed. Once again, Shrike's burlesque is promiscuous in its range, yoking New England allegory to Marxist exhortation and annihilating both in the free play of language and performance. "A young boy wants a violin. It looks simple; all you have to do is get the kid one. But then you discover that he has dictated the letter to his little sister. He is paralyzed and can't even feed himself. He has a toy violin and hugs it to his chest, imitating the sound of playing with his mouth. How pathetic! However, one can learn much from this parable. Label the boy Labor, the violin Capital, and so on" (134). Indirectly, Shrike's allegory also cocks its snook at art; for the boy imitating a violin will become Tod Hackett, imitating a siren at the end of *The Day of the Locust*. Art itself cannot thrive in the kind of supply and demand system that underpins Shrike's control.

For the moment, however, Shrike's immediate target is Miss Lonelyhearts. Shrike's party game is designed to lock him further inside his own head; Shrike himself has blocked off all the exits in a bold piece of living theater. In the guise of a diversion, Shrike secures his employee's isolation, and, indeed, after this game Miss Lonelyhearts, like an outmaneuvered king, resigns from a reality he had initially hoped to control.

Shrike's vocabulary and gestures contaminate the world of the novel. His office is populated by a flock of Shrikelets. His assistant editor, Goldsmith, and his anonymous copy boy, have modeled themselves after their chief, even to the point where they, like their chief, see the end product of the *Post-Dispatch* as *stuff*, a term that all three offer to Miss Lonelyhearts as a measure of their contempt for his activities on the agony column. Goldsmith too has internalized Shrike's professed goal as an editor; he recognizes that his aim is to increase "the circulation of the paper" (98). And when Miss Lonelyhearts finds his colleagues lurking in Delehanty's, all huddled around one all-purpose dirty joke, he is reminded that the great imitator has his own imitators: "Like Shrike, the man they imitated, they were machines for making jokes. A button machine makes buttons, no matter what the power used, foot, steam, or electricity. They, no matter what the motivating force . . . made jokes" (84). The verbal domination that Shrike exerts in the world of *Miss Lonelyhearts* demonstrates the extent to which that world has been subordinated to the resourceful artifice of its chief illusion controller. The godly maker who prevails in *Miss Lonelyhearts*, like the godly maker of John Hawkes's later novel *The Cannibal*, becomes simply the most convincing liar, the man whose language has the most arbitrary relationship with reality.

Confronted by a milieu of exhausted spiritual resources, where power is in the hands of word machines like Shrike, Miss Lonelyhearts gradually withdraws from action and event. His life and his Christ-dream merge, with the result that he becomes a thing who imagines rather than a man who suffers: "He was conscious of two rhythms that were slowly becoming one. When they became one, his identification with God was complete. His heart was the one heart, the heart of God. And his brain was likewise God's. God said, 'Will you accept it, now?' And he replied, 'I accept, I accept.' He immediately began to plan a new life and his future conduct as Miss Lonelyhearts. He submitted drafts of his column to God and God approved them. God approved his every thought" (139).

West's hero had begun with two separate identities existing in uneasy tension. Part New England Puritan, part symbolist seer, Miss Lonelyhearts had wanted to reconcile the moral purpose of the former with the imaginative intensity of the latter. But now these shadow worlds move together, sealing him in a tomblike fantasy of his own design. He becomes morbidly conscientious, repeatedly submitting his columns to God, and God sees that his workmanship is good. In other words, he has managed the seer's transcendence without the seer's unnerving ecstasies; he now clambers inside his own skull, like a mental missionary.

Like Shrike and his cronies (only "machines for making jokes"), like Mrs Doyle (who resembles a giant, life-sized Miss Lonelyhearts letter), West's hero has become reified; he is now a rock rather than a redeemer. Unfortunately for Miss Lonelyhearts, however, his godliness is as self-guaranteeing and self-elected as a symbolist play, and it can no longer even look at the difficulties it was designed to resolve. When it does encounter one of them, in the form of Peter Doyle, who stands enraged with a cuckold's jealousy on Miss Lonelyhearts's doorstep, it is annihilated. Miss Lonelyhearts can survive as a godly artist only for as long as no one else appears in his world; this is not too encouraging for a man whose ancestors were Puritans on a godly errand.

IV.

In *Miss Lonelyhearts*, we watch the authority of the godly maker shift from Miss Lonelyhearts to Willie Shrike. In Shrike's hands the world becomes a resource for a language that consistently bedazzles and defrauds its audience. Consequently, in *A Cool Million*, where the world of Shrike is the sole reality, burlesque and parody, which had vied for control in *Miss Lonelyhearts* with vision and symbol, become both the means and the end of existence. The book's parodic resources are endless: Horatio Alger, *Candide*, leftist agitprop, Oswald Spengler, and Calvin Coolidge are all inserted into the burlesque machinery. But in a sense, the supply of parody has to be endless; for the America of the Great Depression (which is the novel's location) has nothing to reproduce but its own illusions. *A Cool Million* is the precursor of a whole series of books—Elkin's *George Mills*, Coover's *The Universal Baseball Association*, Barthelme's *Snow White*—where art becomes a matter of godly ubiquity rather than godly authority.

Perhaps the book's novelty is the explanation for its poor reception. The observation made by one contemporary critic—"Funny in spots, but there are not enough spots"—stands for many. Not surprisingly, Jay Martin reports that by 1935 the book had found its way to the remainder shelves, where it sold for twenty-five cents.[18] To West, who had planned the book carefully and who considered it an improvement on *Miss Lonelyhearts*, such responses must have been demoralizing.

The book's unfavorable reception may have been due to a simple misunderstanding of its self-created conventions. *A Cool Million* is not, granted, "gravymashpotato realism" like *McTeague* or *Maggie*; but it is, in style and content, entirely suited to a society where illusions are more abundant than gravy and mashed potatoes. In it, we watch the creation of illusion assume the status of a major industry, one that reaches beyond art into commerce, real estate, and, by the end of the novel, even politics. Quite remorselessly, *A Cool Million* turns the clichés of business-class America on their heads. The fluid mobility of American society, so basic an article of faith for business-class apologists in this period, becomes in *A Cool Million* a sort of nationwide vagrancy, so that the Republic begins to look like Burkina Faso (Upper Volta). Mrs. Pitkin's authentically colonial home, for example, becomes a business opportunity for Asa Goldstein, whose "Colonial Exteriors and Interiors" can only be boosted by so handsome an acquisition. Immediately, Mrs. Pitkin's home becomes a mobile one; Goldstein dismantles the residence and moves it to New York. West's novel is underway.

Like all West's heroes, Lemuel Pitkin—whose name, T. R. Steiner tells us, means "belonging to God"—belongs most of all to the past.[19] His naive desire to win back the home he was born in translates into a career of artifice, illusion, and deceit, culminating in his final apotheosis as martyred hero for a new political regime controlled by Shagpoke Whipple. Lem Pitkin is certainly mobile—he performs as stooge, hero, unwitting jewel thief, gold prospector, and agitator—but mobility on this scale constitutes self-dereliction. And sure enough, there remains little of Lem left at the end of the book and none of him at all by the time Shagpoke has recreated him in a mendacious epitaph. Moreover, such mobility (or such chaos) is characteristic of the America West describes in *A Cool Million*. From the unforgettable Goldstein, who tears around in coach and horses, to Wu Fong, whose brothel is by turns colonial and international, to Sylvanus Snodgrasse, whose lyre is tuned with hymns to heroic America one day and lamentations on American atrocities the next, right down to Shagpoke Whipple, whose orbit takes him from the Salvation Army canteen to the White House, there is not a character in the book whose fortunes do not hinge on rapid mobility. But mobility of this Defoe-like magnitude points more to social disintegration than individual opportunity, since it comes to imply that reality, like wealth, is essentially negotiable. The world is, in the gospel according to Shagpoke Whipple, "an oyster that but waits for hands to open it. Bare hands are best, but have you any money?" (149).

It is therefore all the more important for those in pursuit of power to discover some potent image that will consolidate their bid. This search occupies much of the novel. Chief Satinpenny inspires his Indians with visions taken from Spengler, not Manitou; Shagpoke Whipple prophesies a middle-class revolt to his audience of down-and-outs at the Salvation Army; Sylvanus Snodgrasse reads his epic of American heroism as his accomplices pick pockets. None of these images quite fit their audiences; they are essentially short-term expedients rather than lasting symbols. But they do point to a felt need in a society whose economic exhaustion has made political manipulation all the more imperative.

In this light, Lem's career is exemplary. He undertakes the archetypal journey, like Melville's Pierre before him, from rural America to the heart of the city, and is accordingly bilked on his arrival. Following these events, Lem's roles are constantly shifting—from hero to booby, from honest broker to unwitting illusionist: it as if one man were playing Miss Lonelyhearts and Willie Shrike simultaneously. But when the fictions of America collide—as secret policemen battle with Shagpoke's unemployed army—the ensuing friction erodes a little of Lem. Like Hawthorne's Holgrave, Lem's roles are enormously dispersed: from Elmer Hainey, he learns how to follow a script; from Zachary Coates, he learns how to put that talent to political purposes. But all this learning only increases Lem's stupor; the simple soul of the beginning of the novel has become an idiot by its end.

This is all to the good, since the tasks required of Lem become progressively less demanding. In a parodic reversal of the tribute to the career of the self-made man paid in Benjamin Franklin's *Autobiography* or Henry Ford's *Moving Forward*, Lem's identity becomes increasingly a commodity to be manufactured by other people. For Elmer Hainey, Lem must become Mr. Hazleton, and, as Mr. Hazleton, must play his part to the letter. "One more thing," he said, shaking hands at the door, "you may be a little mystified when you read your instructions, but that cannot be helped, for I am unable to give you a complete explanation at this time. However, I want you to know that I own a glass eye factory, and that your duties are part of a sales-promotion campaign" (195). Lem's instructions include the directive that "the slightest deviation on the part of Mr. Hazleton from the prescribed formula must be reported." According to all the authorities—the business-class mythmakers from Alger to Ford—Lem's independence should now increase; instead, even to play a minor part in the success of other people, Lem himself must become more and more a machine that takes orders.

When he stumbles, blind and crippled, into the Golden Gates Employment Bureau, Lem has at last reached the right track for heroism. For he is now inserted into a travestied *Oedipus Rex*. "You almost didn't get the job," Mr. Gates went on, when he had had enough of the mutilated boy's gratitude. "There was a guy in here who heard Moe Riley talking to me, and we had some time preventing him from poking out one of his eyes so that he could qualify for the job. We had to call a cop" (247). Once again, everyone is watching everyone else in this America of illusionists and secret agents. Yet Lem's extreme dismemberment enables him to triumph; it would be hard for the competition, even blinded, to match Lem's wooden leg and false teeth. The oblique allusion to *Oedipus Rex* points to the sorry decline in the status of heroism. Sophocles's hero had maimed himself on attaining tragic self-knowledge; many centuries later, in Depression America, self-maiming becomes the price of survival itself. Suffering defined the classical hero, but for the Lem whose "mental reactions has been slowed by the hardships he had suffered, and it was a heart-rending sight to watch him as he bent over a newspaper to spell the headlines. More than this he could not manage," suffering will dehumanize rather than ennoble. Stripped of dignity and clothing, Lem's nightly performance ends with him being hit over the head "with a wooden mallet labeled 'The Works'" (250).

Throughout the novel, West has shown America as straining for violence. Its heroes are all men of violence; even its stereotypes—like

the Pike County man—are sadistic. Lem's own apotheosis occurs because of Whipple's keen sense of the possibilities of exploiting his role
for military purposes. Unable to shake free of his great taskmaster's
eye, Lem receives a speech written by Shagpoke Whipple himself. As
has been arranged with Zachary Coates, Lem rises to deliver it; within
seconds he is shot and reborn as "Commander Pitkin" in a song composed by Whipple:

> "Who dares?"—this was L. Pitkin's cry,
> As striding on the Bijou stage he came—
> "Surge out with me in Shagpoke's name,
> To live for him, for him to die!"
> A million hands flung up reply,
> A million voices answered, "I!"
>
> Chorus
>
> A million hearts for Pitkin, oh!
> To live and die with Pitkin, oh!
> To live and fight with Pitkin, oh!
> Marching for Pitkin. (253–54)

The violent impulses of Americans have been encased in uniforms;
Shagpoke's triumph, having managed this, is ensured. But the Pitkin
anthem measures the extent to which Shagpoke has swerved from the
truth in the construction of his master symbol. We note first of all that
"striding" is pitching things a bit high, since Lemuel was, at this
point, physically incapable of such an action. Moreover, Lem had
scarcely spoken on stage, except to excuse himself in front of a mob-
like audience that had been anything but transfixed by his presence.
The song fuses all this dissonance into a celebration of social unity
that extends from hero to masses. Martyred, trapped in art like a
quail in aspic, Lem becomes the only godly artist in West who actually
captures the mass audience courted by Miss Lonelyhearts or Tod
Hackett. But he is not a godly maker; rather, dismantled and then
transformed, Lem has been manufactured to fit the political ambitions of Shagpoke Whipple.

V.

The stink of death permeates *The Day of the Locust*. West's original
title for the book, *The Cheated*, had indicated its lines of continuity
with *A Cool Million* as an anatomy of a society betrayed by its illusions. But a series of interesting letters that West wrote while composing the book indicates that West too considered himself one of the

cheated. To Scott Fitzgerald he confessed, "My books meet no needs except my own," a sentiment he also expressed to George Milburn, to whom he wrote that "the only people who seem to like [my books] are other writers." At the same time, he told Edmund Wilson of his sensation of belonging nowhere: "The radical press . . . doesn't like [my work], and thinks it even Fascist sometimes, and the literature boys, whom I detest, detest me in turn. The highbrow press finds that I avoid the important things and the lending library touts in the daily press think me shocking." [20]

Perhaps this was the frame of mind that led to his choice of title. For the focus of the title now shifts from satire to apocalypse, from the everyday fact of swindling to the revenge of an ignored god. In Exodus 10:1–11, Moses and Aaron threaten Pharaoh that the Lord "shall cover the face of the earth" with locusts unless he allows the Hebrews to worship Yahweh. In Revelation 9:3–10, the locusts will threaten "only those men who have not the seal of God upon their foreheads." Taken together, the two scriptural allusions threaten men and land alike, a threat that West's novel appears to fulfill to the utmost in a book that, through its sly but insistent omniscience and its gradual way of distancing itself from its protagonist, comes to take on the shape of a work composed by a slighted godly maker.

West's novel opens on a land that has already been blasted. His California is not as Maybelle Loomis sees it, "a paradise on earth," but a place where "death comes from eating dead things" (360, 362). People come there to die, Tod Hackett thinks. But are they dead already? On a Hollywood lot, Tod sees "a Greek temple dedicated to Eros." Meanwhile, "the god himself lay face downward in a pile of old newspapers and bottles" (352). At Claude Estee's party, Tod discovers "a dead horse, or, rather, a life-size, realistic reproduction of one" (274). In California, art has become compelled by the desire to imitate either that which is not or that which is no longer. Claude Estee makes his body an extension of the make-believe he creates in his art, and teeters "back and forth . . . like a Civil War colonel and made believe he had a large belly." But in fact "he had no belly at all" (271). The pattern repeats itself as if it were a prototype. Earle Shoop pretends to be a cowboy; Abe Kusich sees himself as a giant among dwarves; Tod himself conceives of himself as an American Goya.

Artists imitate negation; nonartists imitate artists. The most efficient imitator of a work of art is probably Faye Greener. And Faye is an invitation to destruction: "If you threw yourself on her," Tod muses, "it would be like throwing yourself from the parapet of a skyscraper. You would do it with a scream. You couldn't expect to rise again"

(271). Faye's utter incapacity to act becomes the spur, not the check, to her pursuit of fame. Unable to perform, Faye makes herself into a work of art, vacant but appealing, a blank that many artists will lust to occupy, like Barth's Jeannine Mack forty years later: "None of them really heard her. They were all too busy watching her smile, laugh, shiver, whisper, grow indignant, cross and uncross her legs, stick out her tongue, widen and narrow her eyes, toss her head so that her platinum hair splashed against the red plush of the chair back. . . . It worked that night; no one even thought of laughing at her. The only move they made was to narrow their circle about her" (387). Faye's art consists of a few physical gestures stripped down to activate a predictable response. It is a method that Marilyn Monroe was to perfect in the 1950s. Yet the dangers of such pared-down efficiency are obvious. As the circle narrows around the starlet, the artist becomes quarry and her audience restless hunters. The obvious analogy is to a blood sport.

In the case of Harry Greener, West shows the capacity of art to victimize even itself. Donald Torchiana has suggested that in Harry "life and art converge," a proposition we might wish to modify.[21] Harry's career shows, rather, the convergence of death and art, a convergence insisted upon throughout the book. Harry carries everywhere with him a cutting describing a vaudeville performance with "The Flying Lings," a family of acrobats whose art becomes increasingly self-absorbed as Harry's becomes increasingly self-annihilating. Toward the end of his act, the *Sunday Times* clipping says, Harry "shows his mettle by finishing his dull story in a recumbent position. When he stands up, the audience, which failed to laugh at his joke, laughs at his limp, so he continues lame" (283). Harry's cutting prophesies his subsequent career in Hollywood: the writer predicts that "Mr. Greener, like certain humble field plants which die when transferred to richer soil, had better be left to bloom in vaudeville" (284). The appearance of a natural metaphor in a life so utterly devoted to bad art momentarily startles us; when we reread it, we are shocked that a prediction offered so offhandedly can be so accurate. Another horror of West's fiction, this: only the unthinking and callous can get it right.

Deprived of his art, Harry peddles it indirectly, as a shoe-polish vendor. His aim in this operation is to get "his man where he wanted him." This he secures, however, by artistic performances over which he has progressively less control: "Harry couldn't stop. He was really sick. . . . Suddenly, like a mechanical toy that had been over wound, something snapped inside of him and he began to spin through his entire repertoire. The effort was purely muscular, like the dance of a paralytic. He jigged, juggled his hat, made believe he had been kicked, tripped, and shook hands with himself. He went through it all in one dizzy spasm, then reeled to the couch and collapsed" (300–301). Without the approval any artist craves, Harry turns his life into a burlesqued victimization. Even the lethal performance he un- wittingly switches on for Homer can only be costed: "He should be able to get five dollars out of the big dope" is all he can think as he recovers from the act that has almost killed him (301).

From the moment Harry moves toward Hollywood, his career points only to his own extinction. If the sum of Harry's performances accelerates his movement toward death, his death, in turn, begets an- other endless series of performances, from the tasteful stage manage- ment of Mrs. Johnson to the clownish interventions of the Gingos, who "moved down the centre aisle of the chapel, bowing and waving to everyone, until they reached the front row" (348). Even Tod gets in on the act; overwhelmed by Faye's beauty, he rails instead at her moral- ity, shouting at her "like a YMCA lecturer on sex hygiene" (346). From his back seat in the everlasting auditorium, Harry can laugh at this fumbled business; every one of these performances is a travesty.

All art is recruited for this universal burlesque. The *Bach Chorale* summons a god who fails to arrive, on which it delights in its own deliciousness, spurning reality for its own self-contemplation. But all this comes to a halt with the intervention of Mrs. Johnson, who can- not allow artistic vision to supplant the proper graveside manner:

> "Now come, O our Saviour," the music begged. Gone was its diffidence and no longer was it polite. Its struggle with the bass had changed it. Even a hint of a threat crept in and a little impatience. Of doubt, however, [Tod] could not detect the slightest trace. . . . impatience disappeared. The treble soared free and tri- umphant and the bass no longer struggled to keep it down. It had become a rich accompaniment. "Come or don't come," the music seemed to say, "I love you and my love is enough." It was a simple statement of fact, neither cry nor serenade, made without ar- rogance or humility.
>
> Perhaps Christ heard. If He did, He gave no sign. The atten- dants heard, for it was their cue to trundle on Harry in his box. Mrs. Johnson followed close behind and saw to it that the casket was properly placed. She raised her hand and Bach was silenced in the middle of a phrase. (349)

Art begins as a cry for God, of the kind that lyric poet Balso Snell had perhaps uttered before inventing his race of imaginary men. Such

a cry going unanswered, art begins its self-asserted path toward fulfillment, taking a Schlegelian delight in its own powers. Tod himself had
based his "Burning of Los Angeles" on this belief in the self-elected
powers of art and, for a time, Bach's *Chorale* glows with the same kind
of magic, basking in its own self-created halo. But when Mrs. Johnson
intervenes, Bach is silenced; the mortician gives command, and all art
ceases. In effect, art shifts from hallowed testimony to neverending
concert turn, where it must perform its piece and be replaced by another act. Where art is ubiquitous, its authority is negated; what remains are a series of increasingly empty performances, from the sani-
tized banalities of Mrs. Johnson to the oafish showmanship of the
Gingos. Tod's art, which aspires to the condition of soliloquy in a milieu of tragic farce, testifies to the artist's recurrent compulsion to become a god. But Tod himself must participate in the shoddy musical
chairs at Harry's funeral; having forfeited his distance, he must join
the clowns.

Harry Greener had in fact acted as a foil for Tod's career. West
introduces Tod to us as a complicated young man who possesses "a
whole set of personalities, one inside the other like a nest of Chinese
boxes" (260). He comes to Hollywood from Yale, where his art had
been jeopardized by a common tendency "toward illustration or mere
handsomeness" (261). That tendency had been fine for his classmates;
but Tod aspires to the art of the visionary satirist, which is why he
conceives of his canvas "The Burning of Los Angeles" as a work drawing on his Hollywood experience and his Yale education. He wants to
create the visual equivalent of Eliot's *Waste Land*, an urban satire bristling with painterly allusions to a multinational tradition that incor-
porates Daumier, Goya, Salvator Rosa, and Monsu Desiderio. Such a
work will make a second Jeremiah of Tod, who will become artist-
prophet to a burning Hollywood.

But West's apocalyptic design consumes even his artist. He draws
Tod into the web that Tod had hoped to capture in art by forcing him
into the pursuit of Faye Greener. From this point, Tod is lost in a chase
where he is inferior to ignorant Earle Shoop in attractiveness and inferior to Homer Simpson in available resources. The pattern of the book
shows Tod as losing what little power he began with. When the apocalypse he has long imagined actually begins, he does not play the part
he had anticipated. On canvas, Tod had been at the head of the mob;
in reality, he becomes a struggling bystander, unable to rescue Homer
Simpson however hard he tries, and only marginally helpful to a
young girl he discovers being sexually assaulted in the scuffle. At the
end of the book, far from orchestrating the great masters in a timeless

art, he stabs ineffectually at the air in a way that suggests he has finally been drawn completely into an illusion he thought he was creating from his own head: "To make his escape still more complete he
stood on a chair and worked at the flames in an upper corner of the
canvas, modeling the tongues of fire so that they licked even more avidly at a corinthian column that held up the palm leaf of a nutburger
stand" (420). A prophet must have a tribe; Tod now blends with his,
and the people who came to Hollywood to die fuse with the artist
who came to Hollywood to create a new kind of art.

As Tod quits his imaginary canvas to imitate a police siren, the
artist deserts vision for function. The end of *Day of the Locust* reveals
no godly maker; the only god left is the unseen Dr. Know-All Pierce-
All, an absent deity for a world about to expire. Perhaps West himself
is this novel's god; if so, he remains a *deus absconditus*.

West's fiction shows us a *topos* being dissolved into its social context. His artists have godly aspirations, but it is the commodity mer-
chants who have godly power, so that the world his artists inhabit
takes on the shape of an unsuccessful concert turn. West shows the
authority of the godly artist in decline and art itself becoming a ubiquitous triviality. For this reason, we cannot leave the *deus artifex topos*
in West without examining more fully the social world within which
his aspiring artists make their diminished way. The next chapter,
therefore, maps out the cultural and social contexts of American life
during the period in which West worked. To untangle the artistic illusions that his characters entertain, we must first understand the social
realities they inhabit.

CHAPTER THREE

Nathanael West: Godly Maker in a Commercial World

> The gains in technics are never registered automatically in
> a society, they require adroit inventions and adaptations in
> politics; and the careless habit of attributing to mechanical im-
> provements a direct role as instruments of culture and civili-
> zations puts a demand upon the machine to which it cannot
> respond . . . no matter how completely technics relies upon the
> objective procedures of the sciences, it does not form an inde-
> pendent system, like the universe: it exists as an element in hu-
> man culture and it promises well or ill as the social groups that
> exploit it promise well or ill. The machine itself makes no de-
> mands and holds out no promises: it is the human spirit that
> makes demands and keeps promises.
> —Lewis Mumford, *Technics and Civilization*

Chapter 2 showed how West used the *deus artifex topos* to measure the changing relationship between artist, audience, and reality in
the America of the 1920s and 1930s. For West, the authority of the artist as a godly maker was under stress at every turn: his artists were
constantly retreating to their own private worlds; his audiences were
always straining over the boundaries of artistic illusion; the reality his
imagination encountered was repeatedly being farmed out to ideologies and powerful vested interests. In West's last book, his visionary
artist, Tod Hackett, had been sure that the masses came to California
to die; in fact, California proved the burial ground for art itself, destroyed by a society that tore down the distance between illusion and
reality. The purpose of this chapter is to bring into greater prominence
the nature of the social and cultural changes that are such powerful
latent forces in West's work and about which West showed such reso-
lute skepticism.

I.

West wrote from and for a world where art and social reality appeared to be moving apart. R. P. Blackmur described the way a new

century heralded a division of realms: "Where in 1800 the capitals of economic, political, and cultural power were the same, sometime between 1900 and 1920 they had become different. London, New York, and Paris made a division of human roles—of human powers or subjection of powers—that has seemed in its present consequence very near fatal to human intelligence."[1] Blackmur's version of the separation of powers at the turn of the century has since been expanded into the full-scale separation of realms described by Malcolm Bradbury: "The American nineteen twenties are a paradoxical decade; and part of that paradox is that a decade most often defined as one of the most conservative in American history, an era of material and business expansion, was also one of the most remarkable periods of American literary experiment, of radical creative exploration and development, and (while extending much that had gone before) the great founding phase of modern American writing."[2] Bradbury's assumptions seem more questionable than Blackmur's. For if there is little disputing the separation of powers that Blackmur outlines, there remains much to object to in Bradbury's separation of realms. Can we really call the era of Henry Ford and Frederick Taylor "one of the most conservative in American history" without twisting the word *conservative* into something that would be unrecognizable to Edmund Burke? Must "an era of material and business expansion" be unquestionably regarded as an era of conservatism? And by what train of thought does T. S. Eliot become radical and Henry Ford conservative?

Recent criticism has begun to look at just how much of "the great founding phase" of modern literature gained its impetus from the technical and commercial revolution that occurred alongside it. Frank Kermode has shown how the early experiments in narrative form conducted by Joseph Conrad and Ford Madox Ford at the beginning of the twentieth century were a direct result of creative opportunities newly opened for novelists by the sudden decline of the three-decker novel.[3] Hugh Kenner has similarly suggested that modernism began with the sense that "early in the century *something external to writing* had changed, and in changing obligated a change in artistic means."[4] In a refinement of Kenner's model, Michael Spindler's study of American literature in the 1920s maps the shifts in social forms that stand behind the period's revolution in literary technique. And the nature of Spindler's thesis, that "social being determines consciousness," leads to conclusions almost the reverse of Bradbury's.[5]

Certainly Spindler accounts most satisfactorily for what seems native to American modernism—an audaciously entrepreneurial thrust toward specialization and innovation. American authors speak with the voice of the time and motion engineer or the expanding entrepreneur: their goal is to produce a new, efficient literature where every word will do its work and where the literary organizations of the past—the weighty *Preludes* and endless *In Memoriams*—can be reduced to the slim operations of the present. Instead of the *Oresteia*, Thornton Wilder will develop the five-minute play; where Clough wrote a sixty-three-page *Dipsychus*, Pound will provide a *Hugh Selwyn Mauberley* at one-fifth of that length. Where Norris and Crane marched behind the banner of natural science, early American modernists rally to the managerial battle cries of efficiency and organization.

II.

Some years ago, Gore Vidal identified the presence of what he called "R + D" literature.[6] Vidal saw this as a spin-off from the professionalism of the academy, with its classes in "creative writing" and its programmed courses on modernism. But the technical revolution in letters surely begins elsewhere, and at a much earlier date, in the programs and manifestos of the 1920s. To look at some of these is to sense the air of a major corporation's research laboratory, its buzz of professionals each perfecting his own special project. Among the white-coated squad of researchers, we can locate John Dos Passos, who told the American Writers' Congress of the role of "the writer as technician"[7] and Gertrude Stein, who sets herself the task of discovering in composition "the excitingness of pure being."[8] Meanwhile, Ezra Pound looked for a "language charged with meaning to the utmost degree,"[9] while T. S. Eliot's task, among many others, was to sniff out "a metaphysical hare-and-hounds" in order to restore "the data of criticism."[10] Whatever the object, the search always aimed to discover phenomena in their most concentrated states. This was what irked Newton Arvin when he recalled a period that he saw as beguiled by an attempt to codify "a tight little Eliotine decalogue."[11]

Many authors adopted for themselves the image of the specialist, the man who could, like one of Frederick Taylor's managers, decide just what counted as optimum verbal efficiency. "We live in an age of science and abundance," Pound told his audience in *ABC of Reading*, and how best should art and its public proceed but by an effort grounded in the former to minimize the accretions of the latter? "Contemporary book-keeping uses a 'loose-leaf' system to keep the active part of a business separate from its archives. That doesn't mean that accounts of new customers are kept apart from accounts of old customers, but that the business still in being is not loaded up with accounts of business that no longer functions."[12] Pound is the progress chaser of literary history, forever looking for ways of making reductions; the idea of a volume like *ABC of Reading* is to write a blueprint for a pared-down literacy. Pound borrows some of his devices from popular culture, where magazines like *Liberty* used to set their readers time limits for finishing their stories. Like them, Pound assigns his readers specific, limited objectives; like them, he is not beyond cozening them with jellies. Just as the typical popular magazine story takes its readers from China to Peru, so Pound rallies his by transporting them to Cathay, Provence, and Florence.

There is considerable businesslike bustle in the way Pound goes about his task, reducing verbal overheads the better to practice the larger economies of scale that will bring Confucius to Idaho: "You are not being asked to decide what theories are correct, but to what degree different writers have been efficient in expressing their thought. . . . It would be a very good exercise to take parallel passages of [Wordsworth and Swinburne] and see how many useless words each uses, how many which contribute nothing very definite."[13] Once you have trimmed down *The Prelude*, you will have time enough to tackle the Provençal troubadours.

Of course, the risk of this trimming, as F. R. Leavis pointed out, is that literature becomes a multinational conglomerate, starved of local traditions. Although hardly a modernist fifth columnist, Leavis worried that this program, so aesthetically ambitious, so culturally promiscuous, would effectively sever literature from social existence. Moreover, he argued, the modern reader faced dangers not merely in "the amount" he had to read but also in "the heterogeneity."[14] Pound's area of cultivation, from Confucius to T. S. Eliot, from Arnaut Daniel to James Joyce, was too wide for anything but a corporation of gardeners to nurture. The danger was that the accumulation of culture would become like the accumulation of capital, a task that somehow forgot human beings. There is also the matter of Pound's tone; he has a habit of addressing his readers as if they were at a board meeting where he presents his chosen authors as so much disposable capital.

And was there not a danger too that such daunting manifestos would deaden the artist, making him into a machine for producing culture? Some of this danger dogs T. S. Eliot's work. For as Eliot presents him in "Four Elizabethan Dramatists: Preface to an Unwritten Book" (symbolist aesthetics harbors many such books), the poet has scarcely more than a functional existence: "No artist produces great art by a deliberate attempt to express his personality. He expresses his personality indirectly through concentrating upon a task in the same sense as the making of an efficient engine or the turning of a jug or a table-leg." [15] Hugh Kenner gave us the invisible poet; Eliot presents him here as a spare part in the art factory. The campaign to expel metaphysics from criticism, which Eliot mounted in "The Perfect Critic," turns the art of criticism into a superior kind of lathe turning.

Where Pound's critical persona is entrepreneurial, and Eliot's mechanical, Gertrude Stein composes sentences the way Henry Ford makes cars. Practicing what she calls "honest enough business methods," [16] Stein rolls out endless lines of sentences with only the most minimal variety; the resemblance to Ford's conveyor belt, which first rolled just four years after the publication of *Three Lives*, is too close to be entirely fortuitous. And if Stein's "rose is a rose is a rose" would not have excited Samuel Johnson, it would surely have found an echo in the breast of Calvin Coolidge, who was certain that the business of America was business. Both Coolidge and Stein thought that achievement relied on an intensified specialization. Accordingly, Stein's attention comes to rest in sentences rather than plots, words rather than meaning. When asked for about the millionth time what she had meant about her famous rose, she answered with a certain weariness, conscious no doubt of the unfortunate potential for technological saws to be endlessly reproduced, that her aim had been to recover the primal intensities that language encrusted, to get back to a prelapsarian vividness.

> Now listen. Can't you see that when the language was new—as it was with Chaucer and Homer—the poet could use the name of a thing and the thing was really there. . . . Now the poet has to work in the excitingness of pure being; he has to get back that intensity into the language. We all know that it's hard to write poetry in a late age; and we know that you have to put in some strangeness, as something unexpected, into the structure of the sentence in order to bring back vitality to the noun. . . . I notice that you all know it; you make fun of it, but you know it. Now listen! I'm no fool. I know that in daily life we don't go around saying ". . . is a . . . is a . . . is a . . . ." Yes, I'm no fool; but I think in that line the rose is red for the first time in English poetry for a hundred years. [17]

Ford, who thought that history was bunk, would have been delighted by Stein's American desire to burn words from their connotations. Her attempt to revive language—"to bring back vitality to the noun"—is peculiarly inward turning. Notice that she says "the noun," not the thing, as if roses were grammar rather than things that grow. She is eager for an audience and rather fearful that what E. H. Gom-

brich has shown to be the most sophisticated of preferences (the preference for the primitive) will be thought naive.[18] But her solution cuts
against the grain of the daily: art and reality make a separate peace.
The effect once again is to send the artist off to his laboratory, all the
easier to perform his experiments.

Stein's means are Fordian, even if her ends are prelapsarian.
There is a great contrast between her goal—to return to a primal intensity—and the purposeful, professional type of resourcefulness
she shows in making so much out of so very little, marshaling her
effects by assembling and reassembling a few basic parts. Ford's materials are valves and gaskets; Steins are words. If he wastes few materials, she wastes few words. Stein's minimal copulatives resemble Ford's
famous Model T, available in any color as long as it was black; Stein,
likewise, can provide any verb as long as it contains *is*. Look, in this
sentence, how she perpetually returns to the same few basic words.
"What is the difference between conversation and writing, oh yes,
what is the difference the difference is that conversation is what is said
and what is said is always led and if it is led then it is said and that is
not written. Written writing should not be led oh no it should not be
led not at all led."[19]

Stein's technique is Fordian, but its purpose seems to be to keep
its own counsel. Writing, indeed, becomes that which is not led, that
which has not fallen into the rut of the prosaic. But outside that rut, it
must perforce swing on its own axis, so that it can excite the rigors of
a mind for whom only the absolute is good enough. "If perfection is
good, then more perfection is better," Stein informs us in *The Geographical History of America*.[20] But Stein's perfection is a monotonous
thing; any aphorism made once becomes automatically worth being
made a hundred times. A reader begins to feel like a Detroit auto
worker watching swarms of identical sentences float past him, as he
reads with an increasingly savage torpor.

Stein's sentence-based intensities became the basis for Thornton
Wilder's attempt to galvanize whole plays with the same kind of energy. In his foreword to *The Angel That Troubled the Waters*, Wilder tells
us he has "discovered a literary form that satisfied my passion for
compression. Since the time when I began to read I had become aware
of the needless repetition, the complacency in most writing."[21] Wilder, too, with his bitter lament on literary monoliths that sprawl along
without the benefit of efficient organization, could easily pass for a
cousin of Frank and Lillian Gilbreth, the work-study experts. His solution takes the form of his famous three-minute prose plays, the first
of which is called, aptly enough, *Nascuntur Poetae*: one of the perpetual dangers of clearing the store so drastically is that self-reference

becomes all that remains. Like Stein, Wilder wrenches idiom to the
point where a reader yelps:

> THE BOY: These are mysteries. Give them no names.
> THE WOMAN IN DEEP RED: This is a leaf of laurel from a tree not
> often plucked. You shall know the pride and the shining of the
> eyes—of that I do not speak long.[22]

Language stripped of complacency is often embarrassingly naked.
Wilder's relentless search for "authoritative moments that all the practice of later maturity cannot explain and cannot recapture"[23] leads him
to take the high road out of common meaning. His laurel trees are
"not often plucked"; his mysteries go unnamed; his protagonists are
anonymous; moreover, the search for the privileged moment conducts Wilder's hero back into the womblike sanctuary of childhood.

The bid to construct fiction on the principle of episodic intensification engenders its corresponding metaphysic, the pursuit of
authenticity that motivates much of the fiction of Hemingway, Fitzgerald, Wilder, and so many other authors during the period. Hemingway makes the clearest statement of their goals at the start of *Death in
the Afternoon*: "The real thing, the sequence of motion and fact which
made the emotion and which would be as valid in a year or in ten
years or, with luck and if you stated it purely enough, always, was
beyond me and I was working very hard to try to get it."[24] Hemingway's ethos is an austere one. It leaves a novelist stripped of everything but those privileged moments when time stops in an intense
epiphany—the vision that underpins the creation of Jay Gatsby, Benjy
Compson, and Nick Adams. Each of these characters appears to be
drenched in Hemingway's kind of authenticity. Yet even in them, we
sometimes suspect that we are confronted by three cases of arrested
development. Dick Diver in *Tender is the Night* and Harry Morgan in *To
Have and Have Not* show the severe restrictions that the pursuit of intensity can impose upon a novelist's vision of adult life. As Leslie
Fiedler has recognized, this pursuit transports the American novelist
outside the world of civil responsibilities, in the direction of ritual
rather than realism.[25]

West has the measure of the artistic developments of his period.
His fiction repeatedly pits the inner compulsions of his protagonists
against the circumstances of urban living. In an episode in *Miss Lonelyhearts*, the hero drifts from a childhood reverie into what dissolves, as
his drunkenness increases, into a meditation on modern art.

> The whisky was good and he felt warm and sure. . . . He forgot
> that his heart was a bomb to remember an incident of his child-
> hood. One winter evening, he had been waiting with his little sis-

ter for their father to come home from church. She was eight years old then, and he was twelve. Made sad by the pause between playing and eating, he had gone to the piano and had begun a piece by Mozart. It was the first time he had ever voluntarily gone to the piano. His sister left her picture book to dance to his music. She had never danced before. She danced gravely and carefully, a simple dance yet formal. . . . As Miss Lonelyhearts stood at the bar, swaying slightly to the remembered music, he thought of children dancing. Square replacing oblong and being replaced by circle. Every child, everywhere; in the whole world there was not one child who was not gravely, sweetly dancing. (84–85)

In this passage West offers a telescoped picture of early twentieth-century aesthetics in its relentless push toward simplicity. There is the snook cocked at the "hard-boiled" school as Miss Lonelyhearts tastes his whisky and "felt sure," only to slide into Proustian (or, more likely, Scott-Moncrieffian) nostalgia. The combined primitivism of the tough-guy and the child-cult together sires an even simpler order as, by degrees, the pastoral of pure art becomes the pastoral of pure form: "Square replacing oblong and being replaced by circle." But as Miss Lonelyhearts's reverie provokes a blow in the mouth, West yokes the dominant aesthetic idiom to the social conditions of Depression America, as the complementary searches of audience and artist for excitement and epiphany meet in a barroom brawl.

Although West's artist-heroes are usually possessed of impeccably up-to-date aesthetic aspirations, West composes a narrative that perpetually thwarts such ambitions. In design, Tod Hackett's "The Burning of Los Angeles" is a visual equivalent of Eliot's *The Waste Land*. To execute it, Tod has situated himself in the city, all the easier to nurture his fastidious distaste at the chaos of modern life. Having taken this necessary step, Tod has assembled his traditions, as a good modernist should; he has merged Goya and Daumier, Winslow Homer and Salvator Rosa. But life leaks into art when he finds himself part of a riot he had intended only to imitate. Tod's final gestures as an artist are comically ineffectual, as he stands "on a chair and worked at the flames in an upper corner of the canvas, modeling the tongues of fire so that they licked even more avidly" (420). Such Nero-like behavior is surely as much a mockery of the modernist enterprise as a fulfillment of it. Tod's next imitation, of a police siren, is much more useful. More important, it vindicates West's recognition of his own role as an artist, as the type of "fellow who yells fire and indicates where some of the smoke is coming from without dragging the hose to the spot." [26] Where West's contemporaries were busily erecting walls between art and society in order to perfect their own autonomous realms, his own fiction, from *Balso Snell* onward, seems determined to reduce the distance between imagination and society. Having suggested how West's privileged perspectives are always trapped within larger social forces, I shall now attempt to indicate the nature of those social forces more precisely.

III.

West's art, I have argued, acknowledges the pressure exerted by social realities upon artistic expectations. What were these "social realities" during the 1920s, the period in which West came to maturity? It is not always easy to identify the main lines of social development during this time, especially since the institutions and technicians who moved into prominence were either invisible (like the "new managers" who pioneered the technical developments of the period), or well disguised (like the advertisers and salesmen who contributed to its vast increases in consumption). But contemporary evidence will provide testimony of their effects on ordinary lives; it is to this evidence that I now turn.

Malcolm Cowley's *Exile's Return* gives us a clear sense of the points of intersection between cultural aspiration and social reality, which Cowley refuses to separate. In the opening pages of his book, Cowley shows instead how culture and commerce grew side by side, in a way that limited cultural possibilities just as they seemed to be expanding. *Exile's Return*, Cowley's reminiscences of his childhood and youth, recalls the whole drift of early twentieth-century America from small-town frugality to cosmopolitan consumership: "Looking backward, I feel that our whole training was involuntarily directed toward destroying whatever roots we had in the soil, toward eradicating our local and regional peculiarities, toward making us homeless citizens of the world."[27] Cowley's account of his generation traces a remarkably familiar path. The process begins with standardization, the creation of like minds: "All but a handful were pupils in the public schools, where they studied the same textbooks, sang the same songs and revolted rather tamely against the same restrictions" (5). The pressure toward standardized conformity provokes standardized revolt, itself productive of no lasting reevaluations. For, as Cowley points out, "There is, however, a practical limit to the series of convolutions. If it leads at one moment to reading Oscar Wilde because other high-school pupils have never heard of him, it leads at the next to disparaging Wilde because you admired him once" (21). Cowley's college boys become the first generation of institutionalized outsiders, as the solitary and almost morbid iconoclasm voiced by Baudelaire's narrator in "The Evil Glazier" becomes the collective disdain of an entire generation.

> Those salesrooms and fitting rooms of culture where we would spend four years were not ground-floor shops, open to the life of the street. They existed, as it were, at the top of very high buildings, looking down at a far panorama of boulevards and Georgian houses and Greek temples of banking—with people outside them the size of gnats—and, vague in the distance, the fields, mines, factories that labored unobtrusively to support us. We never glanced out at them. On the heights, while tailors transformed us into the semblance of cultured men, we exercised happily, studied in moderation, slept soundly and grumbled at our food. There was nothing else to do except pay the bills rendered semi-annually, and our parents attended to that. (33)

Cowley's ironic depiction of the "salesrooms and fitting rooms of culture" forces together what many critics have insisted on separating. His description of these institutions, with their inward-looking remoteness, reminds us of the modern industrial complex, another institution devoted to specialized ends. Cowley's genteel young men, carefully cloistered from their society, are nonetheless part of it. They are only "separate" in that their speciality was culture just as Henry Ford's was cars. Even Cowley's final sentence follows this trend. His readjustment of Villiers de l'Isle-Adam's lofty "As for living—our servants will do that for us" works along distinctly bourgeois lines. By means of a recycling that is canny rather than unworldly, Cowley turns Villiers's aristocratic defiance into a form of subsidized suburban lotus eating. Consequently, his young men are more weary than rebellious: "There was nothing else to do except pay the bills rendered semi-annually, and our parents attended to that." Art no longer sneers at economy but nests in its prosperity, so that the two proceed along separate but parallel tracks toward a common destination—perfect specialization.

By the time of Cowley's youth, such developments were becoming typical. A changing economic structure, one centered on technical perfection, professionalization, and consumerism, formed the basis of American productive power in this period. If we look at the years between 1900 and 1927, we can see the changing economic structure: during 1899–1920, the average rise in output per worker was only 7 percent; the period 1921–1927, however, shows a rise of 47 percent. In 1899 only 5 percent of American factories were run by motors; by 1927 the figure had risen to 78 percent. Large corporations were squeezing out smaller competitors. In 1910 the two hundred largest competitors did 33 percent of the business. By 1930 they owned one-fifth of the total wealth of the United States; in that year, the thirteen largest corporations were nearly twice the size of the three hundred largest at the start of the century.[28]

These massive changes transformed the nature of labor in America. Much of Henry Ford's self-congratulatory *Moving Forward* assures us how inevitable this all was, perhaps most persuasively through the testimony of one of his blacksmiths: "I naturally take most of my impressions from the way they affect my craft. . . . the almost miraculous efficiency of the system is daily rendering what is perhaps the most ancient handicraft obsolete as the methods of transportation." This method, he added, is "the system of production [which] must inevitably become the standard."[29] Although Ford's blacksmith sounds unnervingly like Ford, the pattern of his observations is worth noting.

This period of American history was eager to establish one way of doing things—Ford's way—and to establish this as the "standard." This process—we might call it synecdochical development—was one by which entrepreneurs could supply all needs by transforming them into material wants. Synecdochical development trims down the past to the point where it fits the requirements of the present, steering society toward the glorious future evoked by apologists for technological innovation. At the end of his book, in a finale worthy of Hart Crane, Ford imagines a future that equates his own progress with mankind's: "MANKIND PASSES FROM THE OLD TO THE NEW ON A HUMAN BRIDGE FORMED BY THOSE WHO LABOUR IN THE THREE PRINCIPAL ARTS—AGRICULTURE-MANUFACTURE-TRANSPORTATION."[30] Such happy prospects became *topoi* in the period. The most famous of all belongs to Calvin Coolidge, whose last State of the Union message (delivered ten months before the Wall Street crash) declared that "no Congress of the United States ever assembled, on surveying the state of the Union, has met with a more pleasing prospect than that which appears at the present time. In the domestic field there is tranquillity and contentment . . . and the highest record of years of prosperity. In the foreign field there is peace, the goodwill which comes from mutual understanding."[31]

One of the main sources for this almost Virgilian projection of a new age was the alliance between production and consumption masterminded by Henry Ford. Over only a few years, Ford's methods and products had transformed America. In 1909 he produced his basic Model T, whose "function and design were in spirit a utilitarian creation of rural America."[32] By 1913 Ford had developed the moving production line, an innovation that further simplified the business of manufacturing; some years later, he was to tell admirers that 90 percent of his workmen could learn their jobs in a few hours. But by 1927 Ford's campaign shifted; the production of the Model A, George Mowry tells us, "was but the first step in the ardent wooing of the consumer by means other than price. . . . With the death of the Model T, a part of the tradition of thrift, the pioneer sense of utility, and the nineteenth-century air of sobriety was buried."[33] Ford abandoned the Model T only after much misgiving, and a new phase of American development had begun. Like West's Ada Goldstein, Ford's habit was to collect items of old America for his "pioneer museum," even as his industrial and commercial practices ensured the extinction of that era. The period he helped to create—of installment buying, mass production, and mass advertising—proved unstoppable. America had become a nation of consumers, and abundance had replaced austerity as the basic expectation of most of its population.[34]

By trimming the past and transforming the future, entrepreneurs like Ford hoped to become the "standard." But what were the social consequences of this? One of the features of a conveyor-belt sensibility, if it can be called that, is that it reproduces futures that merely simulate the present. In such conditions, consequences are simply discounted; volume or intensity become all-important. West, however, was keenly aware of the ecological and human effects of the new "standard." Look, for instance, at the episode where Miss Lonelyhearts quits work for the day and takes off for the park.

> He examined the sky and saw that it was canvas-colored and ill-stretched. He examined it like a stupid detective who is searching for a clue to his own exhaustion. When he found nothing, he turned his trained eye on the skyscrapers that menaced the little park from all sides. In their tons of forced rock and tortured steel, he discovered what he thought was a clue.
>
> Americans have dissipated their radical energy in an orgy of stone breaking. In their few years they have broken more stones than did centuries of Egyptians. And they have done their work hysterically, desperately, almost as if they knew that the stones would some day break them. (100)

And so they have. Both Homer and Tod have been cheated by society: Homer into behaving like a machine and Tod (like Miss Lonelyhearts, whose trained eye makes a "quick catalogue" of Mrs. Doyle) into thinking like one: "After she had gone, he wondered what living with her would do to Homer. He thought it might straighten him out. He fooled himself into believing this with an image, as though a man were a piece of iron to be heated and then straightened with hammer blows. He should have known better, for if anyone ever lacked malleability Homer did" (357).

West's analysis reveals the human cost of what Ford's apologia submerges in its rhetorical flood. New York's "skyscrapers" are just that, attempts to graze the sky with the anxious hysteria that had gone into making them. A "trained eye" enables its possessor to reduce human beings to components, to scour environments for clues to its own weariness. West's Americans torture their surroundings to the point where they confess their own anxieties back to them. "Fooled . . . with an image": Tod's meditation is a harsh commentary on the whole effort of business-class apologists to capture the consciousness of the public with images.

One the most important developments of the period was the emergence of two new occupational groups that were to move into key positions in the economy. The first were the specialist managers who were able to organize the increasingly complex business concerns that emerged in the 1920s. In this new business-class environment, constant innovations in products (where Ford's Model T stayed in production for fifteen years, his Model A lasted only five), a drastic reduction in the production cycle (by the end of 1925, Ford's production lines could deliver a completed automobile every ten seconds), and a massive expansion in productive capacity (which almost doubled from 1919–29) all ensured that these experts had plenty to do. Just as important were those "captains of consciousness" who could tempt the new masses to consume the fruits of the newly organized industrial system. One group aimed at control by efficiency, the other by seduction. Both were crucial to the commercial effort of the 1920s.[35]

Stuart Chase's essay "The Heart of Human Industry," published in 1932, summarizes conveniently the goals of the new managers. Their aim, Chase tells us, is to devise a new science of management, which would rationalize the new methods of production, and so act as "the engine at the bottom of the rate of advance."[36] Like Ford's empire of production, this science had its dynastic ambitions. Chase reported that "the technician is constantly undone by a failure to inaugurate a system of super-management," a fact lamented by one of Chase's interviewees, who looked forward to "the lordly science of engineering we might have," if only the rest of us would submit to the sweet voice of coercion.

The widespread reluctance to submit to efficient organization was explained by a witness to a U. S. agency, who commented on his diminishing autonomy under the new conditions of industrial organization: "My trade has been subdivided and those subdivisions have been again subdivided, so that a man never learns the machinist's trade now. Ten years ago he learned, not the whole of the trade, but a fair portion of it. Also, there is more machinery, which again makes machinery. . . . The trade [is] merely laborer's work."[37] "Merely laborer's work": the scientific manager secures his eminence at the expense of the craftsman's independence. If the lords of the new order are the managers and the monarchs the Fords, then the subjects are characters like Peter Doyle, who drags his crippled foot from gas meter to gas meter across New York, and Homer Simpson, whose one illness in a life of ten-hour days costs him his job.

One of West's sharpest insights, however, is his recognition that men of letters cannot avoid such shifts either. Where we expect artists and craftsmen, West gives us day laborers. Where the newspaper of Joyce and Mallarmé is a world of words, West's New York *Post-Dispatch* is rather a world of power, staffed by an efficient, suitably authoritative managing editor (Willie Shrike) and numerous specialists attempting to become as much like Shrike as possible. Miss Lonelyhearts's speciality is misery, to which he cannot respond with the kind of professional detachment he might take to the post of city editor or sports reporter. Instead, his response is "to examine the values by which he lives" (106). The other staff see this as dangerously quirky. For Goldsmith the copyboy and for Shrike himself, the misery is only "stuff" and Miss Lonelyhearts's column a standardized response to a standardized discontent: "On most days," Miss Lonelyhearts "received more than thirty letters, all of them alike, stamped from the dough of suffering with a heart-shaped cookie knife" (66). The newspaper system requires that these little miseries be packaged into one standardized whole known as the New York *Post-Dispatch*. A newspaper is a thoroughfare of columns, ribbons of experience slotted into parcels of "stuff." Miss Lonelyhearts's dilemma is that he cannot see misery in this mass-produced way; what is "stuff" for others is agony for him. But even in torment, he meets an organizational need, since his hysteria testifies to the necessity for the hard-boiled pose adopted by all his colleagues. Scientific societies never lack pigeonholes.

The way to success in West's America must be to become a machine, as Lem Pitkin's career in *A Cool Million* clearly demonstrates. As the book progresses, Lem becomes less and less a person, more of a procedure. He becomes a diamond thief without ever realizing it by virtue of a script provided by Elmer Hainey. Even his martyrdom is carefully prearranged by a thoughtful employer. All Lem has to do to achieve deification as the idol of the masses is to stand up and be shot.

Lem falls victim to one of American capitalism's extreme crises; Miss Lonelyhearts is victimized by its daily casualties. Even daily survival requires anonymity, the ability to blend into surroundings that are not very welcoming, but provide the kind of solidarity that Miss Lonelyhearts observes as abiding among the *Post-Dispatch* employees in the speakeasy: "A button machine makes buttons, no matter what the power used—foot, steam or electricity. . . . They, no matter what the motivating force, death, love, or God, made jokes" (84).

The ubiquitous laughter of Shrike and his henchmen engulfs Miss Lonelyhearts's tragic view of the reality his correspondents endure. Such laughter, originating in hysteria and terminating in brutality, has a larger truth to the nature of West's society, as Frederick Allen's description of a company contest makes clear: "[The company] gave a banquet at which the man with the best [sales record] score was served with oysters, roast turkey and a most elaborate ice; the man with the second best score had the same dinner but without the oysters; and so on down to the man with the worst score, before whom was laid a small plate of boiled beans and a couple of crackers."[38]

This is the world of Shrike's game "Everyman his own Miss Lonelyhearts," where Shrike uses the party spirit to show the incompatibility of Miss Lonelyhearts's dreams with economic fact. West's source for his "Everyman his own Miss Lonelyhearts" may well have been James Joyce. In *Ulysses*, Buck Mulligan proposes the play "Everyman His own Wife or a Honeymoon in the Hand a national immorality in three orgasms."[39] Where Mulligan's customarily heavy-handed satire focuses on Irish linguistic self-abuse, West concentrates less on the abuse of language than the abuse of power; the whole aim of Shrike's burlesque is clearly to contaminate Miss Lonelyhearts's dream to the point where he can no longer function. Such circus barker's rhetoric, designed to reinforce the lines of control within the business organization, rang through West's America. Shrike's mirth works in the spirit of the corporate executives who told Frederick Allen how they had devised a game in which each trainee salesman declared a child from his family as mascot, so that "every one of them would work his head off to make some youngster happy at Christmas."[40]

To secure power by playful means: this was the goal of the second elite that emerged in this period, the persuaders—media, sales, and advertising personnel—whose aim was to translate sizable increases in real income into vast increases in consumption. Jim Potter has provided the evidence for their success: an increase of fourteen million in the number of registered cars, an increase in the number of families with radios from sixty thousand in 1922 to ten million in 1929

says much for their accomplishments.[41] Of course, the persuaders did
not lack persuasion, which came chiefly from a variety of trade publications. Some of these, like *Printer's Ink* and *Selling News*, had circula-
tions as high as 800,000, and they used their circulation as a platform to
educate a newly born industry in all the latest lore in salesmanship,
advertising, and the sister arts. Edward Bok, who has charted the
growth of the research and advertising industries, provides the following figures: "Newspapers, $600,000,000; direct advertising (mail mat-
ters, hand bills etc.), $300,000,000; magazines, $150,000,000; trade
papers, $70,000,000; farm papers, $27,000,000; sign boards $30,000,000;
novelties, $30,000,000; demonstrations, $24,000,000; window displays,
$20,000,000; posters, $12,000,000; street car cards, $11,000,000; motion
pictures, $5,000,000; programs $5,000,000; total, $1,284,000,000."[42] Ad-
vertising employed over 600,000 workers and occupied from 40 to 75
percent of a newspaper's space. Stuart Chase estimated that one dollar
was "spent to educate consumers in what they may or may not want to
buy, for every 70 cents that is spent on other kinds of education—primary, secondary, high school, university."[43]

The executives and entrepreneurs who invested in advertising
knew what they were doing. Clifton Fadiman's comparison of the
reading habits of Americans and Europeans revealed that where
Thomas Mann's *The Magic Mountain* sold one million copies in Germany in ten years, it sold only 13,000 copies in America over the same
period of time, while American daily newspapers sold 44 million copies in aggregate. Where *Miss Lonelyhearts*, after an initial run of 2,200
copies, found itself on the remainder shelf, a popular periodical like
Liberty had a weekly circulation of about 800,000 copies. What does
America read, Fadiman asked? "Certainly not books . . . books are ir-
relevant to its way of life." Newspapers, movies, and films—over
115,000,000 people attended the cinema every week—provided "the
perfect response to the American's desire for what could immediately
be understood."[44] And each of these media knew the aspirations of
their audience, which they fed with great skill.

For West's characters, these desires have come to have the force
of instinctual drives. When Miss Lonelyhearts returns to New York
from the country, among the first sights he spots is "a man who appeared to be on the verge of death stagger into a movie theater that
was showing a picture called *Blonde Beauty*. He saw a ragged woman
with an enormous goiter pick a love story magazine out of a garbage
can and seem very excited by her find" (115). Similarly, Faye Greener
"mixed bits of badly understood advice from the trade papers with
other bits out of the fan magazines and compared these with the leg-

ends that surround the activities of screen stars and executives" (386). West recognizes that these separate journals melt into a seductive hodgepodge that blends third-person know-how (how to be a star, how to tell a story) with a vague *utinam* (how I wish I were a star, how I long to tell a story). Faye herself is a typically unlikely conjunction of dreams and canniness: "They're making a lot of them this year" is a refrain she attaches to any dream, however unlikely, however banal. Her peculiar fusion of the philosophy of Benjamin Franklin, the methods of Frederick Taylor, and the manner of Jean Harlow would not seem unusual to the more avid readers of *Photoplay*.

Ford's blacksmith had regarded the new system as "almost miraculous." Part of the advertiser's task was to convince his audience of the miracle while concealing the mechanism by which the miracle was devised, a procedure at which the industry became increasingly adept. Gradually, advertisers came to present the life of consumption as a little world, as their products subsumed all activities but "involvement in and commitment to patterns of consumption." [45]

Only occasionally does an advertisement offer clues to the means of manipulation. One intriguing example appeared for *Nelson Doubleday's Pocket University*. Notice first of all the title, which promises a whole world of knowledge packed into a small space. Notice, too, in the following extract, how the advertisement crosses the threshold from self-mystification to the mystification of others. Storytelling becomes persuasion and persuasion becomes power; the vignette offers an interesting glimpse into its own procedures:

> "Ali Baba? I sat forward in my chair. I could tell all about this romantic, picturesque figure of fiction.
>
> "I don't know how it happened, but they gathered all around me. And I told them of golden ships that sailed the seven seas, of a famous man and his donkey who wandered unknown ways, of the brute-man from whom we are all descended. I told them things they never knew of Cleopatra, of the eccentric Diogenes, of Romulus and the founding of Rome, I told them of the unfortunate death of Sir Raleigh [*sic*], of the tragic end of poor Anne Boleyn. . . .
>
> "You must have traveled all over the world to know so many things." [46]

From the beginning, the narrator is unassumingly firm about his expertise, an expertise underscored by his knowing epithets: "I could tell all about this romantic, picturesque figure of fiction." At the same time, the speaker is blissfully guileless; he "cannot tell how it happened" that he opens such magical casements of wonder. His range is nothing short of global; from Bagdhad to London, from Athens to Rome, he can transport his audience across space and time and through fact to fiction. All that matters is the telling: it is the tale that turns the trick and wins the admiration of his auditors. Clarence Darrow, who made a study of such techniques, codified the advertiser's cardinal rule as "Do not permit the [consumer] to reason and reflect." [47] The advertiser's magic is to make a captive audience into an etherized audience.

A similar mastery, combining bizarre fantasy and half-baked history in a tone of sober factuality, is part of the repertoire of Willie Shrike, whose opening scenario, conducted on behalf of a distraught Miss Lonelyhearts, does for art what the advertisement above did for knowledge:

> "*Art is a Way Out*.
> "Do not let life overwhelm you. When the old paths are choked with the débris of failure, look for newer and fresher paths. Art is just such a path. Art is distilled from suffering. As Mr. Polnikoff exclaimed through his fine Russian beard, when, at the age of eighty-six, he gave up his business to learn Chinese, 'We are, as yet, only at the beginning. . . .'
> "*Art Is One of Life's Richest Offerings*.
> "For those who have not the talent to create, there is appreciation. For those . . .
> "Go on from there." (69)

Parody again acts as cue for West's social criticism. Shrike has two audiences, both of which his rhetoric aims to subdue. For Miss Lonelyhearts, the initially welcoming "Let me dictate to you" hardens into the more menacing "Go on from there." For the mass audience, Shrike's "way out" is a means of confining it in a virtual blizzard of nonsense. Moreover, the occasion that inspired Shrike's verbal escape bid is something we are not allowed to forget, for the debris of failure, the suffering that catalyzes the achievement of art, and the malaise of the talentless are all active presences that check the flight of Shrike's optimism. At its center and around its edges, Shrike's parable acknowledges the realities his nonsense is designed to evade. West parodies the manner of the persuaders while simultaneously providing a subtext they preferred to ignore.

But Shrike's anecdote also parodies another cliché of American business. Apologists for the new society were fond of new dawns and fresh paths, for these new beginnings and projected leaps into benign futures all suggested ways of consolidating territory not yet possessed. The technique of synecdochical transformation required, of course, that all futures look much like the present. In Earl Purinton's manifesto for a prosperous America, an article called "Big Ideas from Big Business," all the promise of the former must yield to the know-how of the latter. In the eyes of Purinton, big business's big ideas are subsidiaries of one parent company: Big Business. Purinton proceeds by synecdoche, bracketing all the activities (potential and actual) of a country—even the very country itself—under the one all-consuming activity: "Among the nations of the earth today *America* stands for one idea: Business. . . . What is the finest game? Business. The soundest science? Business. The finest opportunity? Business. The cleanest philanthropy? Business. The surest religion? Business." Purinton concedes, "You may not agree," but he does not wait for an answer.[48]

One recurrent feature of the period was for business to annex the language of some other aspect of human activity, depriving it of its authority in the process. When Arlington T. Stone wished to sati-rize this procedure, he turned to education, where he discovered "the dawn of a new science." What this entailed, Stone decided, was a se-ries of curricular changes that added dressmaking, hosiery, and win-dow display to the campus syllabus, for the simple purpose of prof-itability: "All of those shrines of scientific business seem to be making money. Indeed, next to football teams and schools of education, they are probably the biggest money-getters in the world of the intellect."[49] Again, religious and commercial vocabularies join hands as Stone ex-poses the odd frame of mind that makes schools and colleges into "shrines of scientific business."

Business, then, is no longer part of the American way of life; it *becomes* the American way of life. Its panoramic futures are large proleptic leaps, attempts to persuade the public through tempting mirages of pseudoreference to accept the transformation of all that breathes into the standardized requirements of a business class. All the mechanisms of this society roll toward President Coolidge's sub-lime tautology, "The business of America is business."[50] This adage is reechoed in the popular arts, as Arthur Knight's account of *The March of Time* documentary series has shown: "The voice of *Time*, Westbrook Van Voorhis, was the voice of authority—strident, implacable, de-cisive. There was no questioning his figures, his facts, his conclu-sions. Everything had been carefully researched, properly thought out and knowingly packaged. One could not say nay to 'The March . . . of Time!'"[51] These panoramas disguise a society in the making as a fait accompli. They lock present and future into one unchanging epiph-any of progress. Ford can even bludgeon the past into his preferred pattern, as he denounces the nostalgia of those "mischievous, superstitious" people who "believe in 'robots' as they believed in Santa Claus."[52]

West's fiction shows a fascination with the chain of technological production. Where Ford saw a design unrolling from producer to consumer to the stars, and called that design destiny, West's view is very different. The goal of the employees at the *Post-Dispatch*, for example, is simple. They must "increase the circulation of the paper," a requirement that is channeled down the line of command. But West tracks this idea from its deadened source, Willie Shrike (whose "gestures were elaborate" but whose "face was blank"), to its emergence in the public domain, where the newspaper struggles in the air "like a kite with a broken spine" (71). A deadened producer and a crippled product: the life of illusion is maimed in its very procedures. Similarly, when Tod Hackett stares out from his office window at what Hollywood has made of history, West inevitably switches from the spectacle to its source. And again it is conflict, not the all-knowing hand of a beneficent expertise, that West reveals at the controls: "While he watched, a little fat man, wearing a cork sun-helmet, polo shirt and knickers, darted around the corner of the building in pursuit of the army. 'Stage Nine—you bastards—Stage Nine!' he screamed through a small megaphone" (260). The most lasting picture that emerges from West's fiction—a fiction continuously confronting the relationship between imagination and reality—is not that of the artist's shaping hand working mass into form. It is rather of the massive machinery of illusion, slipping out of the control of its manipulators and its audience alike.

IV.

West's fiction contains several clues as to the status of the godly maker in his society and in his work. The first clue comes from *Miss Lonelyhearts* where the hero, suffering from the first of his recurrent fits of anhedonia, finds he can compose neither himself nor his article. Willie Shrike intercedes, and after several lines of blank nonsense concludes that "for those who have not the talent to create, there is appreciation. For those. . . . Go on from there" (69). The second clue comes from *The Day of the Locust*, where Faye's fantasies swell even beyond Shrike's: whole universes revolve and never deviate into sense inside Faye's egglike head. After a particularly unlikely fantasy involving a South Sea island, a girl, a Russian count, a sailor, and a snake, Faye becomes suddenly lost for words: "Tod was to go on from there" (319). The third clue comes from *A Cool Million*, where the one-eyed Lemuel Pitkin is appearing at the Bijou Theatre, in none too promising circumstances, and is rescued by the intervention of Zachary Coates, who wants to use him as a speech maker. When Lem, true heart that he is, professes his incapacity and his possible disloyalty to his employers, Coates replies:

> "Don't worry about those gentlemen. . . . They will be taken care of. As for your other reason, I have a speech in my pocket that was written expressly for you by Mr. Whipple. I have come here to rehearse you in it."
>
> Zachary Coates reached into his pocket and brought out a sheaf of papers.
>
> "Read through this first," he said firmly, "then we will begin to study it." (252)

In each of these situations, the artist becomes trapped in illusion-making machinery he can no longer control. West's importance lies in his early recognition that a godly maker in a commercial world could no longer control even his own illusions. My next chapter shows how this problem becomes still greater for postwar novelists, who must confront a world where the machinery for illusion making has been perfected and the appetite for illusion correspondingly enhanced.

The *Deus Artifex Topos* since 1945:
Everyman His Own Godly Artist

Nothing, in brief, but maudlin confession,
Irresponse to human aggression,
Amid the precipitation, down-float
Of insubstantial manna
Loftily the faint susurrus
Of his subjective hosannah.
  —Ezra Pound, *Hugh Selwyn Mauberley*

We have learned not to insist on meanings, and they are rarely
even looked for now, except in cases involving the simplest,
safest phenomena.
  —Donald Barthleme, "The Balloon"

I.

At this point some backtracking is in order. I have assumed that
the idea of the artist as a kind of god is an aesthetic commonplace continuously subject to redefinition according to social and cultural
change. Since *topoi* such as the godly artist are intended to engage an
audience's attention, to confront it with the shape of a shared reality, it
is no surprise that they should change: as audiences change, so do *topoi.* One of the biggest changes of all, however, turns neither on the
audience nor on its notion of reality, but on the reorientation of the
artist's role that began with the romantic revival. Paradoxically, the
more artists come to see themselves as gods, the more steadily the traditional notion of God as an artist declines. And as the *topos* goes in-
doors, so to speak, artists come to feel common forms as more and
more restrictive, subject not so much to art as to the impoverishing
definitions imposed by economic life. Hence, reality yields less and
less as consciousness craves more and more.

Given this situation, the godly maker encounters two main dangers. First, if he trusts his art too exclusively, he runs the risk of losing
faith with an audience that, according to E. H. Gombrich, has been
coarsened by a daily diet of illusions. As Gombrich points out, in the

modern world "illusion wears off once . . . expectation is stepped up; we take it for granted and want more."[1] To try to satisfy these demands completely is as fatal for an artist as it is to ignore them; in this situation, the artist becomes the hack of Herman Melville's *Pierre* or the martyr-clown of E. T. A. Hoffmann's *Kater Murr*.

The imposing structures of High Modernism were attempts to reopen lines of communication between artist and audience. But the structural complexities of books like Joyce's *Ulysses* and Mann's *Dr. Faustus* are formidable, as likely to daunt audiences as entice them. In the fiction of Nathanael West, the aesthetic of High Modernism goes askew in the context of a commercial culture. West's fiction shows godly artists divested of their authority by social structures that manipulate illusion to increase profit rather than to enrich and delight. West's slim output contains an abundance of godly makers, none of them successful. In *The Dream Life of Balso Snell*, West's lyric poet must contend with the morbid cupidity of the imaginary men he has created; in *Miss Lonelyhearts*, the very authority of religious language has vanished. West's last two novels depict a reality in which nothing but illusion remains; the making of art becomes the tool of certain special interests who use artists as pawns in their own power games. But West's last book, *The Day of the Locust*, threatens this masquerade with the apocalyptic vision of an enraged satirist-god. Like the unseen Dr. Know-all Pierce-all, West peers over the top of his creation with a malign omniscience. Ultimately, West's omnipotence forces him to destroy what he has created.

One of the most exciting attempts to remedy this dilemma is the subject of Albert Camus's *The Fall*. In this novel Camus attempts the difficult task of maintaining the High Modernist impulse toward dialog while simultaneously dismantling its compulsive complexity. In Camus's book, we see an attempt to dramatize and explore a new relationship between *deus artifex* and audience. Camus's narrator, Jean-Baptiste Clamence, can no longer, unlike Joyce's Dedalus or Mann's Serenus Zeitblom, trust in a shared matrix of allusion with his audience. Everyone had an opinion about Shakespeare in *Ulysses*; in *The Fall*, Clamence feigns surprise at a recognition of his Christian name: "You know the Scriptures? Decidedly, you interest me" (9), he tells his silent interlocutor. Where modernist writing from *The Waste Land* to *The Magic Mountain* subtends a Babylonian polyphony of voices, Clamence encounters silence and ignorance. The proprietor of the bar Mexico City is confined to grunts, and anyway "speaks nothing but Dutch" (5). The unexplained suicide of the young girl in black triggers a silence that "as the night suddenly stood still, seemed interminable"

(52). In *Ulysses* Dedalus meditates on *Hamlet* in the midst of an excited, eloquent audience; he and his audience alike are dwarfed by the
resources of the National Museum. Clamence, however, talks to a
mute audience in a Dutch bar called Mexico City. Silence and misunderstanding become active presences in Camus's novel, an exasper-
ated soliloquy that yearns to become a dialog. Where Joyce and Mann
erected monuments, Camus, in a fine display of postwar austerity, is
content with a soapbox. We are on the brink of a new period in the
history of the *topos*, where social structures dissolve into phantas-
magoria, where language and voice must do the work that in earlier
periods came from shared allusions and assumptions.

Camus's fiction, especially *The Fall*, shows an important reorientation in narrative perspective. Things, characters, and places can no
longer be taken for granted; they have to be interrogated before they
can yield even a minimum of coherence, and the coherence they yield
is apt to tell us more about the interrogator than the things themselves. There is an almost palpable air of abstraction about the world
of *The Fall*, a book that seems very much the product of one man's consciousness working in the isolation of an unsought solitude. Camus's
purpose, of course, is to insist on the familiarity of estrangement to
our modern way of life. Jean-Paul Sartre showed this estrangement at
work in the very texture of Camus's fiction, pointing to the way that
his syntax insulated his characters in small private cells, so that "instead of acting as a bridge between past and future," his work "is
merely a small, isolated, self-sufficient substance."[2] While solitude is
certainly nothing new to the novel (we need only recall Defoe or
Sterne), Camus's rendering entraps reader and protagonist alike in a
rhetorical range of confidences that do not appear to form significant
lines of coherence and form without some imposed effort. But Camus's
successors go even further than this; for all its appearance of random
anecdotage, *The Fall* has a clearly defined ethical purpose. Later authors frequently let anecdote go its own self-justifying way.

In *The Fall*, Camus's narrator is preeminent through his equivocal
combination of moral authority and linguistic mastery. Without the
latter he could not articulate his claim to the former, by which he
makes plain our collective malaise, showing us that we are all in the
soup together. Camus's successors, with whom this chapter will deal,
have intensified his conviction that for modern artists the power of
language is the source of godly power; but they have, in the main,
shown less interest in achieving the moral authority that Camus saw
as the goal of any artistic voice. Where *The Fall* proceeds from private

self-scrutiny to public judgment, albeit of a chimeric and phantasmal kind, Camus's successors have focused much more relentlessly on private self-examination. This hypersensitive concern with self-scrutiny, together with a ruthless iconoclasm about forms, has been Camus's main legacy.[3]

Such a shift in technique signals a significant departure from High Modernist perspective. Alan Wilde remarked that "Elkin strives to make the extraordinary ordinary and, more importantly insists that the ordinary is extraordinary."[4] Such a reevaluation will, of course, have its effects on contemporary versions of the *deus artifex topos*. In postwar writing, art is not so much godly in its shaping power as it is godly in its ubiquity; in these books everyman becomes his own godly artist. Postwar godly artists inhabit a world of shadows that they manipulate through their own self-referring artifice. Postwar writing marks the shift from the testimony of special election to the point where testimony exists for its own sake. Although postwar artists reaffirm their belief in the artist as a godly maker, they do so with the implication that he is only one among many in a universe that has become a field for endlessly competing fictions.

Despite its extreme despair, this style has been given a critical name—postmodernism—in recognition of its partial independence from its imposing ancestor. For Irving Howe, postmodernism signals the writer's withdrawal into the normlessness of mass society.[5] Leslie Fiedler, on the other hand, contrasts an olympian, eternal modernism with an aggressively lowbrow and formally slipshod postmodernism.[6] Frank Kermode has tried to discriminate between the "traditional" and "schismatic" wings of modernism, the former "emphatic about its living relation to the past," the latter adrift in a perpetual novelty, continuously discovering the wheel from one day to the next. Kermode's own sympathies are clearly with the former.[7] What he ignores, however, are the social changes that underlie the shifting emphases he so eloquently charts. In the main, these changes have been overlooked by critics of postwar literature: even a critic as attentive to the social context of contemporary fiction as Gerald Graff does not explore in any detail the social shifts that form the counterpart to its immense reflexiveness. With a fuller understanding of these shifts, we can grasp more clearly the willingness of the postmodern author to let everyman become his own godly artist, to be pushed increasingly, as Warner Berthoff commented, to a position aimed at safeguarding "whatever fiction of personal agency he can imagine living by from day to day."[8]

II.

It is just this knowledge of the day-to-day business of living that is missing from most accounts of the social and cultural background of postwar writing. We know about the pervasive insecurity created by a nuclear technology that is not only potentially lethal, but also dauntingly foreign and remote in its operation for the majority of people. We know about the revolution in scientific thought that has made nature take second place to discussion about nature, so that in the words of Werner Heisenberg, "mathematical formulas . . . no longer portray nature, but rather our knowledge of nature."[9] Although our knowledge, or rather our ignorance, of these matters is the context for much discussion of contemporary literature, this section will examine changes much closer to home, the occupational and cultural changes that are the basis of postindustrial, postwar life.

As early as 1940 Colin Clark forecast a large-scale change in the occupational structure of mid-twentieth-century society. Clark identified a labor flow toward the tertiary industries—services, transport, white-collar work—and away from the traditional industrial and agricultural social base. The fact that almost half the working population of the United States, Canada, and Great Britain were already thus engaged led Clark to predict "a gradual elimination of the manual worker, particularly the unskilled, and the rapid growth of the numbers of clerical and professional workers."[10] Nelson N. Foote and Paul K. Hatt, building on Clark's research, suggested that "all industries show a trend toward professionalization." Even in the traditional fields of mining, fishing, and agriculture, "steady increments of specialization and technology are slowly carrying the nature of the work in the direction of a profession practiced in terms of scientific theory rather than empirical skills."[11] By the start of the 1960s, this trend had been consolidated, and *Time* magazine could duly report that "in the highly automated chemical industry, the number of production jobs has fallen 3% since 1956 while output has soared 27%. Though steel capacity has increased 20% since 1955, the number of men needed to operate the industry's plants—even at full capacity—has dropped 17,000. Auto employment slid from a peak of 746,000 in boom 1955 to 614,000 in November [1960]. Since the meat industry's 1956 employment peak, 28,000 workers have lost their jobs despite a production increase of 3%. Bakery jobs have been in a steady decline from 174,000 in 1954 to 163,000 last year."[12]

In the light of these developments, we must ask just how socially stable a postindustrial society can be. The decline of the traditional

industries does not appear to have encouraged the social and economic consolidation of the new. Indeed, as we shall see, the very
thrust of the service industries is toward a dispersion of traditional
social roles and responsibilities. In addition, several developments
not foreseen by either Clark or Hatt and Foote were to modify the picture they presented. First, the emergence of a "cybernetic revolution"
threatened the existence of service occupations, just as the emergence
of service occupations had endangered the traditional occupations.[13]
Instead of a society of professionals, the permanent revolution in occupational patterns promoted a spate of ever-increasing redundan-
cies. At the end of the 1950s, Donald N. Michael reported that service
industries were becoming "self-service, by becoming cybernated and
by being eliminated."[14]

Morever, the nature of professionalization changed as well. It may
be too drastic to argue, along with Richard Sennett and C. Wright
Mills, that the growth of service industries encouraged the production of technicians and quasi secretaries rather than professionals;
nonetheless, the role of the professional did change significantly, as a
brief analysis of the role of the manager will show.[15] In 1941, James
Burnham saw managers as the vanguard of a new elite, a role assured
them because of their control "on the technical side of the actual process of production."[16] But by 1945 communication had replaced technical expertise as the basis of managerial authority. Elton Mayo characterized managerial capacity as the ability "to listen carefully to what
others say. Only he who knows how to help other persons to adequate
expression can develop the many qualities demanded by a real maturity of judgment."[17] Although Mayo stood at the beginning of a new
period for managers, he still saw industry as a machine for producing
goods, products, and tools. But as society moved into its postindustrial phase, management became much more concerned with what
Marshall McLuhan once called helping people in "the process of getting adjusted to what isn't here any longer."[18] And among the things
no longer here, according to Robert Reich, were the traditional responsibilities of the manager to products and processes. Reich characterized the new management as "paper entrepreneurship," an endless reshuffling of organizational feints and gambits for their own
sake.[19] Mayo's moral crusade, which attempted to place the production of goods inside a socially adaptive framework, had now given
way to a peculiarly self-justifying art, with communication as its
means and its end.

The social existence of the new manager became correspondingly free floating. Andrew Hacker reported on the "transience" of

the corporate executives, a group "gypsy-like in their willingness to pursue their careers in whatever part of the country their corporate employer sends them to." Such willingness, Hacker argues, amounts to "a new form of functional, or corporate citizenship . . . arising to replace local or regional citizenship."[20] The new manager's attachment, therefore, is to the fugitive and mobile; he has grounded his values not on Mayo's affective or adaptive norms but on the more slippery goals of perpetual mobility and constant role redefinition. In the same way, although the corporation as an institution can oust the family, the church, or the region, it can provide little of the continuity supplied by these institutions, since corporate advancement is defined by mobility.

The corporate and postindustrial tendency to see the manager as communicator and reality as nothing more than the basis for endless communication plays a prominent part in Joseph Heller's *Something Happened*. Heller's prose reveals the tendency of corporate life to dissolve reality into psychology, and to reduce psychology into a rootless, unfocused anxiety that preys on institutions and people without offering any hope of understanding or sympathy.

> At the important planning sessions that are held out of town every three months at some luxurious resort hotel or plush country club with a well-known golf course, division and department heads (I am told) normally do not argue or complain or express dissatisfaction aloud with each other's work or viewpoint. But Green does: Green criticizes, ridicules, and disparages impatiently, and he always protests vehemently against any cuts in his own budget or any new curtailment of his activities. Then he is sorry. Green rocks the boat impetuously, and is fearful afterward that he is going to sink. He is better read than most people in the company and affects a suave, intellectual superiority that makes even Arthur Baron slightly uncomfortable and makes Andy Kagle and everyone else in the Sales Department feel crude and graceless. (I am much better educated than Green is and, I think, more intelligent, but he is glib and forward, and I am not.) News of Green's repartee and audacious bad behavior at these planning sessions (Green does not even play golf) usually trickles down to us (mainly through Green himself) . . . I know he is tormented each time by the fear that this time he has at last gone too far.[21]

The company's planning sessions are, Bob Slocum assures us, important ones. Nonetheless, their immediate environment is the leisured opulence of the holiday resort or country club, places where it is important not to argue. Their importance, then, is something vague and indefinite, and it is this that provokes Green's irritated but pettish response as he "criticizes, ridicules and disparages impatiently." The situation, so professional in its definition, dissolves into its own opposite, as the atmosphere of impersonality becomes charged with pettishly personal grudges leveled indifferently all around. Implausible in its setting and hysterical in its transactions, the corporate planning session reveals the comic contradictions of postindustrial living. Nothing is quite what it seems: Slocum's executives aspire to authority yet profess a rough equality; Green's heroism is only hysteria; his independence of mind manifests itself as aggression rather than achievement. Here there is nothing to grasp except gossip, about which Bob Slocum shows a trained researcher's skill: know-how is less important than know-who.

There is something qualitatively different here from the social criticism charted in earlier industrial fiction. Where novels like Dickens's *Bleak House* or West's *Miss Lonelyhearts* revealed the capacity of large organizations to grind human needs into mechanized commodities; where Mailer's *Barbary Shore* or Kesey's *One Flew over the Cuckoo's Nest* invested this social machinery with a Manichean metaphysic, the novelists of postindustrial America, the Heller of *Something Happened*, the Pynchon of *The Crying of Lot 49*, or the Hawkes of *Second Skin*, dramatize victimizing mechanisms that are as much the product of their characters' perceptions as they are the world's given conditions. Reality in these books becomes a set of expectations rather than a matrix of objective conditions.

Pynchon's Oedipa Maas wonders "Shall I project a world?" and is buffeted against a whole network of obsessions and counterfeit obsessions; Hawkes's Skipper lives in a perpetual optative mood, projecting a variety of alternative futures, each of which he obliterates through his own permanent sense of disaster; Bob Slocum's hectic present-tense narrative is designed to stop a hole in a world defined only in the last pages of his story, as he clutches his dead son's shoulders. Each of these books renders only a spectral sense of reality and things; each becomes a latter-day ghost story, a testimony to the power of perception to overwhelm a perpetually shrinking reality. It is significant that John Gardner, who called for a "moral fiction" to remedy this state of disintegration, ended his own career with a book called *Mickelsson's Ghosts*. All of these books try to fill the hole that reality once occupied with a stream of talk: communication again becomes an end in itself, to be maintained at any price.

The social thrust from objects to perceptions, from reality to communication about reality, has been backed up by a corresponding cultural reorientation. Hans-Magnus Enzensberger has identified the emergence of a "consciousness industry" in postwar society, a development characterized by the increasing preeminence of the electronic media.[22] Just as the customary functions of a managerial elite have been transformed with the emergence of a postindustrial society, so the rise of the consciousness industries—first, television and radio, then video, cable T.V., and related home-entertainment industries— has threatened the more conventional cultural forms with obsolescence. Indeed, Tony Schwartz has argued that the ubiquity and availability of the new media have made them "a second god" for the mass audience.[23]

Such a revolution has produced its casualties, of course, for the new media have caused a reevaluation of the relationship between artist, audience, and universe that, in turn, has stimulated a new assessment of the relevance and utility of older cultural forms. Marshall McLuhan spoke for a generation of uncompromising new media pundits when he suggested that the day of the more traditional arts— writing, painting, music—was at an end. With not a flicker of regret, McLuhan remarked that "when radar was new it was found necessary to eliminate the balloon system for city protection that had preceded radar. The balloon got in the way of the electric feedback of the new radar system. Such may well come to be the case with much of our existing school curriculum, to say nothing of the generality of the arts. We can afford to use only portions of them that enhance the perceptions of our technologies."[24]

McLuhan's unnerving fusion of William Blake and Henry Ford is a sobering threat for artists working in traditional modes. First, the new media potentially make all art a matter of vision or images, which restricts artists to the messianic mode. Second, there is an implicit social Darwinism in McLuhan's view of culture, which can only see one cultural form existing at another's expense. Third, McLuhan's constant proselytizing on behalf of media that scarcely suffer from neglect elsewhere can make other artists feel neglected and forlorn. John Barth's anonymous narrator in *Lost in the Funhouse* betrays some of these emotions when he moves to attack an audience he is aware may not be there: "The reader! You, dogged, uninsultable, print-oriented bastard, it's you I'm addressing, who else, from inside this monstrous fiction."[25] If modern artists began the century by discovering the imaginary museum, then by the latter part of the century, they were in danger of becoming its latest exhibit.

One of the contemporary author's chief fears is the dwindling of his audience. Charles Newman's essay "The Uses and Abuses of Death" surveyed the social context of literary production in the 1970s, to discover "only the remnants of literary culture." [26] At the same time as publishers' sales projections were rising, the contemporary author's audience appeared to be shrinking at an unprecedented rate. "Five years ago it took 2,500 copies of a first book to break even," Newman reported. "Today the figure is at least 5,000 and trade publications won't look at anything that doesn't have a chance to sell around 10,000." On this scale, the first two novels written by John Barth would stand little chance of publication: *The Floating Opera* initially sold 1,682 copies while *The End of the Road* managed just 3,000. Only with *The Sot-Weed Factor* did Barth reach 5,000 copies. [27]

Where contemporary authors are not neglected, they may (as they are all too aware) become victims of the wrong kind of attention. The dedication to J. D. Salinger's *Raise High the Roof Beams, Carpenters and Seymour, An Introduction* reveals this fear strikingly, declaring that "if there is an amateur reader still left in the world—or anybody who just reads and runs—I ask him or her, with untellable affection and gratitude, to split the dedication of this book four ways with my wife and children." [28] Salinger's amusing story "Franny" shows in more detail the nature of his fears. There can be few more disturbing creations in the age of criticism than that story's Lane Coutell, who wears his literature with the cold pride of a Hester Prynne of the global village.

Just as important as any of these fears is the sense that the electronic media have utterly transformed the style and subject matter of art. These media have, as Richard Sennett has recognized, cultivated a tendency to global abstraction and local impressionism. On television, he argues, "each moment of appearance is a reality," so that seemingly contradictory motions toward concreteness and half-baked "issues" follow each other back-to-back. [29] Television reduces politics to personalities and inflates trivialities into debates. Thus, the electronic media consolidate the thrust of a postindustrial society toward a redefinition of reality.

The social and political effects of this reduction of reality to image are examined in Jerzy Kozinski's *Being There*. When Chauncey Gardiner begins to speak of the garden that is his sole purchase on the real world, he is completely misunderstood by a team of media men and politicians. They translate his simple words into a political allegory, not knowing that he has spent far too long in front of a television screen to mean anything but what he says. In circumstances like these, men become either numbly literal or unscrupulously metaphoric. Either way, the very nerve ends of language become pinched in a manner that can only pain the artist whose authority resides in words.

Clearly, to understand postmodernist literature we must understand the effects of the revolutions in communications media and social organization. When more and more people become locked into a set of social transformations that deprive them of the contact with localities or objects that nourished earlier generations, they come to suffer from the malaise identified by Daniel Bell. "A technocratic society," Bell tells us,

> is not ennobling. Material goods provide only transient satisfaction or an invidious superiority over those with less. Yet one of the deepest human impulses is to *sanctify* their institutions and beliefs in order to find a meaningful purpose in their lives and to deny the meaninglessness of death. A post-industrial society cannot provide a transcendent ethic—except for the few who devote themselves to a temple of science. And the antinomian attitude plunges one into a radical autism, which in the end dirempts the cords of community and sharing with others. The lack of a rooted moral belief system is the cultural contradiction of the society, the deepest challenge to its survival.[30]

Can artists restore such a belief system? John Gardner's *On Moral Fiction* argues that they should, by cultivating and reviving in their audiences the love of virtue that a moral artist knows by instinct. Gardner regards as instinctual drives that may need the nurture of history and circumstance to keep them alive. His is, as we shall see, only the grandest of innumerable attempts made by a series of postwar authors to recreate these two forces inside his own head.[31]

III.

Two main kinds of godly makers emerge in postwar fiction. In the first, postwar novelists have fashioned an artist-deity whose godliness rests in his separation from the real world, and who comes eventually to abstain from the act of making. In the second, the godly maker relinquishes his imaginative and moral authority to savor the delights of a world created by the collision of a swarm of fictions. For writers of the first type of book—Nabokov's *Invitation to a Beheading*, Gass's *In the Heart of the Heart of the Country*, and Sontag's *The Benefactor* are important here—the godly maker must resign from the world of civil responsibilities to examine his aesthetic consciousness. For the second group of authors—Günter Grass, Stanley Elkin, and Robert

Coover—a variety of fictions are piled up in one book by a seemingly neutral author, who appears to concede his authority to the larger political, physiological, or economic systems in which his novel makes its way. The two tendencies in fact form two sides of one coin: they both drift toward a situation where art loses one of its greatest privileges—to create and shape a common world that is recognizable to a variety of people.

Vladimir Nabokov's extravagant commitment to the overwhelming powers of the artist paradoxically results in works that shift symbolist aspiration to farcical form. Nabokov has urged every creative artist to "study carefully the works of his rivals, including the Almighty."[32] Such study distinguishes the master from the artisan, in which class Nabokov brackets "old Tolstoy" for the conscience-stricken cowardice he displays in his unwillingness to trespass "upon the rights of the deity . . . creating, as God creates, perfectly imaginary people."[33] Nabokov himself feels no such misgivings. In an introduction to a revised English edition of *Bend Sinister*, the first novel he published in the United States and one he had originally anticipated calling *The Person from Porlock*, Nabokov announced that "in the second paragraph of Chapter Five comes the first intimation that 'someone is in the know'—a mysterious intruder who takes advantage of Krug's dream to convey his own peculiar code message. The intruder is not the Viennese Quack (all my books should be stamped Freudians, Keep Out), but an anthropomorphic deity impersonated by me."[34]

As a godly artist, Nabokov has already revealed himself as oppressively omniscient. He can tick off Tolstoy, and he can even restructure the plot of his fiction in the interest of "his own peculiar code message." (An odd admission, this, in view of his celebrated assertion that messages belong to Western Union, a restriction that presumably applies even to code messages.) In fact, Nabokov's *deus artifex* becomes something of a deus ex machina; the last-minute reprieve he gives his creation Krug is an act of almost Jansenist arbitrariness. Where in *Bend Sinister* the author tells us "he experiences a pang of pity for his creature and hastens to take over," in a preface to a revised translation of *Despair* published in 1966 he tells us that "Hell shall never parole" that novel's hero, Hermann Hermann.[35] Art has become the domain of the willful for Nabokov, as his much-repeated anecdote about its origins makes clear: "Do you know how poetry started? I always think that it started when a cave boy came running back to the cave, through the tall grass, shouting as he ran, 'Wolf, wolf,' and there was no wolf. His baboonlike parents, great sticklers for the truth, gave him a hiding, no doubt, but poetry had been born—the tall story had been born in the tall grass."[36]

When Nabokov's own godly authority is at stake, art itself can be sacrificed with a lordly wisecrack. Increasingly, what intrigues Nabokov is the artist's godly mind rather than any art he might produce. Such is the thrust of his *Speak Memory*, which begins by lamenting, "How small the cosmos (a kangaroo's pouch would hold it), how paltry and puny, in comparison to human consciousness, to a single individual recollection and its expression in words."[37] Nabokov's fiction shows a persistent concern with men who create their own worlds, from Hermann Hermann in *Despair*, who is enthralled and anguished by resemblances only he can see, to Charles Kinbote in *Pale Fire*, who creates a whole distant northern land that is the mirror image of his own perversions.

Only farce can emerge from the consciousnesses of such extravagantly aberrant artificers, and both Kinbote and Hermann find themselves locked into environments that owe more to Mack Sennett or Anthony Hope than to the kind of high culture that each acknowledges as his official inspiration. But what matters to their creator is the truth of the vision, which is all the more vindicated the farther it deviates from the drab, excessively organized environment of Europe between the wars or Wordsmith College, with its alphabetical streets.

Nabokov's sense of a sovereign consciousness elevated above and progressively remote from any common reality is most strongly expressed in *Invitation to a Beheading*. Here Nabokov creates a world that has suffered a massive cerebral affliction, one where reality is characterized by memory lapses, half-written graffiti, misremembered rhymes, and endless biographies. How audacious then becomes the attempt of his hero Cincinnatus C. to create a world of pure consciousness.

> In my dreams the world was ennobled, spiritualized; people whom in the waking state I feared so much appeared there in a shimmering refraction, just as if they were imbued with and enveloped by that vibration of light which in sultry weather inspires the very outlines of objects with life; their voices, their step, the expressions of their eyes and even of their clothes—acquired an exciting significance; to put it more simply, in my dreams the world would come alive, becoming so captivatingly majestic, free and ethereal, that afterwards it would be oppressive to breathe the dust of this painted life. But then I have long since grown accustomed to the thought that what we call dreams is semi-reality, the promise of reality, a foreglimpse and a whiff of it.[38]

Nabokov himself lines up behind his hero's separation of realms, with the result that his book takes the important step, one repeated explicitly by Susan Sontag and implicitly by William Gass, of transferring the vision of the godly maker to the world of dream and consciousness. In the artist's sovereign mind all is nuance and complexity; in reality, every hand has five gross thumbs. A maladroit stage carpenter has tacked a stage set together that totalitarian society has chosen to call reality; Cincinnatus, on the other hand, is the masterpiece of a master artificer "fashioned so painstakingly . . . so mysteriously" (19). The godly maker no longer occupies a reality accessible to the rest of the world. He belongs to a world of imaginary possibilities that others cannot enter; his desertion of the novel for "that direction where, to judge by the voices, stood beings akin to him" (208) will become a representative step for many postwar godly makers, who have similarly relinquished mimesis for vision.

Where Nabokov locked the artist's godly power inside a single consciousness, William Gass locks it inside a single sentence, arguing that "we can regard the sentences of fiction as separate acts of creation."[39] "Can" is an invitation that Gass steps up into a fiat in his lordly decree that "in the beginning *is* the word, and if the esthetic aim of any fiction is the creation of a world, then the writer is creator—he is god—and the relation of the writer to his work represents in ideal form the relation of the fabled Creator to His creation" (18). The price of Gass's constant linguistic vigilance is, however, the dramatic freedom of his fiction; by viewing "the sentences of fiction as separate acts of creation" (12), Gass stalls his fiction at the stage of reflexive cosmogony, as his protagonists rehearse perpetually the fact of their maker's creation and of their own thwarted creativity. Reading Gass's fiction is like attending a rehearsal for the *theatrum mundi*, a point that did not escape John Gardner, who called Gass's prose a bird "too encrusted with gold to get off the ground," a remark that captures marvelously the Byzantine madness of Gass's fictional method.[40]

But if it cannot fly, Gass's prose can still hover magnificently, and this passage from "Philosophy and the Form of Fiction" provides a representative example of the peculiar way Gass ricochets from reflection to reflection as if he were in the hall of mirrors of some purely imaginary funhouse.

> Beckett tells us that we live in garbage cans; sit at the side of empty roads, in emptiness awaiting emptiness; crawl blindly through mud. My skin is the tattered dirty clothing of a tramp, my body a broken bicycle, my living space is earth to just beneath

my shoulders, my speech the twittering of an unoiled pump. Hasn't he made my world strange, this novelist? No, of course our lives are not a muddy crawl—*apparently*. But that is mere appearance. We're fooled constantly. We think our emotions fine when they are coarse; we think our ideas profound when they are empty, original when commonplace; we think at first we are living richly, deeply, when all we possess is a burlap bag, unopened tins, dirty thoughts, and webby privates.

I cannot help my home still looks well furnished, or my body trim; I cannot help the colors which I seem to come upon, or the unflinching firmness of my chair; I cannot help I glory in my sex or feel and think and act as one and not as a divided community; for I'm incurably naive, incurably in love with deception; still, I can be taught, I can learn suspicion, learn that things aren't really what they seem; I can learn to hate my pleasures, condemn my desires, doubt my motives, deny my eyes, put unseen creatures in the world and then treat them with greater reverence, give them greater powers than those I innocently know—to bow and bow and bow in their direction; I can replace my love for people with a love for principle, and even pursue a life beyond the grave as a program for the proper pursuit of this one. (6–7)

Out of his conviction that reality's "actual home is in the mind. . . . the world I live in, the objects I manipulate are in great part my constructions" (6), Gass sets up a mirage of contradictions. He identifies life's main task as thinking, an activity he mentions six times in the first paragraph. But all that thought leads him only to emptiness (which makes four appearances). For Gass, thinking begins as hygiene and scrupulousness, but it eventually dribbles into the self-delusion from which we construct what we call reality, only to find in it "dirty thoughts and webby privates." But indeed, Gass's rigorously born-again premises had already anticipated what he would find beneath this abstemious cerebral hygiene. If every sentence is a new invention, then revelation loses its godly power to shock: Gass seems to exhaust his subject rather than scrutinize it. The second paragraph reveals the soft underbelly of his resourceful invention most nakedly of all, as it whines with a thrice-chiming "I cannot help," then shrugs into a hand-wringing "incurably." Gass's conviction that reality is a matter for individual initiative means that his second paragraph can proceed innocent of the knowledge of his first; the Swiftian who penetrates the dirty thoughts beneath our tidy mental constructs can protest his innocence in the second, can become the Tom Sawyer who "can learn" the tricks of adult living rather than the Beckett who must empty himself of them.

Gass's prose is suspended in a permanent adolescence, too enticed with the pleasures of potential to adjust to the rigors of refer-
entiality or even a minimal coherence. Is there any way of telling what
these paragraphs mean? Gass does not create a world as much as he
makes one up as he goes along. An aesthetic of dereliction yields a
fiction of pure poverty. Gass's fictional worlds are always miserably
deprived, so scoured of material and company that his characters
must, willy-nilly, project their own anxieties onto them if they are to
survive at all. Certainly, their author gives them little to go on. In story
after story, his characters begin and end in penury: Fender's icicles,
Israbestis's wall, and the insects from which the housewife invents her
order offer little for the imagination to work on. Where Nabokov's idea
of the sovereign power of art starts from a myth of abundance, Gass's
starts from a myth of poverty. In Gass, the *topos* loses all paradigmatic
force, since his imaginative and objective universe, like the ancient inventory of Miss Pimber, is always open to the highest bidder. Starved
of company and reality, his books, like his characters, are always on
the verge of breakdown.

Gass's narrator in "Mrs. Mean" is an artist who creates a community in his own image. All the characters he puts on stage reflect little
reverence for the fact of creation, since their maker's aim is to penetrate them rather than enjoy their independent existence. It is the *idea*
of artifice that attracts the narrator of "Mrs. Mean," not the wonder of
creation. "I have chosen to be idle," he tells us; his isolation in a small
community has allowed him to surround himself "with scenes and
pictures; to conjecture, to rest my life upon a web of theory."[41] He
takes upon himself the power of naming, of asserting by fiat: "I call
her Mrs. Mean," he says of his much-observed, much-maligned adversary. The narrator scoffs at the role in which he imagines his community as casting him: "They expected, I suppose, that I would soon
be round with stories" (83). But the narrator's stories are told for his
own delight, and at the community's expense. He bolsters his self-
esteem by imagining himself as a malign genius, a presiding deity of
evil intent: "The people by me primitively guess that I am enemy and
hate me: not alone for being different, or disdaining work, or worse,
not doing any; but for something that would seem, if spoken for them,
words of magic; for I take their souls away—I know it—and I play
with them; I puppet them up to something; I march them through
strange crowds and passions; I snuffle at their roots" (83). The enormous verbal energy of the narrative "I" almost bullies the reader
into submission. But there is not really much else to go on. To "take
their souls away," the narrator would first have to give them souls and

then show them to us. His magic works best on himself, conveying him through a whole panoply of roles, from magician to mongrel, "snuffl[ing] at the roots" of a community from which he has isolated himself. Indeed, a few pages later he admits that his majesty is self-anointed, and the rhythm of assertion yields, as so often in Gass, to the voice of dereliction. "Except in the case of Mrs. Mean. I am representative of no preternatural power. I am no image, on my porch—no symbol. I don't exist. However I try, I cannot, like the earth, throw out invisible lines to trap her instincts; turn her north or south; fertilize or not her busy womb; cause her to exhibit the tenderness, even, of ruthless wild things for her wild and ruthless brood. And so she burns and burns before me" (88).

Whoever thought the artist could manage any of this anyway? The harsh reaction to the narrator's self-promotion of his godly powers, no sooner made than withdrawn, is one that neither Gass's character nor his creator appear to have entertained. Because the imagination of Gass's narrator is almost liquid, streaming over but never irrigating his stories, the result is a fiction that oscillates between mythology and pathology without ever cultivating the middle ground the novel has typically settled for its own. Characters and creator are trapped in worlds where language becomes premise and conclusion, and can only, like the reader at the end of *Willie Master's Lonesome Wife*, bale out from a narrative too deliquescent for habitation.

Gass's fossil narratives, with stories that heap up like shattered skeletons, work completely differently from the crystalline integrity of Susan Sontag's *The Benefactor*; yet both authors share the sense of the artist as a god formed in his own image, and necessarily severed from company, story, or indeed anything but his own conviction of his self-elected deity. Like Gass's Cincinnatus C., Sontag's Hippolyte has glimpsed a life in dream that he would like to inhabit in reality. Consequently, life itself becomes Hippolyte's artwork as he sets about the task of becoming a dreamer with an almost Weberian sense of vocation. His aim, to narrow to the point of imperceptibility the distance between life and dream, takes him through a storehouse of twentieth-century ideologies. From Professor Bulgaraux he learns of Autogenes, "a self-sufficient male deity," whose most significant act is that "he created no world. . . . He only was."[42] This is just the signal Hippolyte was waiting for; he now deserts theater for the movies, where "there is no audience . . . there is really no acting either" (102). Later, even cinema becomes too oppressively convivial for Hippolyte, who accordingly turns to the diary as a means of recording his path toward self-deification.

Since Hippolyte has become his own artwork, no world exists outside his consciousness. His vision of liberation from reality by attaining "that divine sensation of absence and soaring which rises from the commerce of the flesh to erase the world" (97) becomes the reader's imprisonment at the hands of a narrator for whom nothing concerning himself is ever wasted. "Dreams are the onanism of the spirit" (97), Hippolyte tells us with some relish, and as a narrator he appears to aspire to the status of the Homer of the tribe of Onan. At the end of the book, however, the reader's metaphoric imprisonment becomes Hippolyte's real incarceration, as the narrative unhinges before our eyes like the House of Usher; wives turn into prisoners, mistresses become nurses, apartments are rebuilt as asylums. Hippolyte's dream of destroying boundaries has, in reality, been a progressive immersion into madness and confinement. The bid to live art, to become one's own godly maker, results only in Hippolyte's taking Charles Kinbote's route to the madhouse.

IV.

Not all recent authors who have exploited the *deus artifex topos* have used it in a way that makes it a diminished or burlesqued version of the romantic image maker. Alongside the intense fascination with the creating consciousness that we find in Nabokov, Gass, and Sontag, another group of artists, seeing in postwar reality no more than a congeries of fictions, attempts to create an art godly not so much in its visionary authority as in its exhaustive ubiquity.

Günter Grass's work, initially so grounded in history, has recently revealed this tendency to a marked degree. In his first novel, *The Tin Drum*, Grass created a hero in Oskar Matzerath whose malign omniscience about German history and disturbing musical accomplishments were almost a parody of Mann's *Dr. Faustus*. *The Tin Drum*, which fused a worm's-eye perspective on Nazi Germany with Oskar's own bizarre and protean imagination, made a startlingly original transformation of the *deus artifex topos*; it was as if Shakespeare had collaborated with Falstaff on an alternative *Henry V*.

But Grass's imaginative exuberance has not been maintained. In 1966, he pointed to an important absence in postwar life: "Where is the calendar that would permit the mighty of our day to hold court, to seek utopian advice, or to cleanse themselves from the compromises of everyday life by listening to expositions of preposterous utopias?"[43] Grass's testimony is ambiguous at this point. Although at the end of his lecture he claims that no such utopias exist ("Reality speaks a different language. We have no special advisers or court jesters. All I see—and here I am including myself—is bewildered writers" [52]), his later fiction shows continuing attempts to create them. The nature of this task reveals itself clearly in Grass's third novel, *Local Anaesthetic.* In *The Tin Drum*, Grass obeyed the historical imperative; history supplied his novel's backbone and Oskar Matzerath its wild, all-seeing eyes. But now Grass will obey only the moral imperative: his fiction becomes the kind of bridgework his dentist conducts in the diseased (because historically damaged) mouth of his narrator, Eberhard Starusch. The true nature of Starusch's historical affliction lies in his sense of himself as a godly maker: "You want to create by decree. Ex nihilo. Ridiculous (117)," his dentist tells him. Against the ancient view of a seven-day creation (far too drastic for a nuclear age, this), the dentist argues for a cautious gradualism. Starusch reports on the exchange:

> (When I tried to acquaint him with the demands of the radical wing of my junior class—smokers' corner, a voice in policy making, the right of the student council to dismiss reactionary teachers—he wore me down with clinical reports on EBA No. 2, the dental cement which was to hold my porcelain bridges in place.) "Since EBA No. 2 did not spring from Nothing but may be regarded as the product of many, often unsuccessful series of experiments, we can have full confidence in it; moreover, thanks to its quartz component EBA No. 2 offers insulation even against ice water, which cannot be said of every dental cement that appears on the market. But you despise the evolutionary process." [44]

Grass's own narrative perspective vindicates the dentist's viewpoint. As Starusch himself ruefully acknowledges, "The simultaneity of multiple activities demands to be described" (19). But to achieve this sense of simultaneous action proceeding on different levels, Grass must abandon the *ex alto* (or rather *de profundis* in the case of Oskar Matzerath) perspective of the godly maker. Distance and history are subsidiary to simultaneity and multiplicity; the moral imperatives of art demand no less.

Nonetheless, the exchange between Starusch and his dentist illuminates some of the difficulties Grass has brought upon himself. First, the exchange heaps up grievances and then doles out remedies in stiffly equal measure; the effect is comic here, as Grass must have wished it to be. But the presence of a similar technique in *The Flounder* and *Headbirths* serves only to bury Grass's protagonists in rhetoric. Second, the technique has the effect of stylizing conflict rather than realizing it. Grass's determination to absorb and dissolve Starusch's armchair apocalypticism drains the substance from his moral vision.

We are alienated from the conflict, which we watch as if through a glass or a television screen. Finally, the characters do not seem to be talking to each other: they exchange views rather than absorb each other's ideas. Grass has made mouthpieces of his creation, composing a little postwar morality farce rather than a novel.

These objections are not so important in *Local Anaesthetic*, where the presence of Eberhard Starusch, a first-person narrator with the anxieties of history in his voice, moderates Grass's own tendency toward all-inclusiveness. But the self-conscious desire to force art into right thinking compromises *The Flounder* and *Headbirths*, where Grass chooses to proceed with an almost Gladstonian scrupulousness. In these books the author's aim to cover everything leads him to balance feminist against chauvinist, nun against cameraman, radical against liberal, India against Germany, in a way that suggests his intentions are more to form a cabinet than to make a work of art. The main objection to this procedure is that Grass has replaced the sovereign consciousness of a godly artist with the camera eye of the documentary maker. If the former ran the risk of annihilating his creation in an apocalypse, then the latter can endanger his art through indiscriminate exhaustiveness, or the merely notional intimacy with his characters that informs *Headbirths*.

Grass's overinsistent interventionist policy heaps opposites together for fear that everything might fall apart. The same fear energizes the very different fiction of Stanley Elkin, whose *The Living End* casts God as artist and star turn in his own comic apocalypse. Toward the end of the novel God quizzes his creation on his own motives, motives that the action of the book, an encyclopedia of urban traumata, have revealed as progressively unfathomable. God's accomplices run through an insipid list of orthodoxies before he interrupts them. "Is that what you think?" he asks a saint who suspects fuel is goodness. "Were you born yesterday? You've been in the world. Is that how you explain trial and error, history by increment, God's long Slap and Tickle, His Indian-gift wrath? *Goodness*? No, It was Art! . . . I work by the contrasts and metrics, by beats and the silences. It was all Art. *Because it makes a better story is why.*"[45]

The separation of meaning from human perception is the source of pain for men and art for God. In *The Living End*, the better the story goes for God, the worse the world hangs for men. The result is that Elkin's style celebrates a thorough separation of words from meaning. *Bad* is pressed into service to describe lost change and battered brains; *visitations* and *attentions*, words with connotations of courtship, come to mean liquor-store heists and pistol whippings, while the book's most well-meaning act, Ellerbee's decision to support the wife of his brain-damaged clerk, is described as a deed of utter selfishness.

Because Elkin senses that the world as it is designed falls short of our desires and our capacities, he elevates storytelling into a universal compulsion. So short does reality fall of our expectations that we are compelled to come up with alternatives of our own. The big danger of course is that everyman will become his own godly artist and, in the way initiated by Elkin's spurned artist-god in *The Living End*, make his own lies into rods for everyone else's back.

Friedrich Schlegel could scarcely have imagined that his *universalpoesie* would reach its bizarre destination in the fantastic underclass saga of Elkin's next novel, *George Mills*, which describes a network of victimization and betrayal that invention in turn activates and alleviates. When Mills and Guillalume meet a mysterious figure "whose garments are covered with strange scrolls and devices,"[46] such emblems lead them to expect worlds of wonder and marvel. These expectations are fulfilled when their mysterious stranger turns out to be a master of narrative. Unfortunately, his stories are devised to gull his auditors into the mines, where their bodies will earn their own form of heraldry—the tessellation of scars and wounds that Mills's ancestor discovers as his fellow-workers' very own coat of arms. Storytelling, admits the mysterious merchant, "keeps them down on the farm." Time and again, the book soars into invention only to collide with some bitter cliché that betrays the victimizing designs of its fabricator.

In *The Living End* and *George Mills*, the invention of the oppressor breeds the invention of the oppressed. Neither book has much in the way of structure beyond the projection of a global system of fiction making inspired by, and adding to, a shared universality of pain and poverty. And Elkin's characters, like the janitor Mr. Quiz in *The Living End*, or the merchant of *George Mills*, are in their very different ways too steeped in their own viciousness to allow other people into their inventions as anything other than victims. When Quiz marches his schoolboys around the cemetery to spite Ladlehaus, or when Mills's ancestor discovers a tapestry that weaves in art the same web of victimization that he has witnessed in reality, we realize that the almost tropical profusion of Elkin's narratives conceals one overruling impulse—the desire to cause pain that provokes and maintains the action of both books.

The basis for the world of exploitation that victimizes all Elkin's characters is the story. Elkin himself, fascinated by the arbitrary power of the storyteller, has told Heide Ziegler that his own art is only "controlled whim. Art is the decision of the artist and it can be anything he decides."[47] The result is a fiction that is as shapeless and viscous as life itself, and as seemingly unconditioned by the shaping imagination. Robert Coover, who shares Elkin's sense that his world has become a zone for competing fictions, has an acuter sense of how these fictions inevitably amalgamate into one ruling pattern. But this is not a design made by any mere artist; Coover's world has, like West's, been manufactured rather than designed.

In his novel *The Universal Baseball Association, J. Henry Waugh, Prop.*, Coover records the attempt of one J. Henry Waugh (or Jahweh according to some commentators) to create an authoritative master fiction. Henry's nights are spent with enough dice and average sheets to people his own imaginary baseball league; he has even invented songs with which his imaginary supporters cheer on his fictitious teams. Henry has never had much love for the real game, with its brutal restrictions of time and its arbitrary demands for team loyalty. The songs he invents reveal much about the peculiar resemblance between his solitary vigils and a much more imposing structure: "Funny thing about both country music and baseball with its 'village greens': they weren't really country, not since they got their new names anyway, but urban. Kid stuff, dreams of heroism and innocence, staged by pros and turned into big business."[48] Henry's own game, with its endless columns of averages, its arbitrary dismissals, its nostalgia cycles, and yearlong season, resembles "big business" far more than baseball. As the shape of Henry's game comes clearer, its remarkable resemblance to Henry's real-world employment at Dunkelmann, Zauber and Zifferblatt, Licensed Tax & General Accountants becomes evident. Like Henry, this association aims at expansion: its audits are "Monthly, Quarterly, and Annual"; its turnover is enormous, its activities extensive, its supervision fierce and arbitrary. Like Elkin, Coover gradually reveals how everyman as his own godly artist reduplicates an overruling master fiction. Henry nightly confronts the playful equivalent of the corporate and arithmetical world he dodges during the day. His self-created association is only a replica of the organization he inhabits so unwillingly as an employee.

What emerges from Coover's book is the sense that even the isolated eccentric cannot escape the leveling momentum of American global accountancy. When Henry meets a florist called Mr. Valentine who has devoted himself to the perfection of indestructible plastic roses, he can only snort, "It's not the point." Coover's goal is to fence his godly makers within the fiction created by a greater corporate association—the U.B.A. itself. The U.B.A., as a postindustrial empire, has become as isolated and spectral as the game of a half-insane

middle-aged accountant. Waugh's songs and half-finished biographies
are relics from a time that can now only be reimagined by a solitary
bachelor; Henry himself is so disturbed by his memories that he can
never share them and is compelled to annihilate them. In the battle
between nostalgia and number, Henry favors number—a choice that
may reflect more than personal preference.

Gabriel García Márquez's *One Hundred Years of Solitude* gives perhaps the most decisive commentary on the postwar mythology of everyman his own godly artist. When José Arcadio Buendía, a village
patriarch, sees the metal ingots that a visiting gypsy shows him, he
realizes that "things have a life of their own, it's simply a matter of
waking up their souls."[49] The gypsy's performance, which so cun-
ningly combines animism and science, leads Arcadio to desert his village and reject a shared communal life in pursuit of what is ambigu-
ously called "the spirit of social initiative" (18). Infused with this
spirit, Arcadio is willing to destroy the fabric of his society and the
unity of his family to satisfy a self-devouring quest for gold, gold that
is inextricably linked for him with dreams of wealth and, perhaps
more lingeringly, with the godly capacity to bring matter to life. Because this dream can never be realized, Arcadio squanders his wealth
and spends the remainder of his life devoured by an illusion.

As the book continues, the hivelike structure of Arcadio's village
becomes a set of separated cells, as his descendants take on Arcadio's
own image, becoming increasingly self-absorbed, more and more
trapped in their own illusions. Arcadio's "magic" makes his world disappear; his village accelerates from pastoral to postindustrial without
ever making contact with the things he so desperately wished to bring
to life. The closing pages of the book describe a world of furtive paedo-
philes, religious fanatics, and incestuous lovers. The intensely ener-
getic extended family with which the book begins vanishes completely.

But just as it seems that giants have dwindled and the world has
collapsed into a swarm of isolated destinies, García Márquez reaffirms
the traditional force of the godly artist *topos*. Aureliano Babilonia finds
a manuscript in the shattered remains of his family house. On it he
discovers a prophesy of his own world's destruction. At this moment
magic is revealed as something latent in words not things, and the
words Aureliano reads are uncompromising about the destructive
qualities of self-incarceration: "Before reaching the final line, however,
he had already understood that he would never leave that room, for it
was foreseen that the city of mirrors (or mirages) would be wiped out
by the wind and exiled from the memory of men at the precise moment when Aureliano Babilonia would finish deciphering the parch-

ments, and that everything written on them was unrepeatable since time immemorial and for ever more, because races condemned to one hundred years of solitude did not have a second opportunity on earth" (383).

Where Elkin implies that reality is perpetually open to the negotiations conducted by the eager hands of individual initiative, and Coover sees the authority of all godly makers as subject to the control of one corporate and multinational illusion, García Márquez uses the long perspectives of apocalypse to subdue his ubiquitous godly makers. But what is this parchment that Aureliano Babilonia is reading? Who can have made it? Its conditions are fixed but its contexts cannot be known. García Márquez's book ends here, in an apocalypse unfollowable but also unfathomable. The godly maker in *One Hundred Years of Solitude* moves in ways too mysterious for mere humanity to comprehend.

V.

The godly maker as sovereign consciousness reaches his upper limits in Sontag's Hippolyte, where he ceases to create and is confined in his own private world. A complementary movement closes *One Hundred Years of Solitude*, where García Márquez gradually reveals how a world premised on the idea that reality is no more than a collision of fictions must inevitably suffer one collision too many, with the result that world and book explode simultaneously. On either of these opposing fronts, the idea of the artist as a godly maker endures only under extreme pressure. On the one hand, Sontag, Gass, and Nabokov focus on the artist's sovereign consciousness so much that events wither away, leaving only the artist's report on his own delusions. It is surely no accident that much of *Pale Fire* and *The Benefactor* desert the novel form almost completely; their disguises—scholarly edition and journal—illustrate the fact that their focus is more on the interpreting consciousness than on events. On the other hand, Elkin, Grass, and Coover sacrifice the artist's authority in an effort to realize the potential unleashed by a variety of competing fictions. If the first type of fiction tends to freeze at the point of its maker's conception, then the second buckles under the weight of his accumulations. Neither kind of godly maker can fuse imagination and reality into a continuous narrative. It is to two writers who attempt such a synthesis, albeit in very different ways, that I now turn.

CHAPTER FIVE

John Hawkes's God: The Realist
Malgré Lui

> Imagination, a licentious and vagrant faculty, unsusceptible of
> limitations and impatient of restraint, has always endeavoured to
> baffle the logician, to perplex the confines of distinction, and
> burst the enclosures of regularity.
> —Samuel Johnson, *The Rambler*, May 28, 1751

I.

John Hawkes's work must be approached with caution. Alan
Trachtenberg rightly calls it "hard, original and difficult," adding the
shrewd remark that it is also "metaphysical, odd and self-protective."[1]
Since Hawkes's fiction defies all attempts to apprehend it, perhaps his
interviews will help. They are, after all, remarkably consistent. Over
a thirty-year period Hawkes has insisted on the godly power of
the imagination in a most uncompromising and dogmatic fashion.
Hawkes's credo—that the artist is a sovereign and arbitrary creator
who does not so much represent his fictional world as invent it—has
appeared in many interviews. Similarly, his declaration of war on the
conventional novel, first made to John Enck in 1965, has been repeated many times since.[2] Indeed, two or more Hawkes critics are
rarely gathered together without the master's war cry—"The true ene-
mies of the novel [are] plot, character, setting, and theme"—surfacing
at some stage of the discussion.[3] In a 1975 interview with John Kuehl,
Hawkes was even more uncompromising on the artist's godly powers.
"I write my own authorial visions of what I take to be 'reality,'"
Hawkes told his interviewer, insisting that for him realism was no
more than "pedestrian thinking."[4] Moreover, Hawkes has invested
some of his own imaginative aspirations and ambitions in his characters. Hawkes described Cyril, the sex singer of *The Blood Oranges*, as
"simply a God-like man with infinite capacities for love."[5] About
Larry, gang leader and master plotter in *The Lime Twig*, Hawkes has
been less effusive but more categorical: he told Nancy Levine quite
bluntly that "he's God."[6]

Paul Rosenzweig, in a most illuminating interpretation of

Hawkes's fiction, isolates the tendency of the creator's aesthetic premises to spill over into the consciousnesses of his creations, and identifies a "psychology of control" at work in both. Like their creator, Rosenzweig argues, Hawkes's heroes burst the frame of their narratives, which they attempt to coerce into pure vision through the construction of "non-chronological images or tableaus [in a bid] to frame every aspect and moment of their lives."[7] For both creator and protagonists, what is all-important is the task of subduing reality to the sovereignty of the imagination.

Yet alongside the aspirations of creator and protagonists to elevate the artist to the status of a deity is the somewhat contradictory account Hawkes offers of the *purpose* of the artist as a godly maker. When John Barth visited Stanford University in 1966, Hawkes told his audience that Barth's "purpose is nothing less than to 'reinvent the world' and to restore to contemporary literature a proper Hero." He continued by describing the works in which Barth had managed this: "With *The Sot-Weed Factor* and now *Giles Goat Boy*, John Barth has *twice* reinvented the world, has given shape to a novelistic voice which is unique in this country, and at the same time has about it a fantastic universal appeal. He pierces our most deplorable pretensions—public and private—and amazingly enough, in a disintegrating world, creates for us a new literacy of the imagination."[8]

This mysteriously self-referring testimonial to Barth's imagination is, of course, an authoritative summary of Hawkes's own activity as an artist. Yet Hawkes's godly maker steers his fictional craft into strange waters, where it points in two frankly contradictory ways. If Hawkes's introduction closes conventionally enough, routinely gesturing toward the New Jerusalem created by the sovereign imagination, his initial description of Barth as a godly maker directs us to that writer's satirical and realistic purposes, the way he gains "fantastic universal appeal" by "piercing our most deplorable pretensions—public and private." This confusion gives two contradictory impulses to Hawkes's own fiction. In the first, Hawkes acknowledges the godly maker's capacity to bend the world into the shape he imagines for it, to the point where world, reader, and character disappear in the intense clarity of the Hawksian utterance. Hawkes's second account of the function of the godly maker, however, stresses the artist's mimetic capacity to imitate our everyday evasions and delusions.

If Hawkes's fiction at one level soars toward an autonomous integrity that would shake art free from its slavish dependence on matter and content, then on another, equally crucial level, the godly maker is necessarily laden with cliché, heavy with the oppressions of memory and the burdens of the culture at large. On the one hand,

Hawkes marches to the drum of his own self-begotten view of art; on the other, he colonizes our consciousness like an invading army. In "our disintegrating world," the artist's power rests in his capacity to exaggerate our tricks of habit and to enforce on our attention the disintegrating tedium of our lives and their imminent dislocation. Although the image of the interrupted sleep, a motif in Hawkes's fiction from *The Cannibal* to *The Passion Artist*, testifies to the artist's power to violate our most private experience, it also provides a commentary on the conditions of that experience. For Hawkes, most of us live in a kind of precarious oblivion from which we can be roused only by the unwelcome attentions of a godly maker. The artist's sovereignty rests in a privileged access to "the storehouse of memory" where, as Konrad Vost puts it, "all perception, all psychic life, everything remembered, everything thought, all the products and all the residue whatsoever of the psychological system are retained down to the last drop, the last invisible hair" (43).

The peculiar tension in Hawkes's artistic sympathies between an art godly in its self-sufficiency and one godly in its power to mime the whole panoply of our inner disguises is reflected in critical responses to his work. For one influential group of critics, Hawkes's excellence rests in his language, which is the resource that permits him to release his visionary power. Tony Tanner compares him in this respect to Vladimir Nabokov, finding in both a belief that "style itself becomes the saving assertion" of their work.[9] Earl Rovit, probably Hawkes's best critic, identifies at the center of his work only "the master rhythm of a vast traffic of insane order. . . . his best novels are unattentive to ledger-book balances of commonplace reality." The momentum of this rhythm builds to "a liberating release from rationality itself."[10]

Where critics have failed to jibe with Hawkes's visionary temper, their responses have often been unsympathetic. Perhaps Hawkes's most outspoken adversary has been Roger Sale, who saw *The Blood Oranges* as "the work of a contemptible imagination." With considerable eloquence, Sale marshaled a remarkable case against Hawkes, which rested on the notion that "when horror becomes a pastime it should announce itself," a point that any Hawkes critic must surely confront.[11] To reduce Sale's argument to more neutral terms is in some way to make it even more lethal, since it points to a seeming confusion in Hawkes's loyalties. How far, we might ask, are Hawkes's novels projections of the ambitions of his protagonists and how far are they exposures of these ambitions as delusions? Hawkes himself has consistently entertained the idea of the imagination's godly power; does his fiction unmask this pretension or become fixed in it? If the latter, how can he claim to be a satirist; if the former, what is there in Hawkes's style and technique that makes confusions of the proportions displayed by Sale so common?

Some excavation of the phrase "pierces our most deplorable pretensions" will be necessary to answer this question. The phrase is a favorite with Hawkes, a not at all uncharacteristic self-borrowing—for his work is virtually an echo chamber of horrors—from his description of "Flannery O'Connor's Devil," published in *Sewanee Review* some four years before Hawkes introduced Barth to Stanford students. And this essay too is a mysteriously self-referring document, a work whose methodical eccentricity may help us to understand Hawkes's god, the artistic imagination that he sees as the presiding deity in his fictional world.

In "Flannery O'Connor's Devil," Hawkes remarks that Flannery O'Connor confided to him that the devil was the character in her work who goes about "piercing our pretensions." These kinds of confident orthodoxies are automatically suspect for Hawkes, who, with an alarming critical ingenuity, goes so far as to suggest that the devil's voice in O'Connor's fiction contributed toward piercing the pretensions—or at any rate the orthodoxies—of her stated Catholic belief. Fiction for Hawkes is the realm that disturbs the pieties that the first-person voice of ordinary life mouths unthinkingly. In order to emphasize the distinction he perceives between precept and practice, Hawkes contrasts the typical and shocking clarity of O'Connor's orthodox statement of belief ("I want to be certain that the devil gets identified as the devil and not simply taken for this or that psychological tendency") with the imaginative commitment that he unhooks from her tentacular prose.

> There is an interesting distance between the directness of her statement and profundity of belief, and the shifting, even deceptive substance of what Flannery O'Connor, with disarming humor and understatement, has called her "one-cylinder syntax." My own feeling is that just as the creative process threatens the Holy throughout Flannery O'Connor's fiction by generating a paradoxical fusion of improbability and passion out of the Protestant "do-it-yourself" evangelicism of the South. . . . so too, throughout this fiction, the creative process transforms the writer's objective Catholic knowledge of the devil into an authorial attitude in some measure diabolical.[12]

This account of O'Connor's devil may be no more than a piece of new critical orthodoxy masquerading as an audacious heresy. It was not, after all, so daring for a critic writing in 1962 to separate fiction from belief. But two important points emerge for a reader of Hawkes's fiction. First, once allowed into Hawkes's world, objective event or stated orthodoxy can only function as part of a larger subjective pretension, so that O'Connor's Catholicism becomes a mask, something her imagination must rip off and annihilate. But by the same token, Hawkes's own much-explicated, much-repeated belief in the sovereignty of the imagination may, when the creative process gets to work, be exploded in the course of the narrative. This means that Hawkes's fiction will, all Hawkes's stated opinions notwithstanding, set up "an interesting distance between the directness" of their creator's affirmations on behalf of the imagination and the ambiguous testimony of "the shifting, even deceptive substance" that Hawkes goes about creating in his own work.

Where fiction goes to work, dogma is hurled out of the window. Just what we feel ought to happen. But the case is not always so simple: does Larry, the strongman of *The Lime Twig*, act as a projection of our pretensions or as a satire on them? We cannot reasonably expect Hawkes's protagonists to announce their perfidy to us; their very immersion in the pretense of omnipotence makes this impossible. But if Hawkes's fiction is not merely to luxuriate in what it undertook to explode, we can at least expect to be made aware in the course of the narrative of the actual consequences of these pretensions.

At his best, as this and the next chapter will argue, Hawkes provides these checks to his protagonists' pretensions. Where they reaffirm endlessly their creator's tributes to the unquestionable authority of their own imaginations, Hawkes's narratives show the degree to which the claim to imaginative authority becomes what Rosenzweig so aptly characterized as the "psychology of control." However, one of our most self-deluding devices, Hawkes recognizes, is to disguise our desire for control and power in the language and designs of art. One of the first things Zizendorf in *The Cannibal* captures in his bid for power is a printing press; one of the last expropriations made by Papa in *Travesty* is his theft of Henri's poem, an act that literally takes the words out of the artist's mouth. Hawkes shows us a world where reality has become consciousness's waste product; but although Hawkes's interviews endorse the authority of consciousness to exert its godly will, his fiction does not.

And Hawkes uses some very old-fashioned devices—the plot, character, setting, and theme he disavowed so fiercely to John Enck in 1965—to check these claims. The plots of Hawkes's novels unravel the pretensions of his godly consciousness, which culminate in the highway apocalypse of Papa in *Travesty*. The settings of the fiction, from the asylum of *The Cannibal* to the prisonlike railway station of *The Passion Artist*, bear witness to the power of consciousness to disfigure a whole environment. Moreover, Hawkes's characters repeatedly cross the boundaries from rightful authority to almost Oriental despotism. Finally, Hawkes finds his theme in the pitched battle between imagination and reality that rages at the center of his most important work.

Hawkes, then, like Melville's confidence man, is "quite an original." If we are going to find his kin anywhere, it is surely not with the postmodernist *bricolage* assembled by Albert Guerard—"the rich playfulness of Nabokov; the verbal pyrotechnics of Lawrence Durrell and his humorous relishing of decay; the wilder energies of Donleavy and Bellow; the great poetic myth-making of Andrew Lytle and the visions of Flannery O'Connor; the structural experiments of the later Faulkner and the broken-record repetitions of Beckett." [13] In this company, the distinctively Hawksian—the capacity to entertain and annihilate his own dearest aspirations in a disturbingly unsettled fictional form—is clearly lost. Better, surely, to look for a more distant precedent in the work of Jonathan Swift, for Hawkes and the Swift of *A Tale of a Tub* share the vision of a world whose endlessly circulating, dangerously unauthorized illusions contaminate the attempt of any artist to legislate for their control.

II.

At the very beginning of *The Cannibal*, even before the narrative gets underway, the reader encounters the epigraph, "I have told our story," a boast that puzzles any reader at all familiar with Hawkes's convictions. How can this be, this desire to tell "our story," in a writer who has disowned any truck with mere history or social realism? Hawkes has repeatedly downplayed the amount of history in *The Cannibal*. When Paul Emmett and Richard Vine asked him to reply to Gore Vidal's charge that contemporary American authors had no interest in history, Hawkes replied that he began his novel after reading a high school history textbook. [14] But, of course, there is some history that is too familiar to need research. *The Cannibal* is a book more like *Myra Breckenridge* than *Burr*. Hawkes wants to be true to the shape of our inner histories, for it is there that he can entrap us in a design that will cumulatively reveal itself as "our story." His aim is to record the whole thrust of our lives, from romantic transcendence to bureaucratic totalitarianism, so that the title of his book gradually comes to refer not

merely to the Duke who devours Jutta's child, but to the whole effort
Zizendorf mounts at the end of the novel to devour Germany's consciousness and create a future in his own image.

The book's opening pages track this movement to its origins. The
world of dueling codes, high altitudes, and flashing blades exists only
in Madame Snow's memory now, to be fused with the remnants of a
shell-shocked Germany. Hawkes inspects Madame Snow's mind and
finds all manner of cliché, hope, and wild conjecture.

> Madame Snow could not believe that the worst would come. All
> her faith was in the knuckle bones of a worthless currency, in the
> right of the victorious, a coinage covered with the heads of high-
> spirited men. Bits of gauze were pushed into the clay and women
> wore coats with epaulettes and brass buttons. In the early days
> when the patients had rioted at the institution, it was the women
> who beat them down with clubs, while girls with spirited eyes
> and bare knees lured officers to a night of round-the-world. Arms
> and armies and silver blades were gone, the black had come out
> of the realm of Kings, and butterflies and grass were left for chil-
> dren. Freight trains were hit and burned and no more came, and
> the keys of all machines were welded together. *"Wohin gehen Sie?"*
> cried the devils, and the clatter of boots died out of the barracks.
> (10–11)

Hawkes's prose welds together prewar aspirations and postwar
deprivations in such a way that the past is answerable for the fragments of the present. Madame Snow's belief in "the right of the vic-
torious" is a cliché that dies on her lips, buried with the bits of gauze
and worthless currency that are the remnants of the prewar military
order of armies and silver blades. That time lives on in degraded form
in the ruins of 1939 civil life. The girls who seduced the heroes have
become the women who beat down revolts in the asylum, which itself
is the institutional shell of the prewar Prussian commitment to order
and control. The heroes have all vanished, leaving only the exploitable
fact of their heroism; they provide the heads of a worthless coinage.

Madame Snow's consciousness, half nostalgia and half fantasy,
gives way to the wild surmises of Balamir, who imagines himself to be
the son of the kaiser. But this idea is only Balamir's grandest self-
image. His life is warmed by the friction that results from the collision
of his illusions.

> Balamir came eventually to think of himself as Madame Snow's
> Prince. But for a long while he worked by himself, still smelling
> drugs and fighting with the terrible shapes that leaped from
> drawers. He longed to be in the mountains, to leap from crag to

crag, fly about the snow fields and find gold at the foot of stunted trees. He longed to tend the sheep and be a gangling black dog racing at the herd over green slopes. He longed to live in a cave. Icicles hung between the slats of the cellar window at night, and Balamir began to think of the jewels hanging from the ears of Madame Snow, began to listen for the turning of the key. He listened for the only accordion in the town and the notes travelled down the rain pipe, over the slate, but no voices sang to the crashing of the steins. There was nowhere to eat in *Spitzen-on-the-Dein*, and the tables were piled on one another, chipped with bulletholes. Sometimes Balamir heard sleigh bells that jingled in the valleys of the Alps, and he flung himself on piles of cold rubbish and earth as on a snow heap. He slept on an army cot, longed for the fir trees, and as he grunted and threw his weight every day into the frozen articles of chairs, springs and picture frames, he felt that his strength was falling away. He remembered photographs of the vicious tigers and the days when all men wore spats or silver braid, and from the mountains to the *Brauhaus*, camps and meeting halls sprang up, precision glasses were trained. He thought of a pigtailed donkey and the bones of men ground into food. But now the guardhouse was empty, his father, who had been the Kaiser, was dead, and the nurses had been taken from the institution as corporals. He began to sit at the top of the stairs waiting for the door to open. (11–12)

Hawkes's method is to feed the fabric of public history into the machinery of private illusion. Madame Snow and Balamir are recognizable types—to the point of being stereotypes. They are the romantic lady and the Prussian military officer; but their inner lives overwhelm their typicality, so that, if they begin as all too familiar characters, they soon acquire a disturbing novelty. One grain of obsession—"his father who had been the Kaiser"—yields Balamir a rich harvest of illusions, as he longs for, thinks of, and waits for a host of events that do not occur and a series of identities that do not materialize. The effect is to dissolve reality into the compulsions of consciousness, a process at which Balamir is proficient but unconscious, but one that will be exploited more rationally by Zizendorf later in the novel.

The shape of Balamir's hopes is remarkably like Madame Snow's, indicating that a whole caste is stamped on one die: Madame Snow cannot think the worst could come; Balamir wants to think of himself as Madame Snow's prince. The youthful Madame Snow "seemed the image of the passing swan"; Balamir longs to be "a black dog racing at the head of the herd." Even in his present state of delusion, Balamir wants to command; even as a respected crone, Madame Snow must think back to her days as a grand and desirable young lady. In Balamir's mind, Madame Snow's heroes have declined further; where Stella's heroes were only coinage, to Balamir they have become "the bones of men ground into food." The romantic world of hunters has become the institutional prison where the hunters have become their prey. Cycles of decay, fallen dynasties, ruined careers: Hawkes has packed much into a little here, but we are still unclear how it all happened. All that we await is an explanation.

In their different ways, Madame Snow, now a respected crone, and Balamir, a prince of shadows, form the husks that remain of the compulsion for transcendence that characterized the Germany of 1914. But within that world nests a new elite, just as military in its aspirations, but ballasted by rationality and sophisticated machinery. The futile attempt of Ernst to mount the carriage of Cromwell shows the impossibility of Madame Snow's proud young men ever becoming part of the new world that Cromwell describes.

> Antwerp fell. The Krupp gun, 42 centimeter, took them through and luckily enough, I was able to see the whole thing. It was like Hohenlohe's progress in Africa, more, you see, than just a concentration of men for their own good, more than anything like a unity of states, like the Zolleverein, rather complete success, a mass move greater than a nation, a more pure success than Prussia's in the Schleswig-Holstein affair. We fought, gained in the area of Soissons and they couldn't drive us from Saint Mihiel— glory to the German army! The line is now from the English Channel to Switzerland, and we wait only spring. We extend across Europe in four hundred integrated miles. (92–93)

Once again we come upon a story half told already. We note that in Cromwell's vision machines have come to dwarf men, who are now significant only insofar as they pack into masses: "Four hundred integrated miles, a mass move greater than a nation." Calculation has replaced heroism; we have moved away from a world of silver braid and dueling scars to a world of columns of figures, sweeping statements, and good housekeeping.

Although Cromwell is proud of his regime's precision, we note with with some horror its capacity to compress horror into platitude and its almost ascetic restraint from considering the consequences of its actions. We recognize in Cromwell's language the peculiar combination of a housemaster's enthusiasm and an engineer's precision, a combination that floats clear of its referent, the onward march of a regime committed to wholesale destruction in the name of progress. When Cromwell gasps almost benignly that "luckily enough I was able to see the whole thing," the reader is transported to the world of the holiday snapshot, even though Cromwell's subject is the business of war. Plainly the power to see things as they are not characterizes both the old ruling clique and its successors. But unlike its predecessors, who moved far beyond the concerns of other people, Cromwell's regime wants to work by an unsolicited complicity. This becomes more evident as he slides imperceptibly into a disturbing "we" ("We wait only spring. We extend across Europe in four hundred integrated miles"). In this unexpected shift, he anticipates the lines of a new society that will impose its values collectively. Where Stella Snow's heroes scarcely acknowledged the existence of anything but the "I," Cromwell's military engineers try to impress upon us their unalterable right to make their designs our realities, their pretensions our creeds.

This shift to the first-person plural is, of course, where the narrative began, with Zizendorf's outrageous conjunction of progress and idyll.

> There is a town in Germany today, I cannot say just where, that has, by a great effort, risen above the misery that falls the lot of defeated communities on the continent. It has been slowly bettering itself now, under my guidance, for three years, and I am very nearly satisfied with the progress we have made in civic organization. It is a garden spot; all of our memories are there, and people continually seek it out. . . . I have told our story. The things that remain to be done weigh heavily on my mind, and all the remarkable activity of these foreign cities cannot distract me. At present, even though I enjoy it here, I am waiting, and at the first opportunity, I will, of course, return. (epigraph)

Zizendorf projects the third world of *The Cannibal*. It is one that combines the idea of ease and valor that we saw in Stella's world ("It is a garden spot") with the smug efficiency we saw in Cromwell's ("It has been slowly bettering itself"). Zizendorf is the book's godly maker, for his vision includes past ("all of our memories are there"), present ("the progress we have made in civic organization"), and future in one significant mental landscape where "the things that remain to be done weigh heavily on my mind." When the ordinary universe is as thoroughly routed as this, it falls to men who, like Cromwell or Zizendorf, carry their pretensions in their heads to get things done. Hawkes makes Zizendorf prime mover and *terminus ad quem* for the novel. This is an act of considerable strategic effectiveness, because it ensures that *The Cannibal* comes to us with Zizendorf's vision at its edges, so that

the whole narrative rolls inexorably forward toward the man who purports to be telling "our story," and from whom, for as long as we are
reading this book, there seems to be no escape.

Yet it is in Zizendorf's narrative, paradoxically enough, that
Hawkes reveals the godly maker's propensity for deluding himself.
For Zizendorf has nothing to work with except his own illusions,
which progressively come to entrap the illusionist himself. Toward the
end of the book, Zizendorf's head is full of schemes for a new order of
things, a new world. But when he discloses his plans for this new
world, he invariably betrays the megalomania that rules his inner life.

> Once more I climbed the dark stairs, deciding as I went, that in
> the weeks to come I'd turn the place into the National Headquar-
> ters. I'd use Stintz's rooms as the stenographic bureau, the secre-
> taries would have to be young and blonde. I reached the third
> floor and a gust of cold wind, that only a few hours before had
> swept over the morning already broken in the conquered north,
> made me shiver and cough. My boots thumped on the wooden
> floor, my sharp face was determined, strained. It was a good idea,
> I thought, to make this old house the Headquarters, for I could
> keep Jutta right on the premises. Of course, the children would
> have to go. I'd fill the place with light and cut in a few new win-
> dows. The aristocrat on the second floor, the Duke, would per-
> haps make a good Chancellor, and of course, the Census-Taker
> could be Secretary of State. The town was due prosperity, per-
> haps I could build an open-air pavilion on the hill for the children.
> Of course I'd put the old horse statue back on its feet. Young
> couples would make love beneath it on summer nights. It might
> be better to mount it on blocks of stone, so that visitors drawing
> near the city could say "Look, there's the statue of Germany, given
> by the new Leader to his country." (183)

Zizendorf's bid for power begins with an attempt to capture a
printing press. In his world this is a weapon to be used to capture
minds by reproducing illusions. Finding himself in a postindustrial
society (the Germany he inhabits is too shattered and disunited to
produce anything), Zizendorf quickly determines that his role will be
to manipulate what illusions remain. But the strongest illusion of all in
the Germany described in the book's opening sections is the illusion of
power, and as we watch we become amused by Zizendorf's capacity to
take illusion for event. His "I'd turn the place into . . . I'd use. . . . I'd
put" is relentless, but it gradually wraps around itself, culminating in
Zizendorf's hearty slap on his own back, the vehicle for which is the
imaginary opinions he has projected onto imaginary others: "Visitors

could say, 'Look there's the statue . . . given by the Leader.'" Of course, there are as yet only the fragments of a statue; Zizendorf has no country and is not yet a leader; there are no visitors. Since Zizendorf's world has only illusion to nourish it, his authority rests in his ability to capture the ruling illusion, the will to power that the worlds of 1914 and 1945 both recognize as all-important, that even now is lodged in the maimed brain of Balamir "who had come to think of himself as Madame Snow's Prince." To capture this illusion, Zizendorf must wear the mask of an artist, exploiting the shattered symbols that remain in the town.

Zizendorf's narrative completes the circle of illusion of previous chapters; it does not transform it. The world Zizendorf anticipates is built on the foundations of the old, which he attempts to legislate away through language and technology. Accordingly, Stintz's room, previously the site of a shared guilt, is turned into a "National Headquarters" merely by Zizendorf's fiat. The language of progress—"The town was due prosperity. . . . I'd put the old horse statue back on its feet"—signals us toward a vision of pure regress, a vision clinched by Zizendorf's appointment of the aristocrat on the second floor (who just happens to be a cannibal) to a chancellorship.

Zizendorf's regime promises still worse. Where the first chapter ended in an act of charity, as Stella welcomed the shattered Balamir with "come in, you poor creature" (19), the novel ends with Zizendorf's act of coercion as he bullies Selvaggia so relentlessly that her dazed wonder (a wonder corresponding to the reader's own bafflement) becomes a mute obedience. "Selvaggia opened the door and crept into the room. She looked more thin than ever in the light of day, wild-eyed from watching the night and the birth of the Nation. 'What's the matter, Mother? Has anything happened?' I answered instead of Jutta, without looking up, and my voice was vague and harsh; 'Nothing. Draw those blinds and go back to sleep . . .' She did as she was told" (195).

Zizendorf's language struggles to one last doublethink as his night of slaughter becomes "the birth of the Nation," an assertion that combines megalomania and banality in equal measure. But the last sentences of the book close like a steel trap; in the new world that Zizendorf creates in 1945, coercion will fool itself into believing it is art in order to achieve the power that is its raison d'être. Zizendorf has acquired the means of production and some of the vocabulary; it only remains for him to convince us of his power to tell "our story." For an author not interested in history, Hawkes has excavated pretty thoroughly in the depths of our most inmost pretensions.

III.

"I have told our story": The story of how the fulfillment of Zizendorf's promise becomes a disturbing reality for his audience arises not
so much from the enormity of the horrors he depicts as from the manner of his narration, which establishes an unsettling intimacy with the
reader. Zizendorf himself appears as oblivious of us as he is of almost
everything except his master plan. But his fussy commentaries on his
own performance—"I swung the tuba short. I should have preferred
to have some distance and be able to swing it like a golf club" (173),
his precise specification of his self image—"I answered instead of
Jutta . . . my voice was vague and harsh" (195), and his offhand con-
fessions—"Actually, I had never seen Berlin" (177) accumulate to the
point where we feel like reluctant eavesdroppers, forced to listen to a
story we never wanted to hear and confidences we had no desire to
share. Hence, the story swells into "our story" in two distinct ways:
ours in that it faultlessly maps out the shape of European history from
1914 to 1939, but ours, perhaps more treacherously, in its requiring
our participation for its fulfillment.

The rewards of *Second Skin* and *The Blood Oranges*, where Hawkes
returns to the mind of the godly maker, are perhaps not so great. In
these novels, history, if it is present at all, exists only in parodied or
burlesqued forms. When Skipper signally fails to rescue Catalina Kate
from an iguana and then compares his situation to St. George's legen-
dary bout with the dragon, we are aware of whole vistas of incongruity
that the novel gestures toward but never quite develops. Similarly, as
Cyril, surrounded by sufficient evidence of the history of Western
sexual repression to satisfy Michel Foucault himself, embarks upon
his paean to sexual liberation, the reader again becomes alerted to
some satirical purpose on the part of the author, although the novel
proceeds too obliquely for this potential to explode into action.

Second Skin and *The Blood Oranges*, therefore, do not go as far toward telling "our story" as *The Cannibal* does. What they do achieve is
a powerful penetration into the mind of the godly maker. To Hawkes's
description of Cyril as "simply a God-like man" one can add Thomas
LeClair's characterization of *Second Skin*'s Skipper: "He is, in effect,
a god—the creator of life . . . and a knower of things to come." [15]
Hawkes's narrators, who are hardly short on self-esteem, could say
no more.

For all that, neither book goes very far toward endorsing the
godly claims of its protagonist, as LeClair was quick to recognize.
Where the narrative technique of *The Cannibal* established an uneasy

proximity between audience and narrator, the rhetoric of *Second Skin* and *The Blood Oranges* does just the reverse. Both Cyril and Skipper play star roles in double plots; the two plots in each case fail to mesh in such a way as to incriminate their narrators. In Skipper's case, a godly present crowds out the memories of an abject past; the narrative that purports to liberate its teller entraps him still further. Cyril's narrative, on the other hand, has an almost elegiac cast, as the impotent lyricist intones the tale of the fragmentation of his hot pastoral. In each case the stories do not add up: all kinds of verbal echoes, reminiscences, and parallels point to the likenesses between Skipper's two islands. Similarly, Cyril as a sex singer and automatic seducer has not altered as much as he would like us to believe. All that has changed is the kind of victim he operates upon: an illiterate maid and a catatonic widow now relieve Cyril of the compulsions he used to call his sport.

What propels Skipper is his desire for evasion. His opening words reveal the massive energy he invests in his attempt to evade the actual, and the histrionic gestures he uses to persuade his readers to do likewise.

> Surely I am more than a man of love. It will become clear, I think, that I am a man of courage as well.
>
> Had I been born my mother's daughter instead of son—and the thought is not so improbable, after all, and causes me neither pain, fear nor embarrassment when I give it my casual and interested contemplation—I would not have matured into a muscular and self-willed Clytemnestra but rather into a large and innocent Iphigenia betrayed on the beach. A large and slow-eyed and smiling Iphigenia, to be sure, even more full to the knife than that real girl struck down once on the actual shore. (1–2)

Where Zizendorf projects the state as a work of art, Skipper tries to hammer his personality into one. Yet just as Zizendorf's imagination locks him further into the desire to coerce than was his original intention, so Skipper's imagination shows him progressively more entrapped in his desire to evade. And what Skipper wants to evade is apparent even in his allusions to Clytemnestra, the archetypal betrayer wife, and Iphigenia, the archetypal sacrificial daughter. Skipper's allusions are attempts to distance a fate that paradoxically entraps him further the harder he struggles to transcend it; his aim, to liberate himself from the memory of "the girl struck down on the actual shore," is ill served by the allusions he manages to muster.

Skipper's myth kitty is dangerously poorly stocked. As if to compensate for this, he employs a variety of self-elevating poses, which

range from the self-mystification that leads him to compare himself to
Prospero to the more ordinary gestures of complicity with which he
attempts to convince us that he is more than what he appears: "Surely
I am more. . . . It will be clear. . . . When I give it my casual and interested contemplation." Skipper tries vainly to grow before our very
eyes, as if his language has tapped some magical source.

None of this verbal boasting, however, will stand the test of action. On the contrary, any kind of crisis soon reveals Skipper's limita-
tions. Confronted by an iguana that threatens Catalina Kate, Skipper
runs through an elaborate routine of mantras and benedictions: "I listened until I could disregard no longer the little nun standing there
meekly under the towering wheel. 'Well, Josie,' I said, and stepped
forward briskly, 'Let's go and see what this is all about. OK, Josie?'"
(103). Skipper's rites are designed to fend off danger, not to dominate
it. They are little more than ways of delaying what he has no wish to
confront. His authority is chimeric, the fictive pretension of a sham
hero whose deeds are even less effective than his words: "There at my
feet. Kate. And on her back the monster. So I straddled her—colossus
over the reptile, colossus above the shores of woman—and hearing
the lap and shifting of the sea, and wiping my palms on my thighs
and leaning forward, I prepared to grapple with the monster. . . . I
was in no mood to take advice from Sister Josie and told her so"
(106–7). Only a page later, Skipper, "colossus" though he is, must ad-
mit defeat: " 'Well, Kate,' I said, and let go, stood up, wiped my brow,
'it looks as if he's there for good. Got us licked, hasn't he, Kate? Licked
from the start. He means to stay right where he is until he changes his
mind and crawls off under his own power. So the round goes to the
dragon, Kate. I'm sorry'" (108).

How much of this is comprehensible to Skipper's fellow islanders
is almost impossible to determine. But what is immediately important
is Skipper's distorted self-image. His sense of his own swollen self-
importance ("colossus over the reptile, colossus above the shores of
woman") jars with his petulant "I was in no mood to take advice from
Sister Josie, and told her so." Skipper is a henpecked Hercules, an ineffectual failure who, once he cannot conquer, makes an inconse-
quential joke about St. George and the dragon. The real moment of
self-recognition comes with the bitter self-depreciation of "got us
licked. . . . licked from the start." The gentle island replays only the
same gray deterministic message that Skipper saw inscribed across
the universe beyond the island. Skipper's own destiny, he estimates,
was forecast in a school-room copy book (46); his own daughter had
had "no chance. . . . No chance at all" (175) once she embarked on

her voyage on the *Peter Poor*. In this light, Skipper's language, far from transporting him to a godlike elevation, has a trifling superfluousness about it. For if "history is a dream already dreamt and destroyed" (45), then Skipper's story is an exposure of his own self-delusion. He sees symbols everywhere; his reader sees only cows. Even his gentle island has him "licked from the start." Language is a way to escape the defeats that nature endlessly piles up. At the end of the book, in a faintly onanistic image, Skipper watches "this final flourish of my own hand" and, in a most un-Prospero-like image, he awaits the call from Gloria, his favorite cow. Although he cultivates the illusion of authority, Skipper, like Zizendorf, is waiting only for a call. But in Skipper's case a cow, not a nation, will do the calling. Art in *Second Skin* is Skipper's supreme evasion, his way of miming the kinds of noises he would like to hear reality making.

Cyril, Hawkes's next godly maker, is a far trickier character. The two plots that comprise *The Blood Oranges* both have Cyril at their center as narrator and prime mover. But Cyril seems oblivious to any connection between his role as weaver of love's tapestry and collector of its split threads. He does, to be sure, make a few lugubrious gestures of dismay; but he never reflects on the different roles he plays in what are two essentially contradictory stories. In the first, he is a god, an artist completing the tapestry of love's variousness and promise; in the second, he is merely a pawn in a game played and won long before he began to participate. The first story belongs to the past, when Cyril had hoped to make his life a work of art; the second initiates the action of the novel, as Cyril prepares to seduce what remains of Catherine. The two narrative sequences interpenetrate throughout the novel, souring Cyril's most sweetly lyrical moments, checking even his most inspired flights, mingling the yarn of his erotic tapestry with a coarser cloth. But Cyril presses on, oblivious to all this; for him, as for Skipper, to become a godly maker is to cease to be afflicted by these lesser human complexities.

Cyril's narrative alternates between large boasts and small misgivings. He can at times force his attentions upon us with some of the impact of Zeus himself: "See me as bull, or ram, as man, husband, lover, a tall and heavy stranger in white shorts on a violet tennis court. I was there always. I completed the picture. I took my wife, took her friends, took the wives of my friends and a fair roster of other girls and women, from young to old and old to young, whenever the light was right or the music sounded" (2). "I completed the picture": Cyril's voice is that of an aggressive, defiant artist whose artwork is the great chain of copulation to which he gives his unquestioning allegiance.

He wills us into seeing him as a large, Zeus-like creature who contains
multitudes and can change at will into "bull, ram, husband, lover."

Cyril's language fuses sexuality and art. When he catches sight
of two game birds on his way back from Catherine's sanctuary, he sees
them as "worthy of inclusion in the erotic dreams of the most discrimi-
nating of all sex-aestheticians" (14–15). Cyril's own life aims to satisfy
these twin pleasures. On Illyria, he shares "an idyll" with a beautiful
wife, which he expands into a "quartet" with the help of Catherine
and Hugh. The latter's reluctance to join Cyril's "hot pastoral" leads
Cyril to complain in the language of a disaffected novelist, "When
would he ever respond . . . to my omniscience and Fiona's style?" (92).

Woven into Cyril's vision of a vertical take-off into sexual bliss,
even as he begins his narrative, is the knowledge that his idyll has already been fractured. "Why, after more than eighteen years, does the
soft medieval fabric of my tapestry now hang in shreds—here the
head of a rose, there the amputated hoof of some infant goat?" (3).
Hugh, whose wife Catherine Cyril seduced, is dead; Fiona, Cyril's
wife-accomplice, has left him; Catherine is stupefied, and Cyril is
impotent.

Yet if Cyril's past is tragic, his present is almost comic. The vision
of this cycling lecher en route from his villa to Catherine's sanctuary
is hardly godly; in fact, his automatonlike regularity recalls one of
Bergson's comic persons or Beckett's displaced metaphysicians. When
Cyril explains his motives to Catherine, the account he offers is one
better suited to a machine than a deity. "A steady, methodical un-
designing lover like me really has no choice, Catherine. The eyeglasses
come off in my hands, the skirts of the dressing gown fall open, I fold
the wings of the glasses. No choice. And don't forget you were waiting
for me. You wanted my slow walk, my strong dark shadow, my full
pack of cigarettes, the sound of my soft humming as I approached
your villa. We both knew you were waiting, Catherine. Neither one of
us had any choice that first night. It was inevitable" (11).

The two plots offer opposite views of human destiny. Paralleling
Cyril's tapestry of sexual multiplicity emerges a more impersonal pattern of victimization and humiliation. A metaphysic of naturalism
grows alongside, is woven within, and gradually supplants Cyril's visionary lyricism. Cyril himself is unable to keep this process at bay;
the man who scorned the inarticulate mechanicals who people his island now sits down to a dinner of sparrows' heads in order to ingrati-
ate himself with one of them (52); the velvet-voiced lyricist tries "to
inflame with words she does not understand" (3) an illiterate peasant.

And what brings Catherine back to speech is not Cyril's godlike art but the villagers' boat-launching ceremony, at the center of which is not art but sacrifice, "thickening stains of blood . . . affixed to the high prow of the boat" (126).

As the novel continues, the balance between the two plots shifts. Cyril's own sexual tapestry becomes identified with the larger pattern of sacrifice that is so ubiquitous on Illyria. Toward the end of the book, Hugh, whose photography vies with Cyril's lyricism throughout the book as a rival way to capture reality, discovers a chastity belt. Hugh cannot leave the belt alone. He explains his obsession to Cyril by saying "that damn belt's a work of art" (245). Cyril cannot dissent "because as soon as I pressed thumbs and fingers against the thin pitted surface of the iron band circling Catherine's waist, I realized that Hugh's despairing use of that iron belt must have occasioned a moment more genuinely erotic than any he had known with Catherine, with his nudes, or in his dreams of Fiona" (256–57).

Both men are transfixed by this image of masculine control. In so many ways these characters are participants in a game as old as the church fortress in which Fiona discovers Hugh (who is the image of a maimed St. Peter statue in the church). Gradually, the quartet becomes part of an unnamed ritual in which they must function as counters rather than intelligent agents. When the smoke created by Cyril's rhetoric clears, it becomes evident that his art is almost involuntary, his tapestry little more than animal gratification. Gradually, too, his gods evaporate into an all-enveloping nothingness, a vacancy that perturbs Cyril whenever he acknowledges it, perhaps because it shows the thin air into which his idyll will vanish: "Am I embracing air? . . . Could that be all? Is that what it feels like to discover with absolute certainty that you yourself have simply disappeared from the filmy field?" (34).

Like Skipper or Zizendorf, Cyril is at his most figurative when he is most desperate. In this passage, his "absolute certainty" is revealed as the sophist's unpleasant recognition of absolute doubt. Cyril's love games are played against a perpetually shrinking horizon. Suddenly we are confronted by the image of a man who is no godly maker, but one who merely completes a picture he claimed to create, as artificer freezes into artifact: "I always allowed myself to assume whatever shape was destined to be my own in the silken weave of Love's pink panorama. I always went where the thread wound . . . the gods fashion us to spread the legs of woman, or throw us together for no reason except that we complete the picture, so to speak" (1–2). The deliberate

verbal echo, together with the pronoun shift ("I completed the picture. . . . We complete the picture"), marks the gap between Cyril's
pretension to his status as a god, weaving his life into love's very image, and his situation as an anonymous participant in the ritual sacrifices of Illyria. No wonder Cyril's other speciality is blowing smoke
rings; it is as well to have some release from a vision as bleak as this.

CHAPTER SIX

"Something Like a War Memorial":
John Hawkes's *Travesty*

Your homes the scene, yourselves the actors, here.
—Charles Dickens, Suggested
epigraph to *Martin Chuzzlewit*

I.

When *Travesty* appeared in 1976, Tony Tanner, in a review that was to set the course for future criticism, suggested that it was "disturbing for the same reason that dreams are disturbing . . . we cannot 'frame' it, it contains no markers to indicate how it is to be read."[1] Hawkes himself encouraged such a reading, describing his book as "about a nameless man who sheds guilt, turns perversity into an act of courage, and experiences what it is to be a poet." He also gratefully assented to Heide Zeigler's suggestion in the same interview that the book demonstrates how "if a design is intense enough, conscious enough, it must lead to a debris which originates a new design."[2]

Much recent criticism of *Travesty* has followed an essentially antirational cue. In Donald R. Greiner's essay we notice that the narrator has become "Papa" (evidence of criticism's willingness to assume what Hawkes's protagonist wills us to assume). Greiner, who characterizes *Travesty* as that familiar Hawkes product, the tour de force, suspects that "the other characters and perhaps even the murderously fast drive do not exist except in Papa's obsessed mind."[3] Greiner's dissolution of the characters is extended by Paul Emmett's reading, which dismantles the narrative basis of the novel and places it in a mythic superstructure grounded in Jungian psychology. This is a comfortable procedure, for it removes the reader from what Hawkes's narrator calls "the toneless world of highway tragedy" (11) and places him in more harmless surroundings, amid what Emmett calls the "byways of the theory of fiction." But this interpretation is foreign to the moral topography of the book, and is false even to the experience of reading it. Where *Travesty* insists on the arbitrary necessity of submitting to Papa's godly authority—"You and I," he tells us, "are simply

traveling down that road the rest of the world attempts to hide" (141)—
Emmett offers instead a teacherly plurality: "Although there . . .
seems an infinite number of paths traveled . . . each path traveled is
both enjoyable and enlightening."[4] It is hard to know what Emmett
has in mind here; a book that ends by superimposing a highway
apocalypse upon a hit-and-run killing does not appear to be present-
ing an infinite number of equally pleasurable paths as part of its total
design. There is the same kind of wistful wishing away of the novel's
plot and narrative structure in Heide Zeigler's account of the book,
which finds in Travesty a structure "where the very act of combined
suicide and murder develops into the willed expression of joyfully
embraced artistic design, because the process of narrating, paralleling
the workings of the imagination, creates constant meaning out of impending destruction."[5] Again, Zeigler's interpretation takes no account of the mimetic thrust of the novel. Who joyfully embraces Papa's
design? Certainly not Henri or Chantal, who wheeze and cower their
way through the whole journey. And surely to talk of "impending destruction" without acknowledging Papa's role as the hand that activates this process is misleading and evasive.

Charles Baxter has shown the fallacies in this kind of interpretation. Emmett's reading, Baxter demonstrates, is a typical academic
maneuver, one that conventionalizes authorial aggression in order to
reconstruct the subversive imagination as something "ultimately educational, beneficent, institutionalized." But Baxter's own view of the
book is not without its problems. For, with a feint that is all too typical
of recent academic criticism, he suggests that Travesty asserts the
power of "the imagination at the expense of self and world." Swallow-
ing this assertion quite trustingly, Baxter takes even further the procedure of draining the text of its subject matter and argues that Papa's
"private apocalypse" arises from an aesthetic creating "another world
that entirely supersedes the present one and could care less about
what happens in what passes for the real one. . . . Given enough
rope, the imagination . . . habitually renounces the world to create a
new one from scratch."[6]

Such ideas, however, fail to account for either the pattern or the
action of Travesty. Papa, for instance, is given no rope and creates no
new world; he takes the rope himself—by using his position at the
wheel to direct the controls—and triggers a private apocalypse more
like the destruction of an old world than the creation of a new one.
Moreover, this event is not designed from scratch; like Günter Grass's
Starusch in the dentist's chair, Hawkes's hero has his reasons for want-
ing to blast past and present into an apocalyptic future; both charac-

ters have suffered too many domestic humiliations not to want the pleasures of a spectacular climax. It is this very real commitment to the idea of a vengeful apocalypse that makes Hawkes's *Travesty* so different from the work of his American postmodern apocalyptic contemporaries; where Stanley Elkin's apocalypse in *The Living End* is almost completely a matter of language, Hawkes's is the thing itself, impressed upon us through the persuasive bullying of Papa. The debris of memory provokes the godly mastery of his design. Certainly, any interpretation of *Travesty* ought to account for design *and* debris, something done by none of the commentators cited so far. The problem is that each of them identifies too strongly with Papa's design so that Baxter can even say that "everything turns into consciousness" in the book. It does not; but Papa is masterful at spiriting away even the illusion of the existence of other people.

One of the structural oddities of *Travesty* is this peculiar absence of other people. Papa tells his narrative and *we* become his victims; the silence of Henri and Chantal means, in effect, that *Travesty*, like *The Cannibal*, becomes "our story"; and in the process our postmodern premises about the godly powers of the artist and our postliberationist notions about sex go on trial. Papa is like some great geological fault whose structure reveals flaws in the whole postwar sexual and imaginative landscape. Moreover, the novel shows these flaws to be the product of a series of historical contradictions that range from the authoritarianism of the Victorian father to the morbid nihilism of the existentialist metaphysician. The effect is disturbing, for it makes Papa's voice, like Zizendorf's, timeless. And once again the timelessness is attached to a perpetual despotism rather than a humanist permanence.

If Hawkes uses Papa to attack our own unthinking orthodoxies, it is worth noting that Papa's voice also blows the gaffe on his creator's own rallying cries. In the same way that Flannery O'Connor's imaginative strength was too much for her Catholic orthodoxy, so Hawkes's imagination breaks the bonds of his own commitment to—to imagination itself, no less. Hawkes's book becomes the limiting instance of his much-repeated desire to "create a world," as Papa, propelled by his vision of a "private apocalypse," hurtles his passengers and us toward the future his imagination so desperately craves. At this point, it is difficult for a reader not to have some grave doubts about the authority of the artist to create his own world. Papa's beautifully composed scenario is also remarkably brutal in its practical consequences. Like too few other postwar novels, *Travesty* has the courage of its convictions; and its convictions prove that its creator's orthodoxies are imaginatively exciting but morally and humanly unworkable. It is far more useful to read this book as a case than as a dream; as a case it finds all of us guilty of having hardened our hearts with fine phrases and fantasies. Such is the intensity of the situation that Hawkes invents to house his convictions that his travesty will even bear comparison with the most famous of all travesties, Charles Baudelaire's *Les Fleurs du Mal*. In 1866, Baudelaire wrote that in this book he had "put all my heart, all my tenderness, all my religion (travestied), all my hate."[7] Hawkes himself seems to have written such a book, a book that risks its creator's orthodoxies by making them the source of his audience's imprisonment.

What other markers exist to help us understand the book? A reviewer for the *Chicago Tribune* saw it as "a deliberate and highly sophisticated [parody] of the work and death of Albert Camus."[8] There are indeed relics of Camus's work in Papa's vocabulary and rhetorically the book parallels the narrative structure of *The Fall*. In situation, moreover, the book reruns Camus's famous final drive. But is the point of all this merely parodic? Hawkes seems likely, given the extreme urgency of his novel, to have had more serious concerns, which can perhaps be gauged more precisely through a brief examination of Camus's obituary notice. For the *New York Times*, Camus's career had been exemplary: "There can be no surprise that our era responded to Camus' message. . . . The terrible slaughter of two world wars, the unprecedented menace of the hydrogen bomb, these are part of the modern setting which made Camus' austere philosophy comprehensible and assured his memory such immortality as mere man can give."[9] Camus was, as the *Times*'s tribute implies, primarily an authoritative voice, and it is this authority that Hawkes borrowed for *Travesty*. The typicality of Camus's situation and the authority of his voice give Hawkes's book a layer of familiarity missing since *The Cannibal*, so that his godly artist is no mere islander, but speaks for our whole postwar way of life. Where Skipper is feeble and feebleminded, and Cyril a euphonious vacuum, Papa is authoritative, a godly maker whose testimony it is almost impossible to ignore.

The next marker is more tentative. H. M. McLuhan's *The Mechanical Bride*, a guide to the folklore of industrial man, explores territory very similar to *Travesty*. Both books are concerned with the national inventory of images and pseudomythologies. Both books anatomize societies masking their devotion to power and control with an official commitment to organization and technological expertise. Both books see the highway as the theater of operations that pits public pretense against private obsession. Papa's sleek vehicle transports him to the site of his private obsessions, toward the accidents he tells us he has "always been secretly drawn to" (20). McLuhan, in a passage that could be a gloss on Papa's confidences, suggests that "what draws people to the death shows of the speedways and fills the press and magazines with close-ups of executions, suicides and smashed bodies" is a "metaphysical hunger to experience everything sexually, to pluck out the heart of the mystery for a super-thrill." What the highway embodies for both authors is what McLuhan diagnosed as "a hunger which can be called metaphysical . . . which seeks satisfaction in physical danger, and sometimes in torture, suicide, or murder."[10] And in both books, these lethal desires emerge through "a dominant pattern composed of sex and technology. Amid what otherwise may appear as a mere hodge podge of isolated events, this very consistent pattern stands out" (98). Both books systematize anecdotes to the point where they become cultural indictments. Papa's particular aggressions gradually cohere into a picture of an entire value system of male dominance, just as McLuhan's individual advertisements crystallize into a pattern of cut-price industrial mythmaking.

There is a similarity of pattern rather than a direct source relationship between *Travesty* and *The Mechanical Bride*. There are also some impressive similarities in the rhetorical patterns of the two books. McLuhan, like Hawkes, enlivens his book with bracing challenges to the reader. "Let's all get adjusted to the process of getting adjusted to what isn't here any longer" (126), says McLuhan, in an abrasive attack on his audience that is very similar to Papa's "no, no, Henri. Hands off the wheel. Please. It is too late" (11). Both books shock the reader into a recognition of the inadequacies of a culture of know-how by providing what McLuhan calls "typical visual imagery of our own environment and dislocating it into meaning by inspection" (vi).

The markers so far suggested for *Travesty* appear to move in opposing directions. On the one hand, the narrator has a Camusesque authority of voice; on the other, he is identified with the specious and death-dealing tendencies of industrial society. This opposition constitutes the special life of Hawkes's transformation of the *topos*. His thrust is to realign the godly artist to the society in which he moves and thus make him once again the man with the capacity to tell our story, so that his book taunts the reader with the disastrous social and moral consequences of a whole storehouse of postwar clichés and mythologies. The effect is to unlock what Hawkes found in Barth; in this book he has "pierced our pretensions—public and private" by imposing a vision on us that explodes its creator's articles of faith as systematically as it erodes our own.

128 GOD THE ARTIST

The final marker pushes this interpretation a stage further. The very title of the book does not, by definition, encourage us to read Papa's "private apocalypse" uncritically. *The Oxford English Dictionary* provides these definitions of *travesty*:

A ppl. 1a. Dressed so as to be made ridiculous; burlesqued.
B ob. 1. A literary composition which aims at exciting laughter by burlesque or ludicrous treatment of a serious work; a literary composition of this kind; hence, a grotesque or debased imitation or likeness; a caricature.
B 2. In etymological sense: an alteration of dress or appearance; a disguise. *rare*.

Hawkes uses the idea of travesty as a kind of complex word, the intersection point for a whole collection of public and private masks. Hawkes's fiction has always been possessed by the idea of disguise, and in this book he rips off his own disguises as well as ours. Papa himself is a powerful embodiment of the masquerades of his culture and his creator: his pride in his own expertise is very much a part of the "culture of know-how" that McLuhan identified, while his devotion to his visionary power resembles that of his creator, who, as we have seen, has repeatedly affirmed his desire to "invent" the universe.[11] But *Travesty* lets us inspect the effect of the slogans on our own lives, where we find that efficiency is no longer quite so appealing, and where an imagination answering only to its own authority is in fact lethal. At the end of the book, our efficiency and our visions serve only to transport us on the high road to annihilation. Papa's last words, which promise that "there shall be no survivors. None" (128), pitilessly pierce any pretensions that remain.

II.

Travesty attacks on two fronts. On the one hand, Papa's self-elected visionary power is revealed as only part of a death-dealing machine. On the other, this destructive pattern is gradually disclosed as one that includes us as part of its inexorable fulfillment. If on one level Hawkes encourages us to be judges, on another he ensures that we become victims. One can easily demonstrate the extent to which Papa's illusions are trapped within the system his narrative hopes to explode. Early in the novel Papa describes a scene of "toneless highway tragedy," one of the commonplace, everyday violences that McLuhan saw as the modern equivalent of the medieval pilgrimage. Hawkes's narrator too finds such tragedy irresistible:

> I have always been secretly drawn to the scene of accidents, have
> always paused beside those patches of sand with a certain quick-
> ening of pulse and hardening of concentration. Mere sand, mere
> sand, flung down on a city street and already sponging up the
> blood beneath. But for me these small islands created out of haste,
> pain, death, crudeness, are thoroughly analogous to the symme-
> try of the two or even more machines whose crashing results in
> nothing more than an aftermath of blood and sand. It is like a
> skin, this small area of dusty butchery, that might have been
> peeled from the body of one of the offending cars. I think of the
> shot tiger and the skin in the hall of the dark chateau. (20)

Papa begins, as usual, in confiding intimacy, which he uses as a
springboard to plunge into the vortices of prophesy he sounds out in
"I have always been secretly drawn to." Some hint of revelation is apparent in the portentous "but for me" that follows the emphatically
ordinary "mere sand, mere sand." But the proffered analogy yields
only "the symmetry of two or even more machines"; Papa can multiply, but he cannot transform. His "or even more" reveals him as the
victim of a mistake typical among inmates of a culture of know-how,
the neo-Benthamite fallacy that to increase the amount of pleasure is
to intensify its quality. Papa, coarsened by a staple diet of daily violence, hopes to secure imaginative release by stockpiling more examples of what he already has in abundance.

But his prophesy fades into confining domesticity. Having moved
from "mere sand, mere sand" to the scarcely more epiphanic "blood
and sand," Papa makes a facile little shuffle from highway to home as
"like a skin" leads, by association of ideas, to "shot tiger and the
skin." The highway prophet becomes the armchair hunter; Papa is a
consumer with messianic pretensions. His revelations move us from
an area cordoned off by public necessity (the "small islands") to an
equally cordoned off consciousness, cabined in its "dark chateau"
with its captured dead tiger. His mind is patterned by the ghoulish
expectations of a society that produces endless accidents and casualties—the same society he is struggling to transcend. Eventually too,
like any other postindustrial Mr. Polly, he must confine his desire for
adventure to the well-furnished hearth.

This early passage reveals in miniature the pattern of the novel as
a whole. Papa's "private apocalypse," undertaken to reveal his special
election, instead reveals him as trapped in the same wires as everybody else, another item in what he sneeringly calls "the national inventory." For all his much-vaunted powers of vision, Papa can see
only destruction; his virtuosity lies, if anywhere, in the ingenuity

with which he uncovers this, a gift the first of his simple stories displays in abundance.

> Only yesterday I sat in this very automobile and watched an old couple helping each other down a village street (not La Roche, I have never been in La Roche) toward a life-sized and freshly painted wooden Christ-on-the-Cross mounted on a stone block not far from where I sat in my car. The old man, who was holding the woman's elbow, was a thin and obviously bad-tempered captive of marriage. The old woman was bow-legged. Or at least her short legs angled out from where her knees must have been beneath the heavy skirts, and then jutted together sharply at the ankles. This creature depended for locomotion on the lifetime partner inching along at her side. The old man was wearing a white sporting cap and carrying the woman's new leather sack. The old woman, heavily bandaged about the throat in an atrocious violet muffler, was carrying a little freshly picked bouquet of flowers. Well, it's a simple story. This scowling pair progressed beyond my silent automobile (you must imagine the incongruity of the old married couple, the orange roof tiles, the waiting Christ, the beige-colored lacquer of this automobile gleaming impressively in the bright sunlight) until at last the woman deposited the trim little bouquet of flowers at the feet of the Christ. (25–26)

Papa's "simple story" is deceptively simple. Apparently another fable on the virtues of solitary artifice, Papa's anecdote scarcely grants the old couple humanity. He mates "my silent automobile" with "the scowling pair," his epithets betraying some sympathy for the former. What irks him especially is the awkward reciprocity of the old couple, and in telling his tale he attempts as far as possible to strip down the act of worship into a set of separate incongruities. This, of course, is the narrative technique of Camus's *The Outsider*, which also syntactically imprisons its characters in their actions, thereby making both actions and characters absurd. But Hawkes's book extends this procedure, for he also supplies Papa's consistently evaluating commentary, so that we get the impression of a world where power provides the sole basis of authority. The world of *The Outsider* is absurd; the world of *Travesty* is totalitarian, with Papa its self-elected deity. His parable aims to impress upon us the sense of a natural order in decline, a culture of fractured pieties.

Yet can we trust the teller of this tale? Papa's parable veers alarmingly from the reportorial thrust of "only yesterday I sat in this very automobile," an image that within the total experience of the passage functions as a narrative sprat to catch an ideological mackerel. Papa cannot, for instance, remember where he saw the couple—odd, considering his boasted precision—but the old woman was definitely bow-legged. Then again, was she? The authority of Papa's testimony rests on conjecture, since the woman's "heavy skirts" make it impossible for him to guess the whereabouts of her knees. Papa is developing a parable, and his selection of details is determined by his parabolic purposes. Consider, for instance, the leap of bad faith by which Papa's description of the old couple shuffling down a village street together hardens into the categorization of the old man as "a thin and obviously bad-tempered captive of marriage." How can Papa be so sure? The captured tiger skin, the imprisoned old man, the captive audience in the car—no one can have discovered as many prisoners as Papa, whose mind is warped by the universal projection of a confinement of which he is a victim as well as a diagnostician. His parable beats the couple into a preconceived pattern that Papa applies to whatever he cannot instantly comprehend. As a result Papa's fragments of narrative become, by cumulative effect, self-fulfilling prophecies, attempts to gear himself up for the special project he has designed to prove his own power.

Papa's "simple story" is simple only for as long as we remain within the magic circle the charm of his language hopes to create. Once we step outside it, Papa's interpretation and our own are at loggerheads. What Papa would impress upon us as the subjective pleasures of his godly power, the reader experiences as a world that, in its impoverishment and pain, bears objective testimony to the disastrous ecological and social consequences of unchecked power worship. For Papa's high-speed death wagon is a product of the larger system of victimization he charts on his journey. In this world the Christ-on-the-Cross that awaits the old couple, like West's Christ at Miss Lonelyhearts's bedside, is more victim than redeemer. In both books the representation of Christ in art becomes an emblem of the world as it is—not the promise of redemption from it. Only the hopes of the believers remain; the body of Christ testifies to the extent of human suffering, not to human potential for deliverance.

From the novel's first words, Hawkes plunges his reader into this harsh world, as Papa's opening "no, no, Henri. . . . It is too late" signals his determination to dominate the action, a determination that intensifies as the book progresses. Accordingly, the book's static moral diagram tautens with the intensifying desperation of its protagonist, who is aware that his own authority is only part of a larger pattern, over which on crucial occasions he has been shown to be as powerless as everybody else.

Papa is unhappy with mere expertise, even though he repeatedly draws attention to his own easy control: "At least you are in the hands of an expert driver" (12). Even the fact of his mastery over present and past does not completely satisfy him, for at times he wants nothing less than to subdue time itself: "My mind is bound inside my memory . . . like a fist in glass" (15). He even, for one extraordinary moment, becomes the vehicle for his own revenge plot: "These yellow headlights are the lights of my eyes" (15). On these occasions, his authority exists for its own sweet sake, as he comes to read his designs into the fabric of the universe itself: "You and I are Leos. One more unbreakable thread in the web" (40). Even granting the force of Papa's particular monomania, there seems a definite self-contradiction in the strident insistence with which he attempts to secure our assent to what he has described as inevitable. Papa, like Cyril in *The Blood Oranges*, is a necessitarian who insists on his own godly free will. Like Cyril, he makes his own presence superfluous. What need is there of Papa's eloquence when plainly "all the elements of life coerce each other, force each other instant by instant into that perfect formation which is lofty and the only one possible" (15)? Papa's aim is to become more and more like the god in the machine so that he can achieve what a machine will effect anyway. To do this, he must free himself of contingency and sweep onward and upward to where "You and Chantal and I are simply traveling in purity and extremity down that road the rest of the world attempts to hide from us by heaping up whole forests of the most confusing road signs, detours, barricades" (14).

"Simply travelling": Papa's language gives him away. Papa offers for our inspection a journey where we can abandon road maps and barricades, trivialities and obstacles that are rejected because they will retard a journey in which speed is of the essence. If Papa does not bring things to a quick climax, then there is always the danger that reality will upstage him; the death of little Pascal, at the very moment of acquiring character, has taught Papa that harsh truth. If traffic policemen are wired to the perversities of conventionality, then Papa's web is attached to an equally conventional force, the death that threatens everyone in the book. Papa's own scheme will only accelerate what is inevitable.

Like Elkin's artist-god in *The Living End*, Papa comes to see people as artifacts. But where Elkin's character is virtually defined by his estrangement from a commitment to the everyday, Papa insists on both the estrangement and the affiliation. If Chantal is "a cameo about to be destroyed," she is also his daughter and "must obey [her] Papa" (11). Papa needs the commonplaces of everyday life as raw material for his own imagination; his vocabulary continuously strips the furniture of everyday life to stock the armory of his own special election, so that his murder becomes the act of "some courageous driver [who] falls back on good sense and lunges straight across" (19) the moral commonplaces our own cowardice leads us to honor.

The rationalizations of Papa's imaginative life are violent and domineering. Their principal foe is the ordinary universe, which runs down with a slowness that is the reverse of apocalyptic. Artificial life can dismember these rhythms into units of concentrated efficiency, of which Papa's private apocalypse is only the most spectacular example. Papa's authority has been sapped by the privations of the daily, which took away Pascal and brought Chantal and Honorine to Henri's bed. Papa's apocalypse will, like the work of Elkin's artificer, compensate for a neglect he feels he has suffered over a lifetime.

Yet Papa is not content with manufacturing his own apocalypse; he wants to extend his authority into the future as well. On one occasion, when he projects a happy ending, he finds instead a sorry anticlimax. "Perhaps it would be better for all concerned if just this once I could find you in the right and could hear the shell cracking, so to speak, and all at once find myself overcome with fear and so pull to the side of the road, thus ending our journey, and in rain and in darkness sit sobbing over the wheel. Then I could take Chantal's place back there on the floor and slowly, slowly, you could drive the three of us to Tara. In that case you would take to your bed for two days, Chantal would return to her riding lessons, I would follow your lead to the asylum that effected your famous cure" (83). The gist of Papa's parable is clear enough. Real life is very dull and my mind is very exciting. Accept my inner truths, and you will be liberated from the confinement of the quotidian. Nonetheless, there is an undercurrent less flattering to Papa's sense of self, for his imagined future reveals his own consciousness about its customary task of divide and conquer. His projected future merely reverses and expands the situation in the car: Henri assumes Papa's role, Papa assumes Chantal's. The trip home is the occasion for a mutual imprisonment. Henri takes to solitary confinement in his bed (or at least Papa hopes it will be solitary), Chantal returns to healthier outdoor pursuits; Papa can undergo the convalescence already endured by Henri. Even Papa's anticlimaxes are imprisoning.

Having projected a future of real bathos, Papa next presents one of melodrama: "Little did he" (Papa's doctor, unfamiliar with his projected apocalypse) "know that in several days and on the other side of the city a laboratory technician, unshaven and smoking a

yellow cigarette, would analyze the blood of a man already dead; or
that the hazy image of ribs and single lung on the photographic plate
would represent only as much reality as the white organs lubricating
each other in one of his weekly films" (94). "Little did he know":
Papa's opening words draw attention to his own omniscience. In the
same way, "the hazy image" representing only a minimal reality is to
be contrasted with the fiery images of Papa's apocalypse. Papa's imagination has a melodramatic cast; he wants to cheat death of its capacity
to create images of destruction. But once again, his parable reneges
on his own authority. The image that sticks in the reader's imagination
is of death, death whose utter finality cancels the authority of artist
and technician alike. Little the doctor might know, but Papa—who is
sure he knows much more—can only, for all his godly ambition, concede the game to death.

What of Papa's "private apocalypse"? Considering the number of
tributes he pays to the solitary imagination, it is perhaps odd that it is
shown as bearing the burden of its own bathos. But Papa is artful
here, if nowhere else. For by injecting the future with bathos, he guar-
antees some glory for the present. But this parable, just like Papa's
other exempla, cannot support the interpretation he wants us to make
of it. Inescapably, his own end becomes submerged in just the kind of
bureaucratic inertia it was designed to explode. "It is impossible. It is
not to be. Nothing will prevent our sudden incandescence in the night
sky. And then we shall have blue lights, motorcycles, radio communications, the arrival of several of our little white ambulances. By dawn
they will be hauling apart our wreckage with hooks and chains, and
by noon of that first day there will be nothing left but the smell of
gasoline and the dark signs of a recently extinguished fire. They will
take notes, take photographs, climb through the elbows of hot metal,
and then tow it all away with their clumsy trucks" (60). After the apocalypse, it is time to take stock. Just as Papa inventoried the national culture, the nation inventories what is left of him. His apocalypse existed
outside time, subduing time to its own controlling pattern. Here,
Papa's plan is restored to time, which ticks off the shrinking evidence
of the apocalypse: "By dawn they will be hauling apart. . . . By noon
on the first day there will be nothing left." The passage reverses and
accelerates Genesis, as flesh becomes mere words, bureaucratic words
at that. Where God's time projected more and more of the created universe, Papa's godly power projects waste, "elbows of hot metal" that
are in turn reduced to notes in a police jotter or press photographs.
The sudden "incandescence" of the imagination fragments into one of
Papa's deadened tableaux as his consummate artifice is collated by a

gropingly bureaucratic procedure. The godly artist imagines a world in which he will activate a flaring apocalypse; but in this postwar version of *Bouvard and Pécuchet* that very apocalypse becomes part of a process that can inventory and annul it. For what Papa's imagined future projects is a power switch, as his own seizure of power—"It is too late"—becomes supplanted by "their clumsy trucks." As Papa's world fragments the "we" becomes "they," the officialdom that Papa can neither be interested in nor submit himself to. Papa presents the scene as if his imagination were being deflowered. Reality, after the apocalypse, splits into two worlds: they and we. Papa's Genesis, in other words, has brought together nothing at all. Its supreme achievement has been the destruction of a world already expiring quickly enough of its own accord.

III.

On one level the book sends us crawling toward death; on another, it hurls us toward it. Let us press this polarity further. One of the most disturbing insights to be found in *The Mechanical Bride*, which was suggested earlier as a marker for *Travesty*, was the *collective* nature of the fantasies that the machinery of industrial society generated. The narrative technique of *Travesty* will not let us off this unpleasant hook, for the story is told as what Henry W. Sams defined as a "satire of the second person." Sams explained that where third-person satires ally reader and writer against a distant abuse (in the way that Pope's *Dunciad* makes an alliance with its readers against fools and poseurs), second-person satires direct their attacks "to pierce the defenses of the reader himself," who correspondingly becomes butt, not confidant.[12] Sams's prime example of such a book, Swift's *A Tale of a Tub*, with its unreliably unreliable narrator, its aggressive attack on its audience, and its tendency to thumb its nose at its creator's stated orthodoxies, has many resemblances to *Travesty*.

Few critics have acknowledged the way the dramatic impact of *Travesty* relies on the active engagement of the reader in the book's action. Even Paul Rosenzweig and Brenda Wineapple, who identified the coercive thrust of Hawkes's imagination, fail to acknowledge this important aspect of the book's design. Though Rosenzweig identifies a "psychology of control" in Hawkes's work, he argues that the course of the fiction from *The Cannibal* to *Travesty* is toward a design ever "more absolute and self-referential."[13] Wineapple, on the other hand, recognizes nature as the foe of Papa's artifice: "Rain could make a 'real' accident, not his contrived one, possible."[14] The drift of both these views locks Papa's apocalypse into an autonomous realm, stripping it of its ethical and circumstantial life.

In fact, the narrative structure of *Travesty* seems to have been designed with a very different end in view. The prolonged silence of Henri and Chantal, by a sort of malign proxy, effectively makes us the audience that Papa subjects to the cumulative weight of his ridicule, so that we are the butt of his projected apocalypse. By this device, Hawkes is able to move into a full-scale critical examination of all our social, ethical, and sexual mores. Papa's authority is not really visionary; it is rather a function of his typicality and the way he uses that typicality to inspect the drastically dwindling stock of the national inventory. To say this is to argue that the impact of the book is satiric rather than visionary. And it is as well to remember that it was the satiric capacity of the godly maker that Hawkes stressed when he introduced John Barth at Stanford, in a testimony that is central for understanding his notion of the whole idea of the godly maker.

The narrative technique of *Travesty* forces the reader to confront his own values. Papa allows us two equally unpleasant choices: the Scylla of becoming his accomplices ("You and I are Leos. One more unbreakable thread in the web") or the Charybdis of labeling him guilty and thereby becoming one of his victims: "I cannot accept the idea of 'murder' unless you are able to refuse the illusory comfort of 'reprieve'" (47). This is the technique of the spider and the fly: Papa extends every courtesy to us, but then ensnares us with his hospitality. Everything is subsidiary, ultimately, to his goal of destruction: "The two of us are leaping together, so to speak, from the same bridge" (47). Papa incriminates us in his godly plan: the suicidal leap becomes typical for a world bent on self-annihilation.

Papa constantly presses on us the need to assume what he assumes; these assumptions, which Papa tells us we all share, he then annihilates in some scandalously victimizing anecdote. In this way, Papa's stories simultaneously unmask both himself and us. His description of his affair with Monique, his obedient little sex slave, for instance, begins by reassuring us that "of course she never failed to obey me, and yet even when she conformed to my simplest suggestion (about what to eat, what not to eat, some article of clothing, and so forth), she did so with beautiful vehemence" (65). Papa's "of course" will become very irksome. For the moment it is enough to notice the extent of the control it demands. Women are to be subservient in diet, dress, and behavior: the vague "so forth" gestures down endless vistas of male dominance.

Papa emphasizes, moreover, the typicality of his relationship with Monique, with whom he shared "a familiar and convenient pattern," what he calls a "happy ritual of disruption and reconciliation." He adds, "We relied on it totally, Monique and I" (67). But the effect of Papa's narrative is to break through that familiarity so that what begins as supportive ends in fear and violence. These queerly disorientating shifts begin with the description of Monique's apartment, which is as specialized and functional as a tool shack, and stocked with "every conceivable kind of pornographic or erotic book, magazine, photograph that she was able to discover in our museums, kiosks, bookstalls, establishments devoted to the equipment and stimulation of the sexual drive" (67). Here, "our" culture becomes a universal brothel, its institutions multiplying to serve the one, mechanically attuned end, "stimulation of the sexual drive." Even when memory begets memory there is no shift in plane or focus, as when Papa describes how Monique "thrived on her pornography old and new and liked nothing better than to adorn her own little nude figure in the outlandish black lingerie of those ladies of the boas who in another era so incensed our forefathers" (68). Once again the narrative's thrust is toward a larger system of victimization, as Papa reaches into the past and plucks out only a simpler, but entirely similar, version of the present. Monique, tiny to begin with, shrinks beneath the weight of the desires she is designed to support. Like the "abducted socialite" Chantal (55), she becomes an object in Papa's mechanical parable of power. But the reader too is drawn into this web of force: he too must participate in this design to reduce a woman to a copulating machine, for "it is a familiar and convenient pattern," is it not?

Memory breeds desire breeds violence. Unenthralled by the outmoded delights that Monique offers, Papa rouses his deadened appetites through aggression.

> Suddenly inspired, I spanked Monique. It was not entirely my fault, and it was the only time in my life when I fell so close to being the sadistic villain lurking everywhere in the stories, photographs and fantasies of my little mistress. You will agree that no one wants to find himself becoming nothing more than a familiar type created by a hasty and untalented pornographer. We do not like to think of ourselves as imaginary, salacious and merely one of the ciphers in the bestial horde, to put it somewhat strongly, *cher ami*. But it was not totally my fault, as I must repeat, since the night was rainy and since the hour was late and since there was provocation, a provocation I did not even think to resist. (68)

The episode begins with one of Papa's subtle borrowings from the vocabulary of creativity as "inspired" is travestied by its application to an act of sexual violence. This is a low point in Papa's self-examination. He realizes, with something less than staggering self-knowledge, that he is becoming an expectoration of popular fantasy. From this point he moves to the attack; he is eager to share the stigma of this self-recognition, to expand it into a common acknowledgment of guilt: "We do not like to think of ourselves." The incrimination is made lightly, without any specific charge or personal thrust: we are all of us "ciphers in the bestial horde."

The whole episode swings uneasily between incrimination and evasion. Papa's account begins in the grand style—"suddenly inspired"; in mid-flight, however, it becomes rather timid—"it was not entirely my fault"; by the end it has petered out into self-justification— "there was provocation"; and, most bathetically of all, a weather report—"The night was rainy." The trajectory of exaltation can rarely have dipped so drastically into so vapid an anticlimax. What Papa reveals here is the flabby underbelly of the merciless anatomist of national culture, a man whose violent exhilarations are followed by evasive self-pity. Indeed, by the end of the passage the aggressor has, by a feat of considerable moral agility, become the victim, with Papa not even thinking to "resist" the provocation he insists upon.

Papa's memories, what Paul Emmett calls his "last strong-hold of reality,"[15] reveal him as victim of the strangleholds of victimization and control that are pervasive throughout the novel. Wherever he looks, Papa finds only tableaux of domination and humiliation. One of the most significant of these is the *Chez Lulu* episode, which begins with Papa's customary invitation to the reader to set his bearings against the storyteller's own: "Anyone with a penchant for the ocean and for summers promising a certain harmless decadence will recognize *Chez Lulu* from merely its name" (111). Such mild beginnings are the foundation for Papa's most repulsive anecdote, a rerun of the oldest story of all—the fall into corrupted sexuality—and another demonstration of the narrator's failing godly artistry. As told by Papa, the fall is no *felix culpa* prefiguring the glory of *homo faber*. It is, instead, an *exemplum* of humiliation before a dieu caché, a god whose traps and pulleys give him control but supply his puppets with nothing like love. Papa's description of the *Chez Lulu* episode reveals an almost schizoid split between the manner and matter of his narrative. In a style that recalls the travestied heroics of Baudelaire's "The Evil Glazier," Papa decks his tale of victimization in the most heroic trappings. The hero of his tale, like himself, is a man who exerts "impressive control," and once more that control is seen at its best where a woman is its victim: "The accordianist was not at all in sympathy with his own two awkward girls while Lulu, on the other hand, appeared to be gaining impressive, delicate control over a remarkably responsive Chantal. The black, pointed tip of his shoes was visible between her knees, he crouched behind her like a ventriloquist manipulating an erotic doll" (118). Lulu tames Chantal with expertise, not love. His "impressive delicate control" treats her as an object; she becomes "a remarkably responsive Chantal," a grammatical formulation that seems to equate her with a remarkably bouncy ball. Her dehumanization is one of the novel's bleaker moments, a bleakness intensified by the reader's awareness that, as he mouths Papa's words, his relationship to Papa parallels that of Chantal to Lulu.

Both reader and daughter are performers of a script composed for the gratification of its writer. And once again, Papa himself acknowledges our participation in his game: "You know the rest, the object of the game which was merely the clever excuse for its existence, was to eat the carrot. And while the other two girls nibbled and tossed themselves about and even shed pretty tears, it was Chantal, of course, who finally understood the game" (119). Understanding is what Chantal acquires through participation in the oldest game of all; her knowledge now matches our own ("You know the rest," Papa tells us), the knowledge of the tedious reflexivity of a universe where power exists (as "the object of the game") to feed appetites that, by definition, are insatiable. So it is that Chantal's humiliation secures Lulu's dominance: "[The next day] her companion in the paddleboat was, as you will have guessed, none other than the notorious Lulu. It was plain to Honorine and me that Chantal had quite overcome her shyness and that the gigantic Lulu was enjoying to the full this first day with his little pink and amber Queen" (119–20).

The parodic force of the passage thrusts backward, for it reads as if designed to help a Victorian young person reach maturity without pain. Chantal is cured of shyness, the lovers can "enjoy to the full" their future (to the eternal relief of their worried parents). In a particularly cloying reminiscence of the sugary Victorianism of Ruskin's *Sesame and Lilies*, Chantal becomes a "little pink and amber Queen," while the narrator's "you must obey your Papa," a command heard more than once in this novel, reveals the domineering Victorian father hiding behind the demented godly artist. These small fragments of resemblance between past and present at a time when everything else seems to be falling apart insist on the present as a psychological product of the past. Papa is not a man like Sontag's Hippolyte, whose credentials suggest an impeccably intellectual pedigree; rather, Papa is one of us, his characterization an intensification of resolutely ordinary desires to dominate our female offspring and see them settled with masterful young men.

Where Chantal, in her mute receptivity, would be any sadist's first choice, Honorine represents every consumer's delight. Theodor Adorno commented on a commodity culture's thirst for icons of unlikeness, standardized images that their admirers find attractive because of their difference from their own lives.[16] Honorine, wealthy and static in a society of mobile impoverishment, is just such an icon. Moored in the high walls of her chateau, she belongs to a pretechnological era. Her duties are pastoral (tending gardens) and contemplative (reading) in a world that is just the reverse. No wonder Papa emphasizes her appeal to our secret lives: "At least you have always appreciated Honorine. Yet who would not? In her entire person is she not precisely the incarnation of everything we least expect to find in the woman who appears to reveal herself completely?" (48).

The promise of a woman present "in her entire person" is completely desirable in a novel littered with so many dismembered limbs. But if Chantal's characterization attacks the flaws in our conception of woman, then Honorine's illustrates the psychic inadequacy of our dreams of sexual mystery. For the terrible irony, of course, is that we never see Honorine "in her entire person." She remains a phantom of delight, a taunting question mark in a world of titillating conjecture. Inviting and attractive, she bids us come forward; but as we move toward the trap, we are not shown a woman who lives and breathes, but a decorously packaged luxury item whose taste we never can enjoy. "We see her against a background of yellow cloth on which has been imprinted a tasteful arrangement of tree trunks and little birds; we know that everything in her domain reflects a pleasing light, a texture of familiar elegance; we recognize that she is neither large nor small, neither beautiful nor plain, despite her golden hair cut short and feathery in the mode of the day . . . all these telltale signs we both have scanned too often in the past, have we not?" (48–49). Titillation rubs against familiarity: Papa's "have we not?" draws us further into his web of dream. He is initiating us in the pleasures of the voyeur. But what exactly are we gazing at? The background of "yellow cloth" makes Honorine almost a figure in a tapestry. The negative definition is hardly sensual ("neither . . . neither . . . neither . . . nor"); Honorine is becoming a mirage, enticing but scarcely substantial.

> You sit beside her on the cream-colored leather divan . . . then, like a figure from our wealth of erotic literature, you find yourself

kneeling on that polished stone floor and holding a firm ankle in one hand and in the other the heel of a shoe that appears to have been molded from dark chocolate. And then she leans forward, leans on your shoulder, frees herself of the shoes you could not remove, and then stands up, and, for a moment, experiences girlish difficulty with the zipper of the plum-colored velvet pants. Well, the vision is yours as well as mine. . . . there at eye level, for you are kneeling, there at eye level . . . you see once again the cluster of pale purple grapes on yellow stems—yellow stems!—that coils down from the navel of our Honorine. (50–51)

The reader now takes Papa's route. Just as Papa behaved with Monique like a character "from our wealth of erotic literature," so the reader, attempting to enter (rather too literally) into this world, finds himself worshipping a woman who is commanding (she can remove shoes, we cannot) but somehow unreal (chocolate shoes, grapes on her belly), an image predominantly oral in appeal. And, indeed, the reader becomes increasingly helpless, directed by Papa where to go ("You sit beside her"), how to approach (to kneel in Her Presence), and where to look ("there at eye level"). But these elaborate directions take us nowhere; we shall never possess the grapes. Papa unlocks the storehouses of fantasy ("our wealth of erotic literature") only to show us that our desires can never be satisfied. That shared possession— "our Honorine"—is an impalpable phantom. Papa is testing the ladder of the senses, demonstrating how each rung—from the grossest (his treatment of Monique) to the most authoritarian (his treatment of Chantal) to the most ethereal (the presentation of Honorine)—spans only increasing heights of barren illusion.[17] By participating in the masculine hunt for a disembodied icon, a fox and grapes chase begun by Adam himself, the reader is forced to taste the most bitter illusion of all, the possession of mere vacancy. The mimetic resources of his tale serve to enforce the reader's participation in Papa's own humiliating hunt for illusions that cannot be sustained.

Papa's lordly assumptions of sexual authority are gradually revealed as attempts to master a fantasy empire. His cameo of Honorine is an elegant fragment, polished but unreal. In Papa's telling the life of man becomes a perpetual escalation of illusion; masculine mastery, whether Papa's at the wheel or Pascal's as an imperial infant, is rented on a very short lease indeed.

Papa's "private apocalypse" is a protest against this leveling momentum of biology. His imagination is full of imagery that, in its fiery incandescence, its brilliant *coups de théâtre*, is the very opposite of the progressive decline that affects the body. "Your various nervous and physiological systems are quite determined not to be outdone . . . the whole thing is circular, is it not? The greater the pain, the greater the weight bearing down on your chest, the louder that dreadful rasping sound (it is indeed a curiously annoying sound, *cher ami*), the greater your own fury which, being directed at the self, of course, only gives still greater impetus to the whole wheezing machine" (60–61). The thrust is again outward: we are all afflicted by "the whole wheezing machine," and the sound that Henri makes is only an intensification of our own bodily processes, just as Papa's noises—the text *Travesty*—are only an intensification of our own aesthetic orthodoxies. Papa's godly artistry is a revenge on mortality. Surrounded by death, rage has only one way to go: "The whole thing is circular, is it not?" Papa's cunning use of the rhetoric of solidarity locks us once again in his lethal fantasy scheme.

In the closing pages of the book, Papa remounts his attack on this world of physical decline. His last travesty, with a thrift that argues perhaps for an increasing obsessiveness of imagination, reassembles material used earlier in the novel. Old man with scarf, handclasp, poet as antagonist—many of these we have already encountered in the course of the journey. Nor is Papa's scorn for the awkward reciprocity that exists between old man and young child new to us. "I remember the car, which was powerful despite its size; I remember the street precisely because I was so uninterested in it; I remember the old poet because at the very moment I noticed him I saw that he was gripping the child's hand in lofty possessiveness and was already staring directly into my eyes with shocking anger. But most of all I remember the child. She was a waif with dark hair, dark eyes, an ingenuous little heart-shaped face filled with uncanny trustfulness and simple beauty" (126). "A waif": Papa's sentiments are decidedly Victorian, even if his equipment, a "car powerful despite its size," is slickly up-to-date. His story, as usual, suffers from a congenital desire to transfer epithets. "The lofty possessiveness" of the "old poet"—we have only Papa's word that he is a poet—belongs to Papa, if to anyone: to this reader, at least, the old man is merely protective.

What is novel is the force with which Papa's parable attacks the reader. Richard Chase observed how the shared handclasp became, for nineteenth-century American writers, a token of a solidarity made precarious by the social developments of the period.[18] Papa's parable boldly reverses the angle of vision, so that we watch the vulnerable from the point of view of the threat to its vulnerability; it is as if Twain had offered us the steamboat's view of life on Huck and Jim's raft. It is at this point too that the book, always threatening to dissolve all time into one time, finally manages to do just that. For here, Papa's past and present become nearly identical, fusing Papa, child, and poet into one exalted moment. At this moment, Papa has all the incentive he needs; he has assumed godly power and by an audacious coup, he becomes the arbiter of his own world. Papa now does something highly unusual; he ignores his audience completely in a way that suggests his total immersion in his moment of power. "I accelerated. I saw the tassel flying. The old poet's face was a mass of rage and his umbrella was raised threateningly above his head. I felt nothing, not so much as a hair against the fender, exactly as if the child had been one of tonight's rabbits. I did not turn around or even glance in the rearview mirror. I merely accelerated and went my way" (126).

Since the reader's presence is seldom superfluous in this novel, the effect is to let us escape the fiction momentarily, so that we can observe this remorseless I that subdues everything to its own purpose. It is an *I* completely divorced from moral sympathy, an *I* become, in effect, as impersonal as the vehicle that conveys it. Moreover, it is an *I* that testifies to some of its creator's most coveted beliefs on the power and authority of the imagination. But however imaginatively exhilarating these beliefs may be, we can only see them as disastrous in human terms. The action of the plot defeats the logic of the imagination; no vision is worth the price Papa pays for it. His "I felt nothing" shows how little humanity is left in him.

After this exalted interval, Papa moves back to us, attempting now to secure his audience's assent. "What's that? What's that you say? Can I have heard you correctly? *Imagined life is more exhilarating than remembered life. . . .* Is that what you said? *Imagined life is more exhilarating than remembered life.* Can it be true? But then you agree, you understand, you have submitted after all, Henri! And listen, even your wheezing has died away" (127). Papa's remorseless impulse to incorporate the universe continues apace. "Remembered life," the mutual life of poet and child, is brutally destroyed and that destruction is followed immediately by Papa's attempt to divest Henri of his own aesthetic authority. Having quoted Henri's hymn to absence—the new poetry's new mythology—Papa arrogates it as his own: "I may say it now, Henri, I am extremely fond of these two lines. I might even have written them myself" (127). Were *Travesty* a longer text, I have no doubt that Papa would claim to have written it, so great is the pressure he now exerts toward a total mastery.

Yet the book's closing pages aim at something more than literary theft. The satirical thrust of *Travesty* shifts at this point to the conditions of life itself. "Wheezing machines" may demoralize, but there is only one sure way to escape biology. That way Papa takes—and with a menace that transcends the act itself. Because of Henri's silence, Papa's "there shall be no survivors. None" leaps at his reader's throat, extending his private apocalypse to an attack on the public world. The ending closes the arc of the circle of control that perhaps originated with Papa's "no, no Henri. Hands off the wheel." But we can even extend it back to the beginning of Hawkes's career as a writer, which opened with Zizendorf's threatening "I have told our story" at the beginning of *The Cannibal*. At the end of the book, the texture of the narrative—Papa's repeated assertion of a godlike control over the body (the wheezing machine) and the body politic (a nation of coughers and voyeurs)—has created the "totality of structure" that Hawkes, his creations, and his audience have repeatedly craved. But Hawkes is true to the tale, not to his artist: "There shall be no survivors." In the technological world of illusion that has been Hawkes's consistent focus, the artist who insists on his own authority contributes to the illusion of power that is diminishing the world itself, reducing it to the raw material of manufactured dreams. But the novel seems to imply that the total coherence of this dream will leave nothing to be manipulated. It is not a cheerful thought.

CHAPTER SEVEN

The Nihilist *Deus Artifex*: The Short Fiction of John Barth

Never think in a book: here are truth and all the other capital
letters; but think in a theatre and watch the audience. Here is
the reality, here are human animals. Listen to the words of
heroism and then at the crowded husbands who applaud. All
philosophies are subordinate to this.

> —T. E. Hulme
> *Speculations*

Modern writers should emulate the bees, who not merely return
what they have taken from the flowers, but render this into
marvellous compounds of wax and honey.

> —Petrarch to Boccaccio
> *Familiarum Rerum*

I.

Chapter 6 showed John Hawkes annihilating one of the premises
of the *deus artifex topos*, the idea that the artist could, by force of will
and mastery, create a world of his own against a backdrop of total decline. Hawkes's Papa found imagined life more exhilarating than remembered life, a view bludgeoned into moribundity by William Gass
and Susan Sontag, his postmodern contemporaries, but still alive and
lethal for most of Hawkes's narrators from Zizendorf to Papa. So de-
pressed by the exhausted possibilities of the actual, so scarred by the
contaminations of memory are Hawkes's narrators that each asserts
his right to create his world. But in *Travesty*, the last modern
cliché finally unmasks itself, as the bid for godly omnipotence inevitably expands to include the godly prerogative of destruction as well
as the godly impulse to creation. And the structure of the book ensures the reader's participation in what becomes a mandatory apocalypse, for the silence of Papa's fellow travelers means that we become
his victims. We are hurled into a confrontation with "our story," a
goal that Hawkes set for himself as early as 1949. Moreover, *Travesty*
shows the tragic potential within the idea that everyman must become

his own godly artist. In Papa's case, such artifice is more desperate than exalted: as his memories gradually reveal the events that have brought him to desolation, so his rhetoric insists on the necessity of his private apocalypse. Hawkes's ability to transform the *topos* derives from his need to exploit its possibilities for satirical realism to the utmost together with (in *Travesty* and *The Cannibal*) his power to imagine its most horrific consequences. The apocalypse Camus burlesqued in *The Fall* becomes a reality in *Travesty*, where Hawkes achieves his most fatal marriage of inner compulsion and objective circumstance.

But what of the comic potential of the *topos*? Has any recent writer tapped its comic resources as intensively as Hawkes has mined its satiric possibilities? For many years such has been John Barth's aim. In 1961, he told *Johns Hopkins Magazine* that "the novelist's trade, like God's, is manufacturing universes" and confided to them his hope of joining an eternal vaudeville routine alongside "Shakespeare, Cervantes, and God—hard acts to follow."[1] Nearly twenty years later, he spoke of the godly maker's imperative to "tell the whole story," a requirement that challenged the dissidence and antagonism of his contemporaries and recent precursors. If, Barth argued, "linearity, rationality, consciousness, cause and effect, naive illusionism, transparent language, innocent anecdote, and middle-class moral conventions are not the whole story, then from the perspective of these closing decades of our century we may appreciate that the contraries of these things are not the whole story, either. Disjunction, simultaneity, irrationalism, anti-illusionism, self-reflexiveness, medium-as-message, political olympianism, and a moral pluralism approaching moral entropy—these are not the whole story either."[2]

Barth has voiced these opinions so consistently and for so long that his appearance on an Eastern European lecture tour (with William Gass and John Hawkes) in the guise of "a typical postmodern specimen" seems somewhat unlikely. Is not an author so traditional in his tastes and so conservative in his aims too old-fashioned to be found at the cutting edge of fictional experiment? Jerome Klinkowitz, a longstanding apostate on the matter of Barth's postmodernity, certainly thought so, and in "John Barth Reconsidered" he told *Partisan Review* readers that Barth was an impostor. Klinkowitz charged that Barth, disguised as a postmodernist "solidly aligned with a tenured academic community," had for years furthered the aims of his "vested interest in representational literary art" through the composition of fiction that merely went through the postmodernist motions.[3]

This is a verdict that is difficult to dispute. Throughout his career, Barth has acknowledged the inheritance of the past in a way that many of his contemporaries have not. In his first published story the young author made routine homage not only to James Joyce, but also to Homer and the *Arabian Nights*, all of which merged in the drowsing consciousness of Ronnie Kahn, a young Jewish boy on the eve of his bar mitzvah.[4] Similarly, where Barth's colleagues on the postmodern lecture tour acknowledged only the authority of the mind that would reduce reality to the raw material for a sovereign consciousness, Barth has, as Leslie Fiedler argued, made Maryland his own.[5] It is worth noting that one of the earliest critical essays on Barth, John M. Bradbury's "Absurd Insurrection: The Barth-Percy Affair," viewed Barth as a southern novelist, albeit of a peculiarly newfangled kind.[6] This is not simply a matter of geography: a concern with narrative form as a way to mediate past and present, an appalled fascination with abstract thought and its tortuous relationship with social mores, an elegiac sense of a passing order—these are qualities that describe *Absalom, Absalom!* or *All the King's Men* as well as *The End of the Road*. Perhaps too the author of *Jurgen* would have understood *The Sot-Weed Factor* better than some of its earliest reviewers did. As a godly maker, Barth draws on a bulkier stock than some of his contemporaries, whom in 1961 he admitted he spent little time reading. The sense of being at the elbow of Shakespeare, Cervantes, and God would not, I suspect, come easily to William Gass or Bernard Malamud. On the other hand, the intimate and almost claustrophobic sense of small town living that characterizes Barth's earliest fiction would not be accessible to Susan Sontag or Donald Barthelme, either. Barth has roots in traditions—learned and lived—that are not available to some of his contemporaries.

But Barth recognized the burden of the past as well as its legacy. No author of the later part of this century—particularly in the late 1960s, which Barth remembers as a time of "tear-gassed protesters"— could have done otherwise.[7] One of Barth's recurrent fears is that the tradition in which he was born and reared has been used up. By about 1960, the call that the novel was dead had transcended cliché to become a real problem for creative artists; and Barth, like other writers, was forced to confront the threat of the new intermedia arts. These, as Barth pointed out, "eliminate the most traditional notion of the artist."[8] In such a context, the desire to tell the whole story, to be postwar America's godly maker, becomes vulnerable and problematic.

As a self-styled "traditionalist innovator," Barth was forced to confront the possibility that the latter desire might drive out the former. From his first novel onward, however, Barth has acknowledged this impulse toward novelty as an inescapable aspect of modern life, one not to be denied in his fiction. In 1960 he told John Enck that he had been intrigued by the idea of a new comic fiction because "I thought I had invented it"; likewise nihilism, which, he told Enck, "I thought I had invented . . . in 1953."[9] In Barth's fiction, this mistaken sense of novelty is dramatized by characters like Jacob Horner and Henry Burlingame who see the world as their own godlike creation and reality as a neutral zone to be transformed by the masquerade of art.

Barth's fictional world then celebrates two rival impulses. On one side, he creates characters who aspire to the comic virtues of variety and multiplicity; on the other, he recognizes the impulse toward self-creation and the exercise of arbitrary will that motivates men like Ambrose M——— and women like Marsha Blank. The first set of characters want to invent a world; the second are sure they have already done so. This duality results in two very different kinds of story. Todd Andrews tells the first kind, and the site for his narration is a flat, open-decked showboat that will float up- and downstream to audiences on either side of the river. The story will depend for its existence on the participation of its audience, and what it lacks in unity it will compensate for in variety. Todd promises "a floating opera . . . fraught with curiosities, spectacle, melodrama, instruction and entertainment" (7), a narrative godly in its heterogeneity and multiplicity. Todd's narrative exploits the mimetic responsibilities of narration: "That's how much of life works," he admits, readily conceding the priority of life over art.

These storytellers, of whom Todd Andrews and Capt. Osborn are the chief examples, come to us as voices, detached from the reality they describe but able to bring it to life by their modulations of tone and the variety of their narrative techniques. Their rivals do not really tell stories at all; unwilling to concede the priority of reality, they substitute the authority of their own performances, which they manipulate according to their particular whim. For Henry Burlingame, "the captor's sole expedient" (373) is the stance any artist must take toward life; for Jake Horner, "mythoplastic razors" (119) are the weapons with which to have at reality. By the time Barth reaches *The Sot-Weed Factor*, he has come to recognize such godlike desires to transcend reality as an all-important part of American identity. The Americans of that novel begin every day as if it were the first of creation; the result is the same "contamination of reality by dream" that Barth noticed as pervasive in the fiction of Jorge Luis Borges, one of his later enthusiasms.[10] In *Lost in the Funhouse* Barth's "series" begins with a sperm narrator whose hatred for the "official heritage" gets the narrative in motion; the book ends, without ever having proceeded very far, with the invention of "fiction" by a misplaced bard. At this point, locked in a world that makes a daily discovery of the wheel, Barth's self-deifying solipsists appear to have stifled his imaginative life. But in 1979, with the publication of *LETTERS*, Barth makes his most sustained bid to emerge from this ever-closing circle of experimental fiction. By pitting his narrators against his self-absorbed performers Barth goes as far toward telling "the whole story" as he has so far managed.

II.

The facts concerning the publication and subject matter of Barth's first two novels have, to some degree, determined the critical responses to them. We know that *The Floating Opera* occupied the first three months of Barth's 1955; we know that *The End of the Road* took up the last three. We also know that both novels were originally designed to form part of a cycle of books on nihilism that Barth subsequently abandoned. Armed with such knowledge, it is hard not to weave the two novels into a composite text, and to make the subject matter of that text the nihilism the author has so obligingly identified for us as his major pursuit.

Richard Noland saw nihilism at work in the way these novels present manners and mores, discerning in them a widespread postwar malaise rooted in "a failure of contact of the members of a whole society on the most basic level possible. . . . only abstract systems are left by which people attempt to communicate with each other."[11] Barth's fiction continuously exposes the failure of these abstractions, however, whether they be the abstractions of Marxist-Leninism (Harrison Mack's subsidized socialism) or psychoanalysis (Jake Horner's mythotherapy). He begins his fiction with very little and pares it down to almost nothing at all.

But critics have rarely been content with such a bleak vision. Campbell Tatham, who acknowledges that Barth's fiction "resolutely denies the primacy of engagement with the moral imperative," and Beverly Gross, who thinks that Barth's fiction shows how "all issues . . . come down to some sort of game," both attempt to renovate their author's nihilism.[12] After making a formidable inventory of Barth's dismantlings and deconstructions, Tatham remarks that "by insisting on aesthetic artifice [Todd] is able to construct a bulwark against the acceptance of personal and universal irrationality; art posits a momentary stay against encroaching confusion." Rather differently, Gross acknowledges that with a fine disregard for the performative, Barth includes a real corpse in his imaginary lexical field: "Having reduced everything to comedy, the book suddenly reduces its comedy to loath-someness. . . . Barth's novels are comic masks for a tragic face."

These were the very characterizations that Thomas LeClair took issue with in his brilliant article "John Barth's *The Floating Opera*: Death and the Craft of Fiction." LeClair acknowledged that Barth's canon amounted to a cumulative attempt to cope with mortality through the consoling fictions of art. But LeClair could see neither the tragic potential discerned by Gross nor the humanist impulses identi-fied by Tatham. For LeClair, Barth's fiction evaded mortality rather than controlled it, so that his artists were liars, "protean fictionalizers who compromise the novelistic conflict between imagination of the purely possible and recognition of the unfortunately necessary by adopting disguises or illusions, which they recognize as such, to con-trol their lives and thus survive." [13] The prototype for this pattern was, LeClair argued, Barth's Todd Andrews, whom he saw as a radically unreliable narrator, attempting at all costs to evade a mortality that troubled all Barth's subsequent artificers. LeClair saw the course of the fiction as a movement toward a militant affirmation of artifice, requiring "ever greater claims to the control and transmutation of life itself." At the same time, Barth's heroes become "progressively impotent," a predicament that dramatizes the utter severance of art from life.

In such a context, it scarcely seems relevant to speak of Barth as a comic *deus artifex*. But has criticism asked the right questions of Barth's first two novels? Does Barth's fiction move on an ever-ascend-ing scale of artifice from *The Floating Opera* onward? Is it true that he occupies forms only to invert them, imagines lives only to avoid life itself? Is Todd Andrews as unreliable as LeClair suggests? The charac-terization LeClair offers is of a kind of minstrel-show Faust who has bought his imaginative virtuosity at the cost of becoming a moral idiot. What LeClair ignores is Todd's aspiration to create a work that will celebrate a common world, a task requiring that he unpeel his mask of mastery and replace it with a more hesitant and less absolute point of view. Jake Horner, who never manages to make this renuncia-tion, brings about the destruction of a world in his story. The differ-ence cannot be accidental. Barth's first two books show the activities of two very different kinds of godly artist; the way to get a clearer sense of the nature of Barth's imagination is surely to begin to discrim-inate between them.

Barth's first hero, Todd Andrews, is a godchild of the new cen-tury. Indeed, he seems to belong to that type prophesied by Henry Adams, who thought that the child born in 1900 would be born into a new world, and "must be a sort of God compared with any former creation of nature." [14] Adams saw the twentieth-century child's godly status as resting on the force generated by machine power; Todd's authority, however, rests rather on the peculiarly negative power of being able to see around the contradictions of his society. In his compromised ability to reveal the absurdities of power, he is simultaneously a typically modern outsider and a participant in society's neverending switches of alliance—a sort of God by virtue of his superior rationality. And in his daunting capacity to project scenarios that will assure him complete dominance he is a kind of artist as well—though not too happy an artist in not too happy a century. Until he writes his *Floating Opera*, Todd's godliness is a matter of pure power, of using real people as pawns on his private chessboard. It is Capt. Adam's floating opera, which celebrates the human capacity for change rather than the will to power, that inspires Todd's rebirth as a *deus artifex* in its traditional sense, as well as the composition of the many voiced, multi-layered text that constitutes the book as we read it.

Where *The Floating Opera* moves from mastery to wonder, *The End of the Road* remains fixed in mastery. *The Floating Opera* is a comedy of ideas; *The End of the Road* is a tragedy of ideas. And the tragedy is that in *The End of the Road* ideas are the sole source of authority. At one point in the book, Rennie Morgan tells Jake Horner that "sometimes I think that nothing Joe could think about would ever be worth the sharpness of his mind. This will sound ridiculous to you, Jake, but I think of Joe as I'd think of God" (62). The narrative never explores the possibility of thought unfreezing into kindness; here, the godly artist is a perpetual plotter, always rehearsing the ways his mastery can best be deployed. Once Jake has learned the principles of a mythotherapy that enables him to reduce reality to a series of considered performances, he can perfect his act in private, monitor it all the easier to annihilate the assumptions and expectations of other people: "My moods were little men, and when I killed them they stayed completely dead" (30). The casual brutality Jake takes to his own emotional life is transferred to his treatment of the emotions of others, as he tortures Joe and destroys Rennie Morgan.

In *The End of the Road*, the godly artist is the manipulator of a life scenario, the olympian who "sees all the arbitrariness of the rules and social conventions, but who has such a great scorn or disregard for the society he lives in that he embraces the whole wagonload of nonsense with a smile" (136). But the smile is that of a Mephistopheles, not of a Jacob R. Adam; Jake's manipulativeness is that of a man who treats the world as if it has been invented for his solitary delight. As

Peggy Rankin tells him after a particularly unpleasant episode, "You're so wrapped up in yourself that you don't have a shred of respect for anyone else on earth!" (96). Respect, the acknowledgment of the existence of other people, would be foreign to the very premises of the world described in *The End of the Road*, a world where reality is only a basis for negotiation, and not, as in the eyes of Osborn or Jacob R. Adam, a source of wonder.

Most of *The Floating Opera* is also concerned with this world of role play and control. Harrison Mack Senior and Colonel Morton are the entrepreneurs whose enterprises control the world of Cambridge. The motto of the latter is "don't feel obligated," while the former rules from the grave by force of will. Todd's own form of mastery, which he practices for most of the book, imitates this chain of absolute authority. His artistry at this point is largely a result of the inventive imaginativeness with which he devises scenarios to get what he wants. But a brief summary of his last day, which he planned to live "as ordinarily as possible" (16), establishes how much like his sponsors Todd actually is. What does he do on his last day on earth? He sleeps with Jane Mack and presides over a meeting of the Dorchester Explorers' Club. The two events lead him to set a test for Jane that will leave one of the Club members—his favorite—in his debt (47). He lunches with Harrison Mack, all the time subjecting Harrison to a silent examination (142). He is examined by Mr. Haecker and, with rough justice, examines Haecker in turn (158–65). Finally, he is examined by Marvin Rose, from whom he exacts a final act of obedience (135). Life for Todd, from the events recounted in the novel, consists less of a grand series of masks than a thousand little tests, which cumulatively but precariously underpin his sense of absolute authority. But his decision to commit suicide shows how his endlessly examined life is not worth living.

When Jake Horner begins as a teacher of prescriptive grammar at Wicomico College, this scenario of domination is just the kind of script he writes for himself. Jake's description of his class is full of godly imagery, but it is clear that Jake is an unpredictable and harsh deity. He reports that his students "wrote my name and office number as frowningly as if I'd pronounced the Key to the Mystery" (94). In the high places of the lecture hall, the self easily imagines that it has created the world. "Perched high on my desk," Jake reports, "I had nothing at all to do but spin indolent daydreams of absolute authority" (94–95). Jake eventually comes to see the razor-sharp articulations of language as the only way to achieve an absolute, although he recognizes that "to turn experience into speech . . . is always a betrayal of experience, a falsification of it." But as he also admits, "only so betrayed can it be dealt with at all, and only in so dealing with it did I ever feel a man, alive and kicking" (119).

It is tempting—and he tempts us to see it that way—to regard Jake's mythotherapy as a necessary fiction in a value-free world. But Jake's description of himself, his "mythoplastic razors sharply honed [ready] to have at reality" (119), ought to disillusion us. In terms of the book's action, such self-derived authority is inevitably victimizing. One of Jake's first classroom confrontations is with a diminutive visionary called, appropriately enough, Blakesley. Jake hopes to crucify him in the educational process. In the pedagogical world of *The End of the Road*, the *deus artifex topos*—even the idea of a God—is a dead metaphor, deadened as much by the omnipresence of performance as by the characters' lack of belief. But it can still kill, even where it is only a fiction as the case of Rennie Morgan, who dies aspiring to Joe Morgan's godlike self-sufficiency, shows clearly enough.

Both of Barth's first two books deal with worlds that have shriveled into abstraction. The power of entrepreneurship has dwindled, leaving only Harrison Mack, Jr., who changes ideologies like lounge suits, and Colonel Morton who maintains his authority through a desperate marriage. Even the life of the mind is but poorly represented by the aged, role-playing, suicidal school superintendent, Mr. Haecker, whose acting is as compulsive as Mack Sr.'s will changes, and every bit as death ridden. In *The End of the Road* the whole world dwindles into a classroom where a phalanx of pedagogues apes the language of drama and imagination.

> "You drill and drill," Jake tells his interview committee, "and talk yourself blue in the face, and all the time you see that boy's mind groping, stumbling, stretching, making false steps. And then, just when you're ready to chuck the whole thing. . . ."
>
> "I know!" Miss Banning breathed. "One day, just like all the rest, you say the same thing for the tenth time—and *click!*" She snapped her fingers jubilantly at Dr. Schott. "He's got it! *Why, there's nothing to it!* he says. *It's plain as day!*"
>
> "That's what we're here for!" Dr. Schott said quietly, with some pride.
>
> "That's what we all live for. A little thing, isn't it?"
>
> "Little," Dr. Carter agreed, "but it's the greatest miracle on God's green earth! And the most mysterious, too." (17)

"Mystery and miracle; plain as day; what we live for": this is clearly a pedagogue's version of theophany. From the language of revelation and epiphany that is so freely bandied around, we might expect a godly artist here. But Miss Banning's *"click!"* dissolves the whole charade; in *The End of the Road* men and women are only machines that think. The whole thrust of this book is away from imaginative creation. The godly maker is the man who, like the Doctor or Joe Morgan or Jake himself, can manipulate others into thinking his way as Jake does by the careful construction of this schoolroom masquerade.

The novel gradually moves from a parody of ubiquitous artistry to a tragic recognition of the consequences of imagining oneself to be a god. Role play, the sense of self as the sole authority in a universe of power, is revealed as imprisoning rather than liberating. After a riding class, Jake and Rennie discover a Joe Morgan who seems locked into the notion of his own authority, unable to distance himself from his own role. Jake reflects:

> Joe wasn't reading. He was standing in the exact center of the bare room, fully dressed, smartly executing military commands. About *face*! Right *dress*! 'Ten-*shun*! Parade *rest*! He saluted briskly, his cheeks blown out and his tongue extended, and then proceeded to cavort about the room—spinning, pirouetting, bowing, leaping, kicking. I watched entranced by his performance, for I cannot say that in my strangest moments (and a bachelor has strange ones) I have surpassed him. Rennie trembled from head to foot. (70)

Joe's performance is no more than Joe magnified. The idea of a godly authority has established in Joe a despotism that he cannot put off even in privacy. Joe's desire to be a god has overwhelmed his life as a man. It is the same unchangeable conviction—to be herself and no one else—that leads Rennie Morgan to her death. Rennie wants to be like everyone else in the book; she wants, that is, to be at last herself. But the way she defines herself is so narrow that it leads her to her own annihilation.

If *The End of the Road* shows a commitment to godly control as gradually imprisoning and finally destructive, then *The Floating Opera* explores the liberating potential of a godly artistry. *The End of the Road* depicts a world of abstraction makers and pedagogues; *The Floating Opera* has plenty of these, but it also has a brace of seamen who bring tales that do more than assert mastery and authority. The first of these is told by Capt. Osborn in "A Chorus of Oysters" to an audience described dryly by Todd as "Osborn and his colleagues of the loafers' bench" (109). Theirs is a life of collective storytelling. Immobilized by their age, they participate in a shared fumbling, a joint attempt to reconstruct life through memory.

> "Whose funeral?" [Todd] asked.
> "Why, that's Clarence Wampler's wife, ain't it, Osborn?" offered my neighbor, watching the hearse move off.
> "Yep," assented Capt. Osborn. "Died Monday night."
> "That the Henry Street one, come from Golden Hill?" asked the third.
> "Naw, that's *Lewis* Wampler's wife yer thinkin' of," Capt. Osborn declared.
> "Yer thinkin' of ol' Jenny Fairwell."
> "Ol' Jenny?" the first cackled. "Ol' Jenny?"
> "Ol' Jenny," Capt. Osborn grinned, stretching his leg. "There was a hot one." (110)

Osborn may gasp, but his story is a collective inspiration for his fellow loafers, as a memory of one woman elicits recollections of a host of them. This in turn jogs Osborn's memory of his own past, and a narrative of a long-vanished world of oyster dredgers crowds out this present world of pickle factories, sinuses, and old wheezers. The comparison is never made explicitly, but the course of Osborn's narrative—which has an audience, which involves other people, and which creates a world with all the unfinished, faltering, quivering life of memory—is clearly the inspiration for Todd's final narrative design. Todd devoted the earlier part of his life to a solitary accumulation of facts with which to master the business of living; he has become the self-crowned deity of Cambridge through his capacity to shape reality into a pattern that makes him an authority to be reckoned with. Osborn's narrative, a confession of and appeal to a necessary imperfection in memories and audiences, is just the reverse of this. Todd's life scenarios require other people for their fulfillment, but only in the same way that a chess set needs a full set of pieces; Osborn's narrative needs other people as participants, contributors to a shared attempt at reviving the present by remembering the past. Osborn's story, faltering and halting as it is, holds a promise of an artistry that will be godly in its capacity to recreate a common world; his story restores the common sources of the *topos* that were tapped by Thomas Mann and James Joyce in the twentieth century, or Sir Philip Sidney in the sixteenth.

This is the kind of narrative Todd wants to write when he speaks of a tale like a floating opera that "wouldn't be moored, but would drift up and down the river on the tide, and the audience would sit along both banks. They could catch whatever part of the plot happened to unfold as the boat floated past, and then they'd have to wait until the tide ran back again to catch another snatch of it, if they still happened to be sitting there. To fill in the gaps they'd have to use their imaginations, or ask more attentive neighbors, or hear the word passed on from upriver or downriver" (7). This is the kind of tale that Osborn tells, and it is also the kind of performance Capt. Adam enacts on his actual floating opera. Where Todd collates a journal devoted to the impossibility of knowing anything, Capt. Adam's opera mocks the very business of knowledge, and strikes at its self-inflating roots:

> "Good evening, Mr. Tambo; you look a little down in the mouth tonight."
> "Mist' Interlocutor, ah ain't down in de mouf; ah's down in de pocketbook. New hat fo' de wife, new shoes fo' de baby. Now dat no-good boy ob mine is done pesterin' me to buy him a 'cyclopedia. Say he needs 'em fo' de school."
> "An encyclopedia! Ah, there's a wise lad, Tambo! No schoolboy should be without a good encyclopedia. I trust you'll purchase one for the lad?"
> "No, sah!"
> "No!"
> "No, sah! Ah say to dat boy, ah say, 'Cyclopedia nuffin'! Y'all gwine walk like de other chillun!" (234–35)

Where Todd has devoted a career of solitary evenings to evaluating the worth of existence, T. Wallace Whittaker's soliloquy on this matter is laughed offstage in a matter of seconds on Capt. Adam's opera. Where Todd's masks are assumed for power by a self that remains unalterably Todd, Capt. Adam as Mr. Interlocutor is "transformed into an entirely different person—grammatical, florid, effusive—so that one doubted the authenticity of his original character" (234). Where Jake, Todd, Joe, and Mr. Haecker all don their masks from a sense of inauthenticity, Capt. Adam revels in a multiplicity that only confirms his unique individuality. The potential for an art godly in its variety as well as its intensity has at last returned to contemporary literature.

But it is potential rather than achievement that emerges as the overriding impression of the book. For one thing, Todd's narrative voice—the vehicle for a solicitous regard for otherness—remains a voice; the novel ends with Todd's celebration of the event that leads to his adoption of this voice, which is never, for this reason, inserted into the action of the book. Todd recollects a world—he does not create one. Consequently, the action of the novel is distanced by being placed in the past; it has none of the hectic vitality of a Rabelais or a Cervantes, where the vision of the godly artificer makes its presence felt directly in the action of the narrative. Moreover, the voices of

Capt. Osborn and Jacob R. Adam belong to a past that is superseded during the course of the novel. If Barth is going to tell the whole story, then the roles of these two characters cannot retain the prominence they have kept here. The old dilemma of the comic novelist—whether to be true to Falstaff or England, to Huck or the South—has made an unexpectedly early appearance in Barth's career.

Barth's first two novels turn on the career of the godly artist in a nihilist world; but in *The Floating Opera* the artist escapes his nihilism through a gentler artifice, benign in its tenets but scarcely shown as operating in the action of the novel. In *The End of the Road*, however, the godly artist merely pursues the designs of his own will. It is interesting to note the results: *The Floating Opera* ends with the aversion of catastrophe; *The End of the Road* ends with the engineering of one. Barth's godly artists, however different their roles, clearly possess important responsibilities and dangerous powers.

Even so, the voice of an Adam or an Osborn has only limited potential for a novelist. In effect, the action on the floating opera obliterates the preoccupations of the earlier part of the novel. Where Shakespeare, Cervantes, and God—the "hard acts" Barth wants to follow—merge comedy and tragedy in one all-absorbing movement, Barth merely sweeps tragedy away with the clean broom of farce. His genres collide; they do not interfuse. Todd returns from the floating opera to encounter Haecker's attempted suicide; the effect is Dickensian streaky bacon rather than cosmic comedy. Barth has administered his coup de grâce to tragedy with undiscriminating inclusiveness. That intensity is often no more than affectation in postwar writing is no doubt true, but Barth's overwhelming urge at the end of this novel, to see life as a river that drifts and passes, is more reminiscent of the philistine's complacency than the comic muse's wisdom. For two miragelike moments—Osborn's oyster chorus and Adam's opera—Barth restores the *topos* to its early vitality. But how will he organize his two star turns into a performance, how will he integrate their voices into the action of an entire novel? How will a young man put to imaginative use the kind of vision reserved in this novel for the very old? How can a minstrel-show interlude inform the voice and action of a novelist writing in a nihilistic world? [15]

III.

When Barth's *Lost in the Funhouse* appeared in 1968, critical responses were often sharp. Barth's reviewers have always been tempted to regard each of his books as worse than the last; *Lost in the Funhouse,* a labyrinthine combination of pop mythology, multiple allusion, and electronic voice games, appeared to invite these very responses. Accordingly, Guy Davenport found the book "thoroughly confusing" while the *Book World's* critic dismissed it as "blitheringly sophomoric," a verdict echoed by the *Library Journal's* reviewer, who damned it as "pseudo-Homeric." [16] But it was Tony Tanner, in what remains the best criticism of Barth, who argued that the book's underlying theme was anguish, and that *Lost in the Funhouse* was "a story of loss, a demonstration of how we lose what we don't believe in, how we can never again be sure of [what] we called into question." Tanner recognized the spirit of anguished Pyrrhonism in the book, which he saw as representative of the way we live now; but he also pointed to the possibility of a creative malaise in Barth, a "corrosive doubt about identity and its relation to language." The result is that Barth's fiction continuously eludes his control; *Lost in the Funhouse* is a book where words "drift on in self-canceling and self-undermining recessions." [17]

Certainly, Tanner's account is justified by results; in the decade after *Lost in the Funhouse*, Barth produced only *Chimera*, suggesting a Homer not so much nodding as defunct. It was to be 1979 before Barth would publish *LETTERS*, proof that whatever he was up to in *Lost in the Funhouse*, it was not to be a fructifying affair. A vocal minority among Barth's critics, however, saw *Lost in the Funhouse* as a passport to a new irrealist tradition. These critics insisted that the author had dislodged himself from the burden of a modernist past and opened new lines of communication for himself and his audience. Edgar H. Knapp's Barth is a new Icarus, one presumably capable of avoiding his potent progenitor's fate as he plots "the mirror maze of a new fiction." [18] Similarly, Michael Hinden argues that *Lost in the Funhouse* is a manifesto urging "the writers and critics of contemporary fiction to cut the coils that bind them to the recent past." By one of those fortunate falls that occurs from time to time in literary history, this past has "already . . . furnished Barth with new materials for art." [19] But these arguments cut against the grain of the book, where Barth's Ambrose is overwhelmed and undernourished by a past he is unable to master. And even if we distinguish Barth from Ambrose, our interpretation must take account of Ambrose's anxieties, which are crucial to *Lost in the Funhouse* as a whole. To read the novel as a triumphantly visionary work, largely on the basis of carefully selected passages from "The Literature of Exhaustion," is like reading Donne's "Twicknam Garden" as a devotional poem on the basis of a reading of his sermons.

Beverly Bienstock's stridently affirmative "Lingering on the Au-

tognostic Verge: John Barth's *Lost in the Funhouse*" presses on in bliss-
ful disregard of the book's basic conflicts. At the center of the book,
surely, are the identity crises of its protagonists. Menelaus is in endless pursuit of an identity; Ambrose is agnostic about the existence of
his own; even the unnamed, unborn sperm cell of "Night Sea Journey" is embittered by his sense of inauthenticity. Any view of *Lost in
the Funhouse* must surely take these anxieties into account. But Bienstock shrugs them off so that she can end her essay in a burst of effu-
siveness that seems foreign to the irritated, nettled self-questioning
that informs her source: "We go on forever exchanging masks in a fantastic hall of mirrors," she concludes, "and one shouldn't try to tell
the dancer from the dance."[20] One problem with this interpretation is
that it makes *Lost in the Funhouse* scarcely a book about loss at all.

The same is true of Linda Westervelt's incisive account of the
book.[21] Westervelt recognizes how this novel constantly frustrates, in
typically postmodernist fashion, a reader's expectations about coherence and design. But Westervelt overlooks how far Barth's narrators
and protagonists entertain similar expectations; it is not only Barth's
readers who are disappointed. By ignoring this important fact, Westervelt is able to transform a problem into a "how-to" textbook. Barth
is not Robert Coover, whose *Pricksongs and Descants* baffles his reader's
desire for coherence by overwhelming him with choices. When Barth
presents his audience with a set of alternatives, as in "Life Story," he is
apologetic that he cannot provide the coherence that his narrator feels
is necessary. Where Coover's "The Elevator" suggests rapture at the
sublime possibilities of a multiple universe, Barth's narrators find it all
a little ragged. Moreover, Barth's self-conscious tricks are void of content. When the spouse of "Title" remarks to the narrator that she is
"sorry if [she's] interrupting the Progress of Literature," he duly cate-
gorizes her remark (as any good teacher should) as "good-humored
irony" (102). After hinting at more human griefs behind the quip (he
suggests that his wife's words are "defensively and imperfectly masking a taunt" [102]), Barth again dons his writing instructor's cap: "The
conflict is established though as yet unclear in detail" (102). By now,
"the unusual analytic ability" that Westervelt sees at work in these
stories is clearly paralyzing any attempt at narrating a story worth listening to.

In *Lost in the Funhouse*, as Carol Shloss and Khachig Totolyan recognized, the world has become a text.[22] The result is the inevitable demise of the *deus artifex topos,* summarily disposed of in "Life Story" as
the narrator announces: "He'd been about to append to his own tale
inasmúch as the old analogy between Author and God, novel and

world, can no longer be employed unless deliberately as a false analogy, certain things follow: 1) fiction must acknowledge its fictitiousness and metaphoric invalidity or 2) choose to ignore the question or deny its relevance or 3) establish some other, acceptable relation between itself, its author, its reader" (125).

To see the world as no longer the creation of an artist-god is to see it through the lenses of self-conscious rationalism. Accordingly, Barth reverts to a diction that belongs more to the classroom or the law court than the fiction maker. His legalistic "inasmuch as" and his precise subheadings (cast-iron boxes to deposit used checks in) recall Todd Andrews's *Inquiry*, that opus magnum of futility, and like that *Inquiry*, are destined to become an overdetermined, self-justifying activity.

The shift in Barth's voice, from poet to unacknowledged legislator, indicates the shift in authority that is at the center of *Lost in the Funhouse*. The world of *Lost in the Funhouse* sounds like a parody of a world created by a godly maker. Its repeated echoes, recurrent situations, and set pieces from world literature (the adolescence of a sensitive hero, the disenchantment of a middle-aged spouse, the displacement of a tribal bard) all point to the existence of a common maker whom none of the book's characters can penetrate or even acknowledge, for none of them can recognize the existence of others or even perform a meaningful action on their own. In this, a book saturated with artists but quite void of an authorizing imagination, Barth has created a world of anxious solitaries and irritated solipsists; the book's structural parallels and allusive echoes ultimately have an imprisoning effect. Moreover, messages written on water cannot last. The most important evidence the narrator of "Anonymiad" can muster of a living presence in the world (other than his own) is a message that is illegible enough to be construed according to his own purposes. All the world consists of writers, but all its texts are indecipherable. Unlike Capt. Osborn of *The Floating Opera*, Barth's anonymous narrator brings no knowledge of the larger world of destinies outside of his own into his narrative. We have already met the Thalia who is his first muse in "Petition"; Menelaus has already been cited in "Menelaid"; messages inscribed "YOURS TRULY" have floated from the Ambrose story "Water-Message." But these similarities go unnoticed by the narrator; they are not marshaled into any significant design by any of the protagonists in the series, and the stories therefore stay sturdily separate. The effect of repetition and variation is oblivion, not interanimation: "Telling the story over," we hear in "Echo," makes it "lose sense" (95). Like *The Crying of Lot 49*, published two years before it, *Lost in the Funhouse* is the product of a culture where number is beginning to supplant narrative. Further, in both books hysteria—not rationality—is one surprising result of this shift in power.

There are, in effect, three distinct universes described in *Lost in the Funhouse*, and each attempts to cope in its own way with a life without a godly maker. In the first, Ambrose searches a commodity-exhausted America for a sign. In the second, electronic voices try to establish new relations between audience and universe. The mythic stories that close the book try to ignore the question by simulating claims to originality and ultimacy that the text has not borne out. (Neither Menelaus nor the narrator of "Anonymaid" can claim priority in the matter of identity crises; it is the blight man was born for, as the narrator of "Night-Sea Journey" knows.) And behind all the thrashing toward new fictional seas is the depressing circularity of the "Frame Tale" that wheels back and forth within the oldest narrative model of all: "Once upon a time" (1–2).

Such prolonged stasis perhaps lies behind the aggression of "Night-Sea Journey," where the ocean, which Barth has so often associated with the liberating potential of story, becomes the location for an ontological self-examination of the kind that provoked Todd Andrews's planned suicide and Mr. Haecker's completed one. It was the sea that brought Todd Andrews the voice of Jacob R. Adam; but on this sea journey, told by a sperm on its way to birth, we can find no sign of the neighborly reciprocity of a tale. What the story exhibits, rather, is the anxious cerebration of a head-piece. As a godly maker, an artist peoples a world with destinies different from his own; Barth's narrator in "Night-Sea Journey" is submerged in multiple varieties of his own destiny. In fact, his story presents him as a victim of that persistent Barthian illusion, the idea that the self creates the ground for its own story, that the world is created in the single image of the narrator: "Numberless the number of the dead! Thousands drown as I think this thought, millions as I rest before returning to the swim. And scores, hundreds of millions have expired since we surged forth, brave in our innocence, upon our dreadful way. 'Love! Love!' we sang then, a quarter-billion strong, and churned the warm sea white with joy of swimming! Now all are gone down—the buoyant, the sodden, leaders and followers, all gone under, while wretched I swim on" (4).

Barth's narrator peoples his world with an ever-diminishing shoal of swimmers, each motivated by an indefinable goal whose worth is by turns all-important and unimportant. The sea, Barth's region of free-floating abundance, has become a zone of endless self-questioning where those trained to swim come to doubt and reject the task for which they are trained: "What has fetched me across this dreadful sea," Barth's sperm cell confesses, is "a private legacy of awful recollection and negative resolve" (11). The impulse to sea voyaging that Barth had previously seen as liberating becomes in this context cruelly confining, as the incarceration of Ambrose M——'s father in Eastern Shore asylum makes clear.

"Night-Sea Journey," then, prepares us for a world where individuals will be a burden not a boon, the past an anxiety not an inheritance. The Ambrose stories—"Ambrose His Mark," "Water-Message," and "Lost in the Funhouse"—systematically deface and destroy the series of realistic conventions in which they initially seem to be lodged, in the same way that the narrator of "Night-Sea Journey" hopes to annihilate the tradition that gives him life. In addition, these stories imply that the exhaustion of narrative conventions complements the greater exhaustion of reality itself. Ocean City and realistic fiction are allowed to rot together. A heroic name and a golden tongue, a knowledge of the best in the literary past, are not enough to make Ambrose the kind of artist he would like to be; he is deafened by the echoes of literary history all around him, drowned in the multiple tides of solipsism he must swim against. When he travels to Ocean City, "strive as he might to be transported, he heard his mind take notes upon the scene" (81). However much Ambrose wants to become a mythmaker, he can only write like a stenographer. One of the proposed names for him had been Hector; but his mother's pet name Christine—in memory of the role of the movie star who had above all wanted to be alone—is a cannier assessment of the shape of his psyche and his culture. Not for nothing is his nation's principal secular holiday "Independence Day": the signs of an anxious desire to be left alone, together with self-loathing and disgust at one's own aloneness, are everywhere in these stories. Ambrose's family go "about their separate pleasures" (21) on Sunday quite heedless of their familial bond. Both Uncle Konrad, whose aim was "to see things in their context . . . to harmonize part with part, time with time" (15), and Ambrose, who had hoped to write a family romance, are overlooked, even ridiculed, by their household. In LETTERS, which provides a retrospective account of the Mensch family, we learn that one of their most outstanding achievements was a jerry-built wall. Ambrose lacks the resources to make a common universe, or even to master his own interior life, which he believes was created and even lived by other people.

In trying to scour the universe for signs of his heroic origins, Ambrose can only find a withered material reality. Visiting his den he reflects, "In years to come the Jungle would be gone entirely . . . his children, he supposed, might miss the winding paths and secret places—but, of course, you didn't miss what you'd never had or known of" (49). An old saw, but unfortunately—like so many of the received ideas in this book—an unhelpful one, since Ambrose searches, fails to find, and agonizes about failing to find a whole set of things he has never had, knows of only by reputation, but still misses terribly.

What he does discover are signs of commodity manufacturing, not signs of special election.

> He even recalled how, standing beside himself with awed imper-
> sonality in the reeky heat, he'd stared the while at an empty cigar
> box in which Uncle Karl kept stone-cutting chisels: beneath the
> words *El Producto,* a laureled, loose-toga'd lady regarded the sea
> from a marble bench; beside her, forgotten or not yet turned to,
> was a five-stringed lyre. Her chin reposed on the back of her right
> hand; her left depended negligently from the bench-arm. The
> lower half of scene and lady was peeled away; the words EXAM-
> INED BY __ were inked there into the wood. Nowadays cigar boxes
> are made of pasteboard. (74–75)

No longer an ocean of metaphors, the world has become a region of manufactured emptiness. A would-be man of letters, Ambrose must read what has now become a hopelessly corrupt and unauthorized text. First, his world is bewilderingly polyglottal—always a problem for the tale teller, whose medium is so incorrigibly a matter of language. In Ambrose's world, Uncle Karl jostles against El Producto, Italian Magda pushes out German Menschen, the Irish Hurleys battle with the English Coopers. Such plurality may well further the party of humanity (and America is indeed a creation of the Enlightenment), but it is all very confusing for the would-be writer yearning to belong creatively to someone or some place. Second, Ambrose must scan his destiny from the imperfect signs that a world of commodity can manage. Ambrose learns too that commodities can only recreate the world in the consumer's self-image. When Ambrose searches for romance, he confronts only a distorted mirror-image, a woman who appears as self-absorbed and passive as he is. "Standing beside himself," Ambrose observes a lady with "a five-stringed lyre forgotten or not yet turned to." Suffocated by "the reeky heat," Ambrose is exposed to the incomplete charms of no femme fatale, no mermaid, but a dismembered creature whose image is superimposed on an empty cigar box. As Ambrose scrutinizes with increasing anxiety the unyielding object, he discovers the words "EXAMINED BY" where the vitals should be! Like Winston Smith in Orwell's *1984,* Ambrose has discovered a man-made commodity that promises entry to a forgotten past; but unlike Winston's coral paperweight, which is commonplace but memorable, uniting beauty and utility, Ambrose's cigar box is only a container; it has lost its purpose and its promise. In this context, narrator and audience take on the shape of the Arnie twins of "Water-Message," who spend their nights "exploring garbage" (40). The world is on the slide. When Ambrose crawls beyond the funhouse boardwalk, he discovers only "a small old man . . . nodding upon a stool beneath a bare, speckled bulb" (84). The machinery is running down; in an exhausted world, life draws wearily toward an anxiously expected, perpetually deferred point of extinction; it is as if reality cannot bear too much of mankind.

"Lost in the Funhouse" shows Ambrose's attempt to imagine a new world in the midst of the wreckage of the old. In a commodity-conscious world, Ambrose's hope is to imagine a wonder-working gadget that will elevate his own power at the same time as it eases the plight of his nation. His technical solution will ease his personal dilemma, making him a sort of push-button *deus artifex*. "He envisions a truly astonishing funhouse, incredibly complex yet utterly controlled from a great central switchboard like the console of a pipe organ. Nobody had enough imagination. He could design such a place himself, wiring and all, and he's only thirteen years old. He would be its operator: panel lights would show what was up in every cranny of its cunning of its multifarious vastness; a switch-flick would ease this fellow's way, complicate that's, to balance things out; if anyone seemed lost or frightened, all the operator had to do was" (93). The idea is not a novel one. Ambrose's envisioned electronic world, its coil of cords and switches illuminating a fading Ocean City, had in fact been mapped out as Barth wrote in Marshall McLuhan's pioneering books of the 1960s— *The Gutenberg Galaxy* (1962), *Understanding Media* (1964), *The Medium is the Massage* (1967), and *War and Peace in the Global Village* (1968).[23] Like Ambrose, McLuhan relinquished printed literature for the electronic media; his conviction of the moribundity of a "print-oriented culture" is implicit in the way the very title *War and Peace in the Global Village* merges Tolstoy's masterpiece into McLuhan's multinational conglomerate. Indeed, McLuhan's global village would be godly in its omnipresence, a place where electronic media would provide simultaneous contact between past and present across five continents.

In "Autobiography," "Echo," and "Title," Barth answers Ambrose's call by providing an electronic world in the style that his protagonist imagined. Unfortunately, these stories are nothing like McLuhan's utopias or Ambrose's global social work. Rather, they sound like a parody of Samuel Beckett's *The Unnameable.* Instead of offering a push-button solution to the problems of communication in a silent world, they intensify and multiply what Ambrose has already found unbearable. In these stories too fathers disappoint sons, and wives become cynical about their ineffectual husbands. In a mirror-image of the Ambrose narratives, these tales buckle under the weight of conventions that now overwhelm the narration they were meant to sustain. But the electronic stories lack the skeletal presence of human beings that inform the Ambrose narratives; all they have are voices— sometimes wry, sometimes aggressive but always elusive and ultimately incomprehensible. Even the most ordinary utterance in this context becomes perplexingly uninterpretable. "You who listen give me life" (33) can be read as a plea or a command, but without a speaker to attach it to, we have no way to tell which. Whoever the source, he (or she or it) is as confused as we are and is forever blurting into unfocused aggression: "Is it over? Can't you read between the lines?" (110). By assigning McLuhan's devices and slogans to Beckett-like unnameables and lost ones, Barth reduces the global village to desolation row. These voices read like a misprogrammed computer printout or an urgent telegram from an unidentifiable source.

Where Ambrose's language was constantly on the point of sinking under the weight of literary precedent—how did the Mensch family ever get to Ocean City with that five-foot shelf of world literature in their boot?—the puns of the electronic stories either expire into cliché or become wrapped up in their own entrails. The narrator's reflection that his father has "found himself by himself . . . a novel device" suggests a pun that fidgets with itself without ever managing to throw off a certain frigid artifice. Such creation has only "a posthumous cautionary value, like gibbeted corpses, pickled freaks. Self-preservation, it seems, may smell of formaldehyde" (36). Once again, the call is not to prolong the world but to terminate it: "Put an end to this, for pity's sake!" The electronic universe is stillborn.

Barth's last two stories, for all their mythic possibilities, remain locked in the cycle of self-searching. In "Anonymiad" Barth tracks this solipsistic impulse to its source: the creation of fiction by a displaced bard. Having lost his tribe, Barth's bard now sheds his subject matter to the point where his tale, like so many of these stories, points back to the head of its maker. Once again, as in the cases of Ambrose (isolated from family and friends) and the speaker of "Autobiography" (who must "compose himself," but knows he "won't last long"), the overall effect of solitude on the storyteller is one of loss. Barth's narrator loses his muse, his innocence, and his big subjects. War, lust,

and conquest—the raw material of the mythmaker—have to be rejected. Adultery and psychology—the stock in trade of the novelist—
must also be jettisoned so that the narrator, through a mixture of com-
putation and exposition, can simulate an ultimacy denied by the
evidence he himself compiles and an originality his position in the
series denies.

On these occasions the fiction maker falls victim to his own invention. When he at last discovers decisive evidence of some world
outside his own invention in the form of a blank parchment marked in
ink, his first response is to people it with another like himself. His
hope is for a world that "might be astrew with islèd souls, become
minstrels perforce, and the sea a-clink with literature!" (189). The discovery of this manuscript recalls the similar discovery made in the last
pages of one of Barth's favorite books, Gabriel García Márquez's One
Hundred Years of Solitude (first published in Argentina a year before
Lost in the Funhouse). But Aureliano Babilonia's discovery of the gypsy's
manuscript annihilates a century of solipsism; in "Anoymiad" the discovery wheels the book around to its point of origin, where we met
the night sea voyager peopling a universe in his anxious self-image.
Barth has exhausted his theme rather than transformed it. The three
main types of story—realistic, electronic, and mythic—point only to
a common loss in narrative energy and objective resources in Barth's
universe.

The best account of the phenomenon dramatized in Lost in the
Funhouse came from Arnold Schoenberg, who described how in battling with musical innovation he "had the feeling as if I had fallen into
an ocean of boiling water and not knowing how to swim or get out I
tried with my legs and arms as best I could. . . . I never gave up. But
how could I give up in the middle of an ocean?"[24] The narrator of "Autobiography" must have had just such a feeling when, after battling
with a series of exhausted literary conventions, he concluded that
"the odds against a wireless deus ex machina aren't encouraging" (35).

CHAPTER EIGHT

The Global *Deus Artifex*: John Barth's *The Sot-Weed Factor* and *LETTERS*

> I have often had a fancy for writing a romance about an English
> yachtsman who slightly miscalculated his course and discovered
> England under the impression it was a new island in the South
> Seas. I always find, however, that I am too busy or too lazy to
> write this fine work, so I may as well give it away for the purposes
> of philosophical illustration.
>
> —G. K. Chesterton, *Orthodoxy*

Barth has made two extended bids to capture the career of the
godly maker in America. In *The Sot-Weed Factor*, Ebenezer Cooke sails
to Maryland convinced that a poet's godly vision will ennoble his new-
found land. After a host of swindles, a threatened holocaust, and a
marriage to an exhausted whore with a "social disease," Ebenezer ex-
changes the voice of the idealist for the voice of the satirist. By the
end, Maryland's laureate has become a bitter jester of the type familiar
to American literature from Mark Twain onward. Moreover, he has
lost his authority, his voice now becoming only a part of the larger
American polyphony (or cacophony) celebrated by that master of
masquerade, Henry Burlingame. Ebenezer had fashioned in his imagination an America in the form of Plato's *Republic*; he finds one that resembles Samuel Butler's *Hudibras*. And the sum of the voices that comprise Maryland does not make a whole; each of the performances
Ebenezer witnesses is self-canceling and self-enclosed. The result is
more like a masquerade than a novel.

In *LETTERS*, however, the past enlivens Barth's project. The
novel, Barth tells us, was initially planned to appear in the year of the
Bicentennial, an occasion that afforded Barth the opportunity to review his own career as well as the nation's. Accordingly, Barth has
suffused his book with the elegiac realism that enriched *The Floating
Opera*, becoming his own retrospective godly maker, as he recreates
characters from his fiction-writing past, refashions figures from
American and European history, and invents new people to reveal his

vision of postindustrial, post-Nixon America. The past that Barth annihilated in *Sot-Weed* he replenishes in *LETTERS*. History and form, the targets for a global satire in the earlier book, become the sources for the enrichment of the later one.

I.

Some critics have exaggerated the degree to which *Sot-Weed* marks a reorientation in Barth's concerns and techniques. David Morrell, for instance, speaks of the book as Barth's liberation from realism, noting that "while [Barth] prepared to write the book his ideas about the nature of fiction changed drastically." Yet however drastic the change, the kinds of concerns Morrell discovers in *Sot-Weed*—"not Reality itself but what we make—or what people have made—of Reality"—do not appear to be so drastic.[1] Does not the whole of *The Floating Opera* converge on just this theme? Admittedly, *The End of the Road* appears confined in the present tense; but Jake's narrative is surely a retrospective view of "what people have made" of their own particular portion of reality.

The difference between *Sot-Weed* and Barth's earlier fiction then is in degree rather than kind. Barth's mirror on reality now extends through space and time; it is no longer confined to a small group of educated individuals. Yet the underlying metaphysic of Barth's characters is not very different; the impulses toward role play and control that Barth had identified in Todd Andrews are also the driving force for Henry Burlingame. But to spread this pattern across so vast a time scale and so broad a canvas was perforce to transform the pattern so that a comic novelist necessarily became a parodic one. It was here that Barth and his critics parted company. Earl Rovit, in a sympathetic and astute account of the book, suggests that "the novel ends in the last analysis as a shallow parody, an intellectual gymnastic, a mechanical puzzle in which Barth can flex the muscles of his extraordinary dexterity. The reader admires the labor and the craft, enjoys the well-wrought gimcrack, but finds his world unchanged, his experience unenhanced."[2] Barth's shifting relationship with realism, what appears to be his unequivocal endorsement of the mythomania articulated by Jake Horner and enacted by Henry Burlingame, drains his novel, for all its stylistic vitality, of any moral life.

Sot-Weed began, Barth confided to John Enck, in the "impulse to imagine alternatives to the world."[3] This is an impulse that many of the book's characters share: it takes Ebenezer Cooke to Maryland; it leads Henry Burlingame on a universal quest; it underpins the new science that ousts the old cosmology as the book progresses; and not least, it explains the existence of Maryland and, by extension, America itself. But it also leads to the frightening impermanence of the forms and existences that the novel as a whole unfolds, for the sheer multiplicity of the alternatives to reality that Maryland offers means that every identity will become a mask and every institution a masquerade. The alternative to reality that Ebenezer Cooke, for instance, brings to Maryland is the ideal of a poetocracy; for Cooke's fellow Marylanders the alternative to reality takes the form of endless exploitation. What moral life the book has comes from the collision of these two rival attempts to imagine alternatives to the world; the first belongs to an ancient tradition, the second to the new conditions that will supersede that tradition. The former is driven out by the latter, which transforms an aspiring Homer to an enraged *poète maudit*.

Barth's treatment of one of his main sources, Ebenezer Cooke's poem "The Sot-Weed Factor," makes this relationship clearer. The poem turns on the swindling of its narrator, an honest traveler who goes to Maryland to open a store. What was merely a swindle in the source becomes in the novel the endless contamination of reality by double-dealing. Where Ebenezer Cooke's loss is material—the loss of his goods and his profits—Barth's hero loses his illusions about poetry and about reality. Cooke arrives in Maryland convinced that it is ripe for the poet's godly vision. His very unidealizing servant, Bertrand Burton, is Ebenezer's audience for his opening paean to poetry. "Who more so than the poet needs every godlike gift? He hath the painter's eye, the musician's ear, the philosopher's mind, the barrister's persuasion; like a god he sees the secret souls of things, the essence 'neath their forms, their priviest connections. Godlike he knows the springs of good and evil" (234). Ebenezer hopes to open the store of the world's goodness so that his poem will be an inventory of its several excellences. The alternative that he discovers, however, is the sot-weed factor, a tobacco trance that is certainly not inspired by poetry, but by the opium that is the religion of the Maryland people. Their sense of a perpetually changing universe in which reality is a parcel of illusions to be traded inspires an alternative aesthetic, the one promulgated by Henry Burlingame. Confronted by Ebenezer's idealistic qualms, Burlingame urges him to cast scrupulousness aside: "Who knows what manner of sloven huts the real Troy was composed of. . . . 'Tis the genius of the poet to transcend his material" (418). For Burlingame, Achilles's shield would reflect only Homer. Burlingame's is an aesthetic of burlesque, Ebenezer's one of idealization; Burlingame is godly in his ubiquity, Ebenezer in his transcendence. Such drastic

divisions have the effect of making Cooke and Burlingame two parts
in search of a whole: Burlingame hunts for his past, Cooke pursues
his future; Burlingame ransacks documents, Cooke dreams poems;
Cooke wants a bride, Burlingame is missing a father; Burlingame is a
rational debauchée, Cooke a passionate virgin. Cooke and Burlingame
are complementary; they become the Tambo and Bones of the new
world Barth explores in *Sot-Weed*.

Parody is not so much a style as a metaphysic in this work,
where reality becomes a matter of constant improvisation, a sort of
challenge to creative invention. The world withers under the godlike
assertion of the individual consciousness, what Burlingame calls the
captor's expedient.

> The truth that drives men mad must be sought for ere it's found,
> and it eludes the doltish or myopic hunter. But once 'tis caught
> and looked on, whether by insight or instruction, the captor's sole
> expedient is to force his will upon't ere it work his ruin! One must
> needs make and seize his soul and then cleave fast to 't, or go bab-
> bling in the corner; one must choose his gods and devils on the
> run, quill his own name upon the universe, and declare "'Tis *I*
> and the world stands such-a-way!" One must *assert, assert, assert,*
> or go screaming mad. What other course remains?" (373)

"Quill his own name upon the universe": Burlingame clearly
represents an alternative godly maker, one toward whom Barth, judg-
ing from the imaginative energy with which he invests him, feels considerable attraction. The force that drives Burlingame obviously motivates his creator, who exercises a captor's prerogative over a variety of
literary forms and narrative voices during the course of the novel.
Ebenezer's adventures with his servant recall Smollett's *Roderick Random*, but the mission he undertakes on behalf of a Maryland threatened by holocaust resembles an existentialist version of the Leather-
stocking saga or a frontier *The Plague*; likewise, his panegyrics to his
new colony are dislodged by an aesthetic that belongs in *Axel's Castle*.
The novel resembles *Tom Jones* in its size and the complexity of its plot.
But where Fielding's narrator provides all manner of disquisitions on
matters worldly and learned, the most this book can aspire to in this
vein are the bitter proverbs of some of its protagonists: "A good post is
worth a long wait" (49); "Anger begins with folly and ends with re-
pentance" (122).

This kind of drastically curtailed sententiousness, the very reverse of Fielding's leisurely wisdom, reminds us how different *Sot-
Weed* is from *Tom Jones*. Indeed, many of the book's parodies and allu-

sions swerve away from their sources in a slightly disturbing fashion. The lines from Cooke's poem—"Figures, so strange, no God designed / To be a part of humankind; / But wanton nature, void of rest, / Moulded the brittle clay in jest"[4]—nest without disturbance in the cautionary narrative that the eighteenth-century poet composes. But in the world Barth creates, where restlessness seems always on the point of exhausting "the brittle clay" of his characters, where reality seems on the point of shattering its God-designed frame, the same words take on a more sinister resonance, rather like Pierre Menard's rewriting of *Don Quixote* in Borges's famous story. The sum of all these parodies that rewrite their originators is a universe constructed in the pattern that Burlingame imagines, a field of force rather than an image of ideal forms. The world of *Sot-Weed* cannot be expected to stay with any one form for very long; Burlingame's restless virtuosity has been injected into the very structure of the novel.

But the burlesque energy of the book is not its whole story. Burlingame's philosophy of energy, by which everyman becomes his own godly artist and reduces the world to his own infinitely variable artwork, is governed by the subject's capacity "to force his will upon't" (373). Barth's book, however, allows the metaphor to become hideously alive: the disfigured skin of Drepacca, the withered face of Joan Toast, Ebenezer's "social malady," and Burlingame's gradual exhaustion all result from the frantic *universalpoesie* that originates in the increasingly desperate effort to "imagine alternatives" to reality that begins with Sir Isaac Newton's revolutionary discoveries. Maryland itself is one such alternative and Ebenezer hopes to make poetry out of it. But he does not reckon with the fact that in a world created by will, prostitution, not poetry, becomes the typical condition of man. In Maryland we hear so much of the word *whore* because the modern spirit celebrated by Burlingame ensures that we shall have so much of the thing as well.

How important then Ebenezer's last-ditch attempts to save Maryland—and his own imagination—by playing the angel of light become. His adoption of Burlingame's aesthetic had taken him to the brink of self-annihilation and to the creation of a work of self-begetting malice (499). When he feels his community threatened, he has a vision of a new poetry, one that will trade mastery for reciprocity, bind present to past, and end the universal masquerade of the Maryland to which he has elected himself poet in residence: "A kind of insight . . . glowed in his mind . . . he beheld the homeless ghosts of a thousand joys and sorrows meant to live in the public heart till the end of time: feast days, fast days, monuments and rites, all dedicated to glories that dwarfed his own" (655).

But the nobility of Ebenezer's vision does not guarantee his authority. It is only under the threat of apocalypse that Ebenezer can function as a *deus artifex*, making plots that reconcile men rather than separate them (624). The book's major structural pattern—the dislodgement of certainties and the ubiquitous role play that results— reasserts itself in the last pages as characters are swept from the stage by disease, disappearance, or death while Ebenezer himself suffers from neglect, then uncomprehending acceptance at the hands of the community he has saved in action and blasted in verse.

Toward the end of the book, Barth appears totally dissatisfied with both story and language, untrusting of the capacity of either to resist the redefinitions of an endlessly circulating reality. At the end of the seemingly interminable narrative of "The Tale of the Invulnerable Castle," Henrietta Russecks remarks on the discrepancy between story (where all ends happily ever after) and history (where all is ongoing bloody crisis), a situation insisted upon almost dogmatically in the book's final chapter as in an explosive parody of realistic conventions we revisit *Sot-Weed*'s characters only to watch them rot. In that chapter too the language of the poet loses whatever scraps of authority it had retained. Instead of Ebenezer Cooke's self-lacerating attacks on his bad faith ("Here moulds a posing foppish Actor / Author of THE SOT-WEED FACTOR"), his heirs have "his head stone graved with the usual piffle" (819). Once again an inheritance is squandered; once again a possibility of real moral development is sacrificed to civic self-esteem or local expediency.

By the last page of *Sot-Weed*, no reader can be confident of any author's capacity to render reality accurately. The godly artist has been worn down by an America that has already wasted its potential even in the first hours of its creation; the attempts to imagine an alternative reality end the way they began, with the utterance of a few lies over an unwholesome swamp; the voices that the comic godly maker has so endlessly ventriloquized, from Smollett and Fielding to Jean-Paul Sartre and Norman O. Brown, are no longer audible; reality itself has been exhausted.

II.

The appearance of *LETTERS* in 1979 provoked a host of reviews that were (at best) respectful in a chilly fashion. Barth's attempt to tell "the whole story" overwhelmed his audience. Not all his reviewers were as blunt as Joseph Epstein, who confessed "when a reviewer of *LETTERS* calls it triumphantly labyrinthine, that is all the hint I need to step aside." But many hinted that the book's length was due less to its creator's endless invention than his compulsive inability to stop writing.[5]

By the time many of Barth's first reviewers reached the end of his book, they had come to have doubts about his principle of selection and his manner of presentation. These doubts were voiced less concisely than Epstein's, but their drift was similar. For instance, both David Lodge and Philip Stevick found fault with the modified epistolary form that Barth had adopted for the novel. Stevick commented that "old-time epistolary novels . . . develop an almost embarrassing intimacy, [through] plots at once simple and astoundingly intricate. . . . Barth's book, however, does not invite us to enter a world: there are seven different and incongruent worlds."[6] But Stevick overlooks how Barth's narrative embeds each of these different worlds in one common plot, so that destinies as different as those of Jerome Bonaparte Bray and Germaine Pitt Amherst are woven into a composite narrative. The effect is now to allow Barth to reconcile the intimacy of epistolary fiction with the larger judiciousness of a Fielding, to combine what Ian Watt called "the realism of assessment" with "the realism of presentation."[7]

For David Lodge too, means and ends were at cross purposes in the narrative of *LETTERS*. Lodge's judgment, like Stevick's, invoked a literary history that Barth was assumed not to have the liberty of changing. "The great epistolary novels," said Lodge, "are not, on the whole, novels of action and adventure, but novels of sentiment and sensibility in which the development of a single situation or relationship is scrutinized from various angles."[8] This commentary offers a useful summary of epistolary fiction, but it overlooks one of Barth's central pursuits in this novel, the aim he describes in "The Literature of Replenishment" of acknowledging the inheritance of the past without buckling under its sheer weight. Lodge would have Barth reproduce the form and the function of the epistolary novel; Barth wants us to acknowledge that the permanence of forms depends on their capacity to fulfill different functions. It is Lodge perhaps who is being dictatorial here, for all his attempts at historical understanding. Barth's own commitments are encyclopedic; his aim, as "The Literature of Replenishment" makes plain, is to tell the whole story; to do this, as the history of the novel from *Don Quixote* to *The Counterfeiters* suggests, requires a certain irreverence on the subject of form. Without the confidence that will lead him to penetrate forms so that he can realize his own purposes, no novelist can create a world beyond words.

Josephine Hendin extended Lodge's criticism. For her, Barth's use of epistolary conventions unmasked his solipsism; she saw the book as his "love letter to *belles lettres*" and as such declared it to be "entirely self-referential and self-limiting." Her final judgment was more like an obituary: "One of the great human tragedies is self-enclosure."[9] Our author, imprisoned by epistolary conventions, breaks down and confesses his utter self-reflexiveness. Hendin failed to recognize that Barth takes great pains not merely to lay his subjective selves end to end, but also to allow interplay between his various subjectivities, so that, for instance, Lady Amherst's desire for a child catches a glow from Andrew Cook's exasperation with his own. Moreover, many of the characters begin the book imprisoned in self-enclosure; at the end of the novel, however, Barth has secured the release of even such long-term solipsists as Jacob Horner and Ambrose Mensch. If the origins of *LETTERS* and its means of narration are the subjectivities of its multiple correspondents, then subjectivity is not the sustaining metaphysic of its plot. The "J. B." or "the Author" who gets the action in motion by relaying correspondence from one character to another, is a plot maker made more in the image of Jacob R. Adam than Antoine Roquentin, spinning a story more in the manner of Scheherazade than Henry James, as he tells us himself at one point (53). In other words, the energies of the novel are occupied with survival, not the exploration of a solitary consciousness. Hendin's interpretation is closet drama, not criticism.

The same impulse to honor the interplay between permanence and change motivated Barth's adoption of his second major experiment, his recycling of characters and events from earlier fiction. If, as Todd Andrews tells a funeral party gathered to mourn the mad Harrison Mack, Jr., *praeteritas futuras stercorant* (the past fertilizes the future) then perhaps Barth, in the way of Balzac or Zola, can revive his own career through the presence of voices from his narrative past. Justly irritated by Barth's misleading comments about his revived characters' self-sufficient status in this novel (they self-evidently do not have that status), several reviewers pounced on the least creative reason for Barth's *retour de personnages*. Their diagnosis—failure of creative nerve—was made with the hasty air of surgeons in search of more interesting patients. In *Newsweek*, Peter Prescott suggested that Barth "long ago gave us all that Todd and Jacob can offer."[10] For Josephine Hendin and George Steiner, it was Homer who nodded, not his creatures. Hendin saw the recycling as Barth's latest contribution to the literature of exhaustion: "Wading through the plots and people of his past novels, Barth seems to search for some fresh emotion."[11] Steiner was more cruelly witty, implying that Barth's was an undertaking at once risky and tame, "a highwire leap into the safety net of the self."[12]

Such comments, however, completely ignore Barth's interest in the creation of a *comedie humaine*; they suggest, instead, that his fiction is a self-regarding scrutiny of his own navel. What they overlook, moreover, is the elegiac quality of Barth's revival of the past; in a world where the dwindling stock of natural resources and the intense avarice of human nature pretty well assures that the planet is on its way to becoming "used up," Barth's raid of his own imagination is a daring act. It is not a bid for novelty, as Hendin seems to suggest, nor is it the act of an impoverished imagination, as Steiner alleges. Rather, it is an act of imaginative conservation, a bid to make the past replenish the present. And its audacity ought not to be underrated. The book's American precedents are not encouraging ones: Mark Twain's repeated attempts to revive Tom and Huck are case studies in American failure, while the European experiments made by Balzac and Zola proceed from the premise that reality presents a solid palpable backdrop to the realist novelist's activity—the very assumption that Barth's sense of the "used-upness" of forms and realities cannot make. Behind the Europeans lies the weight of tradition and the authority of natural science; behind Barth lies only his stubborn conviction that for a writer "to tell the whole story" he must acknowledge his own past as well as his country's.

Not many reviewers saw it that way, however. George Steiner briskly cut the book down to size for *New Yorker* readers, telling them that the author, far from being a narrative conservationist, was more like an incapable home economics tutor, who had devised a "more or less indigestible classroom souffle."[13] David Lodge, more willing to concede the exoticism of Barth's stockpot, concurred with Steiner's verdict on the recipe: "*LETTERS* can scarcely be approached except by way of Barth's previous books, since it cannibalizes them all." Lodge's attack, in fact, was the severest of them all, since he queried the whole structure of the book, which he called a "folly . . . an eccentric and extravagant production . . . mixing incompatible styles . . . parasitic upon the past and sterile as regards the future."[14] All these reviewers agree that Barth's self-regarding subjectivity overwhelmed his design so that *LETTERS* never pulls its considerable weight. Peter Prescott remarked that the book "rises like a monument—a monument being, of course, a construction that demands attention but is not itself liked." [15] Such verdicts leave the book looking like Johnson's pyramids, an imposing erection designed as a testimony to human folly.

Even the book's defenders have been hard put to identify its purpose. Max Schulz's investigation of its sources and contexts suggested that LETTERS was Barth's bid for synthesis, "an attempt to establish on its own terms a fusion of American experience and Anglo-American European epistolary and confessional tradition." [16] But if we grant that Barth has done this, we still need to know why. It is not inconceivable to imagine a book that will fuse Boolean algebra and Thomist theology in the course of its narrative. Yet any critic will still have to explain the purpose of such a fusion. It was just this lack of purpose that Gerald Graff, in an important essay, found in LETTERS. In Graff's view the book proceeded by inventory rather than synthesis, with the result that its "symmetries are all pointless—or rather their point is precisely in their pointlessness. To put it more charitably, their point is not in any ultimate synthesis that we can make out of history, but in the process of trying, even of trying and failing." [17]

Graff's fiercely argued critique of the book seems to go to its heart. Is the journey through LETTERS taken for its own sake, or is so long a journey really necessary? Is Barth's journey back through his own fiction-making past a folly or a revival? Much of the book is occupied with the manufacturing and marketing of illusion; is the book as a whole only one or more postmodernist illusion? Does LETTERS, like Jane Mack's frozen-food empire, mask its shoddiness through the enormity of its ambition?

Barth hints at his purpose through a series of allusions to Karl Marx's oracular threat that "tragic history repeats itself as farce" (255, 332, 385). These are repeated in Barth's postpublication interviews with George Reilly and Heide Ziegler. [18] The cumulative thrust of these allusions propels us to a new interpretation of LETTERS. Marx's bitter mock epic Reflections on the 18th Brumaire underscored how farcical conditions need not rule out apocalyptic consequences. Barth's challenge, as a tragic humanist, must be to transform farce into humane comedy. Where Marx insists on the necessary and unchallengeable dominance of aesthetic possibilities by social forces, Barth tries to create a novel that will allow both to coexist. Where Marx sees history as moving steadily toward the "ultimate synthesis" of an apocalypse (an idea shared, after their fashion, by each of the illusionists and image makers in Prinz's crew), Barth, as a godly maker bent on telling "the whole story" and preserving it intact, collates contingencies that are to be shaped into form with the help of his audience. Such a design is undoubtedly not perfect, but its imperfections do accommodate change and development; Marx's vision, meant presumably to blast itself into perfection, cannot ultimately accommodate these.

In "Tales within Tales within Tales," Barth described the impossibility of predicting the actions of God's artistry. His "story's not done yet, who knows what plot reversals the Author may have up his/her sleeve for the dénouement?"[19] Such a conviction becomes part of the narrative technique of *LETTERS*, where Barth "the Author" must consistently try to block the headlong rush of his characters to conclusion. (Lady Amherst, for instance, nearly stops the narrative before it begins.) "The whole story" as Barth tells it reveals a series of factions that try to reduce multiplicity to their particular preference, whether that preference is for Drew Mack's dictatorship of the proletariat or the supply-side tsardom of the industrialist proposed by old Jane Mack. Attractive people both, Drew and Jane; but it is the balding and harassed J. B. who composes a narrative that will divert and absorb the explosive impulses of American society.

I have described the principle behind Barth's *retour de personnages* as an elegiac attempt to knit together past and present. Similar motives underpin Barth's repeated allusions to the *18th Brumaire*. For Marx's voice is one that, in a variety of travestied guises to be sure, plays an all-important role in *LETTERS*. Marx's is the voice from the past that seeks to annihilate the future. Barth's debate with Marx's work becomes a test of the comic imagination, so that a brief examination of his book here will enable us to understand the nature of its claims and challenges to Barth's vision. Marx insists that art must be pressed into social service, the "ultimate synthesis" that Graff had called for. Moreover, he also dictates how this is to be done. Not for him any reconciliation between past and present, for even in matters of literary history, "the tradition of all dead generations weigh like a nightmare on the brain of the living." Memory for Marx is an affliction, a matter of "anxiously conjur[ing] up the spirits of the past," spirits arriving in "time-honored disguise and . . . borrowed language" (15). Marx's aim is revolution, and revolution, by definition, severs past from present to clear a space for the future: "The social revolution of the nineteenth century cannot draw its poetry from the past, but only from the future. It cannot begin with itself before it has stripped off all superstition in regard to the past. . . . it has in truth first to create for itself the revolutionary point of departure"—a point of departure, we might add, that is frozen in an uncompromisingly iconoclastic posture: "All that exists deserves to perish."[20]

Marx's unnerving and probably unconscious reminiscence of Guarini, who as a Renaissance *deus artifex*, thought that "nothing that lives will perish," illustrates the apocalyptic view of history that Barth chose to confront.[21] Not only does Marx snatch back any crumbs of comfort he allows himself to grant so that his opening "men make their own history" quickly becomes "but they do not make it as they please," but he is also grimly deterministic, permitting the world in its unpurged state only an inevitable decline. Bourgeois history hiccoughs along, but the first belch comes from plentitude, the second from emptiness. It is at this point that Marx voices the maxim that intrigued Barth so much: "Hegel remarks somewhere that all facts and personages of great importance in world history occur, as it were, twice. He forgot to add: the first time as tragedy, the second as farce" (15).

III.

LETTERS is full of characters who think like Marx, from Reg Prinz with "the world in [his] pocket" (381) to the Jane Mack whose revised logo for her fast-food chain is "Tomorrow now." Joe Morgan, once a history man, now has one foot in the future and one aimed at the past, the kind of acrobatics possible only for a space traveler. And Joe has indeed embraced space because of the outrages that time has inflicted on him. The book dramatizes the universal tendency for ideals to become commodities in conglomerate America. Yet *LETTERS* shows that, eventually if not ultimately, it is Guarini's idea of a *deus artifex* that will abide, not Marx's notion of a global travesty. For *LETTERS* shows how writing can humanize a society brutalized by the seductions of the electronic image and technological power. Barth's postindustrial society, a world of tycoons in culture and hamburgers, entrepreneurs in pedagogy and revolution, is one made habitable by the writer, who charts the common bearings of his correspondents in a way that will reveal "the whole story" to his creations and his audience.

Once again, Barth's metaphor for this kind of all-encompassing movement is the ocean. But on this occasion, he presents the ocean as a place of endless fusion and separation; *LETTERS*, he says, will be a work where "several narratives will become one; like waves of a rising tide, the plot will surge forward, recede, surge farther forward, recede less far, et cetera to climax and dénouement" (49). Where *Sot-Weed* fused past and present only to dissolve both in one Pyrrhonist apocalypse, *LETTERS* attempts to make form a rendezvous for both. A book that stalks the big game of history with the small arms of comedy, *LETTERS* is Barth's attempt to trade the lake of self-reflection for the ocean of story.

LETTERS is Barth's most sustained reconciliation of social satire and imaginative possibility. As in *The Sot-Weed Factor*, Barth recognizes that the structure of American life is nothing but a web of illusions. But where *Sot-Weed* explored the consequences of this masquerade only fitfully, *LETTERS* mounts a much more sustained attack, exploring its psychological and institutional repercussions. The first letter of the book, which begins in stiff officialese, emphasizes the colonizing powers of the education business, its capacity to cramp the style of even the very civilized Germaine G. Pitt (Amherst). When Germaine poker-facedly writes that Marshyhope State has undergone "annexation as a four-year college in the state university system" (3), we are reminded of how far educational goals have stretched to fit the imperial aims of administrators. Empire building is no longer the prerogative of emperors alone; administrators now practice in 1969 the annexations that were previously attempted by politicians. At the start of the novel, then, power has knowledge in a headlock.

But power has also usurped the functions of art; Germaine's conviction that Marshyhope is only a make-believe university leads, naturally, to the enrollment of hosts of make-believe students. These students crib their knowledge from sets of "Monarch Notes," fake learning designed to keep the institutional machinery going. In the same way entrepreneur Jane Mack calls on the literary Germaine as a "resource person" in the expansion of her business empire. "Acting President" John Schott wants to take his act to a different theater: he has his eye on Washington. These alliances between power and knowledge present a much more damaging diagnosis of the world as university than the one developed in *Giles Goat-Boy*. That novel heaped up similarities like a catalog; in *LETTERS*, the similarities are also evaluations, crushing critiques of the equivocations and pretensions of campus and world alike. Marshyhope State, for instance, is for Lady Amherst a "Factory of Letters" (5). As a factory, it produces attractively packaged commodities, such as the degrees awarded to worthies most likely to advertise the college to the community. As a factory it expects a certain impersonality in the conduct of its affairs. When Lady Amherst reveals signs (of all things!) of excess emotion, she is treated as an employee, not as a shareholder in the enterprise of knowledge, and is summarily dismissed. The "Diploma Mill" is a place of desperate expediency, a sweatshop of ideas where the most powerful agent is the copying machine. In *Giles Goat-Boy*, the relationship between the world and the university was one of identity, verbally asserted at inordinate length; *LETTERS* investigates the areas of tension and exploitation between the two.

For example, business and university are, in a postindustrial society, conducted more like works of art. Both are headed by entrepreneur impresarios whose imaginative leadership provides leverage to all the corridors of power. Where business requires university-trained know-how to acquire respectability, so too the university must borrow from business its capacity to package shoddy as excellence. "Not so much pretentious as pretending" is Lady Amherst's characterization of Marshyhope: "A toadstool blown overnight from this ordurous swamp to broadcast doctorates like spores, before the stationer can amend our letterhead" (5). This chimeric conjunction of waste product, natural resource, writing, and broadcast journalism shows, as does much of *LETTERS*, the monstrous consequences of pretension financed and supervised by corporate means.

In fact, one of the central truths of *LETTERS* is that a society run on the lines of technological capitalism is devoted to pretense, to the unending manufacture of illusions. Nothing is what it appears in this book, which shows us again and again that art is not the only institution dedicated to illusion. Business can pretend too, so that the formidable organizational and technical resources of Mack Enterprises, with its R + D departments and resource persons, are coordinated to produce "Cap'n Chick," a product held together on a popsicle stick by "less crabmeat and more Fillers and Binders" (458) than any of its rivals. Expansion and changes of state are the goals of education and business alike, with the methods of production and distribution of the latter ("quick-frozen" and "cold storage") making a wry commentary on the aspirations of both. The inedible synthesis of Cap'n Chick, which blends various indigestibles on a mass-produced popsicle, is the brainchild of Jane Mack. Jane's Mack Enterprises becomes characteristically telescoped into the threatening acronym *me*, at the same time as it diversifies its products to include "chemical fertilizer and freeze-dried food [and] certain research in the chemical warfare way" (86). Barth captures this kind of imperial subjectivity in all its squalid and sprawling pretensiousness. Harrison Mack, who comes to think he is George III, and Jane Mack, amnesiac and ageless, are only the limiting instances of what Todd Andrews calls "U. S. imperialism and isolationism at once: US become *me* and inflated to a global insularity" (394).

Such an enterprise is the very opposite of J. B.'s role as a godly maker since it shrinks and freezes "the whole story" into one mass-marketed illusion, a pattern that is stamped throughout the book like a counterfeited designer's trademark. Cap'n Chick, synthetic, unwholesome, and pseudotraditional, forms the culmination of a chain of events that leads Todd Andrews to contemplate suicide, just as Capt. Jacob R. Adam, populist and fabulist, helped to deliver him from the same malaise some thirty-two years before. Cap'n Chick, in fact, is the technological counterpart of the very world of abstractions and entrepreneurs that Todd found unbearable in 1937.

Imitation is pervasive in Barth's America; but it is also tracked to its origins at the beginning of the modern world. For Barth, modernity begins in Bonapartism—the sense of the self as its own deity—a fallacy that he explodes throughout the book. One of the most impressive exposures comes in the presentation of a Napoleon who, no longer the hero who stormed Europe but a taunting, aging showman, "turns his surrender into a diplomatic and theatrical coup" (599). Napoleon, in fact, has become a Cap'n Chick, an industry supporting "any number of Channel fishermen" and surrounded by an audience and concession stands: "A thousand small spectator boats jam Plymouth Sound; the quays and breakwaters are thronged. Bands play French military airs; vendors sell Bonapartist carnations; cheers go up whenever the emperor appears on deck or when, to placate the crowd in his absence, Bellerophon's crew obligingly post notice of his whereabouts" (602).

The more of modern life we are offered, the greater our sense of its inauthenticity. If John Schott is acting president, Bonaparte, now accompanied by trumpets rather than muskets, is an acting Napoleon. When Todd Andrews confronts a ghetto-talking bomb thrower on Choptank Bridge, he discovers yet another illusionist, for "Tank Top" "turned out to be the child of third-generation-affluent New England educators; he had discovered his negritude as a twelfth-former at the Phillips Exeter Academy, become a militant at Magdalen College (Oxford) and exquisitely exchanged his natural Boston-Oxbridge accent and wardrobe for what we heard and saw above. His major passions in student days had been rugby and the novels of William Dean Howells" (95). Tank Top's present has forgotten his past. As so often in this book, political careers are seen as combining the histrionic and the pedagogic. Tank Top discovers a pedagogic abstraction—"negritude"—that is found not in ghettos but in classrooms. He then acts out his own improvisation of a role without a social referent.

But Barth does not reveal only the social illusions of a postindustrial America. He also investigates the personal illusions of a cluster of artists, each of whom attempts to become a god of his own making, either through an all-consuming exhaustiveness or by intensive cultivation of his own personality. These are characters for whom illusion is more end than means; insofar as their aims have a dangerous resemblance to their creator's, their characterization is a risk for Barth. But it is a risk that if he is to achieve his godly goal of telling "the whole story," he must inevitably take, for that story will be incomplete if it does not include the "everyman his own godly artist" phenomenon that the book reveals as so pervasive in Bicentennial America.

Through Jeannine Mack, whose limited charms and limitless self-absorption have merged into one massive neurosis, Barth examines this fallacy in its coarsest form. None of the available evidence shows any reason why Jeannine Mack should consider herself an artist or in any way a deity. Yet she has lived her life on the premise that she is both, so that she has become a woman who exists only through the reflection of her image as a spouse for a series of fading showmen. The Jeannine introduced to us in *The Floating Opera* as a girl who wanted to know why and who had a yearning for ice cream becomes in *LETTERS* a woman who has made ice cream her why, and her desire for stardom an almost metaphysical pursuit. As Todd reflects, the dream has exhausted the dreamer: "She's staler at 35 than her mother at 63. The very obverse of her brother, Jeannine has, I am confident, never in her incoherent life voluntarily read a newspaper, much less a book, or been moved by a work of art or a bit of history, reflected on life beyond her own botch of it, felt compassion for the oppressed, or loved a fellow human being. I'm told she's divorcing again, and feels the charmless Prinz to be her great chance" (17).

Barth's investigation of art and society shows how both are expected to reveal themselves by apocalyptic means. So it is that Jeannine, like Drew Mack on the Choptank Bridge or Jane Mack expecting "tomorrow now," awaits "the great chance" that will justify a life devoted to illusions. The husks of a religious vocabulary persist, attaching themselves to secular lives of fragmentation and waste. For all her devotedly rehearsed self-concern, Jeannine has played a poor range of roles. She begins as the wife of Barry Singer, a charming and cultured Jew who has "part-ownership of a chain of small-town movie houses" (82). When Jeannine meets the film and stage people Singer has befriended, Singer's own reign is curtailed. Her next husband is a vaudeville Tank Top, an impostor whose "real name had been Mel Miller; as an apprentice borscht-circuit comic he'd changed it to sound more Jewish; later, when he moved into 'straight' acting, he regretted not having kept the low-profile original, but couldn't bring himself to sacrifice the small and no longer quite appropriate celebrity of his stage name" (85). Barth's language, again, becomes charged with evaluation: "sacrifice" is not what one can expect from lives devoted to inauthenticity, where names float separately from identities to be assumed as occupational requirements think fit. It is impossible to run quite fast enough to keep up with this image-conscious world; Miller, like so many of these characters, is afflicted by the backward glance of desire that his choice of life had precluded. He wants to hoard what he undertook to spend.

Jeannine renounces the failing Miller for Louis Golden, a "producer of B—and blue movies." For her promise of instant celebrity, Jeannine has accumulated a lifetime of worthlessness. Her audiences are now the diners at family restaurants for whom her four-letter expletives will, no doubt, secure the greatest possible attention. Seduced by images, Jeannine has attempted to become one.

If Jeannine's attempt to become an image leaves her the victim of an illusion, then Ambrose Mensch attacks the problem as a godly seer, "a slightly astigmatic visionary" (50) whose business becomes the "all" in its varying guises. But Ambrose lives in a postindustrial society, not a romantic one; he is forced to inventory the whole rather than inhabit it. His career begins with a Defoe-like ambition. His hope, he tells us, was "to render the entire quotidian into prose," to which end he claims "to have set himself even then the grand objective . . . of filling in the whole world's blanks" (240). Like so many of the artists in *LETTERS*, Ambrose sees life only as a less shapely version of Lana Turner, something hanging around just to be discovered by art, and he fastens on a priceless opportunity in his encounter with a real-life Blank: "It was her *name*, Ambrose now maintains, most drew him to her twenty years ago, when he was an undergraduate apprentice and she a young typist . . . possessed of a fetching figure and a face with the peculiar virtue of being so regularly, generally *pretty* as to defy particular description. . . . And her personality matched her face; and there she sat, nine-to-fiving those reams of empty paper through her machine day after day, like a stenographic Echo, giving back the words of others at 25¢ the page plus 5¢ the carbon" (239–40).

Here was a marriage, he adds, "made in the heaven of self-reflexion." Because Ambrose sees reality as a hollow to be filled by artifice, it is not surprising that his personal revelation should be an illusion as well. He is looking for blanks when—voilà, a real-life Blank appears. Ambrose's idea of Marsha Blank does not expand into a sense of her outside the terms of his project. Yet in an odd way, she is more of a commentary on his aspirations than a fulfillment of them. Reproducing material she does not control, Marsha is a paid copyist in whom work ("empty paper"), life (her "generally pretty" face), and art (as "stenographic Echo") have coalesced into the significant vacuity that awaits Ambrose himself as inventorist of the ordinary. That Marsha's drudgery ("nine-to-fiving reams of empty paper") will soon become Ambrose's becomes clear when his "major literary endeavour" becomes "bogged in bathos" (242). Lives of illusion can at best aspire to farce.

Ambrose and Jeannine are both in search of the "all" as performers, but it is the filmmaker who, in a postmodern, postindustrial society, has the world in his pocket. Barth's filmmaker, Reg Prinz, like Nabokov's Hermann Hermann or Hawkes's Papa, embodies the desires of the postmodern *deus artifex*. Like Papa, he possesses the technology to make his own apocalypse. Like Hermann, he takes advantage of social circumstance to pursue his self-serving end. Just as Hermann knows every beggar wants a handout, so Prinz knows every American wants to star in his very own illusions. Prinz himself, like Nabokov's hero, is as inscrutable as any deity; but if his motives are unfathomable, his actions are not. He wants to make a movie of J. B.'s work. Again, the language used to describe the movie is obliquely threatening. Prinz will, we hear, "execute a film" (192).

Prinz has a part for all the novel's main characters. He ensures their participation by a prolonged silence, a silence that seduces them because it represents the lucid transparency into which each of them reads the likeness of his own obsessions. For them, Prinz is an enigmatic artist whose very remoteness provokes interpretation, who for all "he will not write letters" (192) can still correspond with his audience's hopes. Prinz, the novel's postindustrial Napoleon, is a vacuum; and postindustrial men and women adore a vacuum.

His project begins modestly. He and Mensch will attempt to "execute a film" (192) based on the author's "recent work, but echoing its predecessors" (662). Disturbingly simple this, in its easy and unquestioning acceptance of the relationship between past and present and the necessary priority of the parent work. Can the Prinz who calls literature "a mildly interesting historical phenomenon of no present importance" and who has "absorbed and put behind him all the ideology of contemporary film making" (217) mean no more than this? Before long, Prinz has revealed himself as a true image maker and has begun to preempt the authority of the author at every turn. Significantly, the first shift alters the relationship of past and present. Prinz wants to anticipate as well as echo his author's work. Gradually, it is revealed that he will alter, willy-nilly, since Germaine tells J. B. that he has " 'kept his imagination pure' by *not even reading* your books" (356), just as Ebenezer Cooke kept himself pure of Maryland by reducing it to merely abstract status.

The purity of Prinz's imagination requires a certain rough-handedness with events, chronology, and actors. Prinz is an artist who constantly steps over the borders—geographical, temporal, or ethical—to boost the authority of his own projects. His scenario, Lady Amherst complains, is one where "1969 and 1812 (and 1669, 1776, and 1976) are tossed together like salad greens" (445). Like Mack Enterprises, Prinz's scenario rolls inexorably on, with no real purpose but its own fulfillment.

Eventually, Prinz's film can only double back on itself. Once he has incorporated as much of the past as he needs, once he has stripped away the last "discernible boundary between that wretched film and our lives" (368), he can only, like the "streamlined logo" proposed for the reorganized Mack Enterprises, rewind it back on itself. The suggestion for this change comes from Jerome Bray, who proposes that "inasmuch as the movie reenacts and re-creates events and images from 'the books,' which do likewise from life and history and even among themselves, why should it not also reenact and echo its *own* events and images?" (383). The film set is, as Lady Amherst recognizes, a chain of command, not a network of reciprocation: "Ambrose is enchanted, Bray is willing, Bea is appalled, Prinz is boss" (383). Prinz's project now bursts out of its container as "the *fight* is the thing now, the armature of a drama which has clearly outgrown its original subject" (445). Barth's fiction, Lady Amherst tells him, "is at most the *occasion* of the film these days" (445). Barth's method here is like Nabokov's in *Despair* or Hawkes's in *Travesty*. Like them, he reduces a work of art to the status of the malevolent motivation that inspired it. The Prinz who began his adaptation of J. B.'s work convinced that literature was "a mildly interesting phenomenon" has projected his artwork to reflect his own power, as Papa projected *Travesty* or Hermann *Despair*. Like them, Prinz ends with a work celebrating his own will to power, a will that, as Germaine says, threatens to remove "all reference to your works . . . which are only a sort of serial cues for Prinz and Ambrose to improvise upon and organise their hostilities" (445–46). Barth constantly exposes the pretensions of Prinz's enterprise, which is damned both in its design and in its trade talk. Jake Horner has the best comment on the kind of epic that Prinz has created: "Bayreuth by Lever Brothers. . . . Procter & Gamble's production of the Bathtub Ring" (404). Such an art, endlessly incorporating reality in a quasimilitary set of "takes" or capturing it through hidden "bugs," becomes, like Jane Mack's cold storage or fast freezing, a trade in death not creation. By the end of his shooting (another "ominously terminal" phrase), Prinz has not only eliminated traditional notions of artist and audience, but he has also eliminated the artwork itself, leaving only a situation of empty antagonism on which, his "imagination pure," he may expand endlessly.

Ambrose M—, Reg Prinz, and Jeannine Mack, not Barth, are the cannibals David Lodge identified as populating *LETTERS*. These artists are hungry for illusion, willing to exhaust all emotional and physical resources to make contact with a transcendent "all." Each of these characters is a self-elected deity pushing *LETTERS* toward either farce or apocalypse. It remains, however, to account for the careers of another set of characters in *LETTERS*—the "writers" whose participation in Barth's effort to tell the whole story enables him to achieve at last his goal of reviving the idea of the godly maker and investing in it something like its traditional force.

IV.

Just as everything appears to be mobilized toward explosion, Barth's book makes its move toward a reconciling synthesis. In a society of instant intimacies, he shows the power of narrative to mediate between self and world. The quietly stated serenity of Germaine Amherst's final epistle testifies to the benigner capacities of storytelling: "My husband loves me devotedly, I believe. And I him, though (since my little Vision) with a certain new serene detachment, which I can imagine persisting whatever Dr. Rosen finds on Tuesday" (691). It is characteristic of the best of Barth's work that this passage should have an understated grace. Like Lady Amherst's hard-won "little Vision" (of a possible child and heir), the prose makes no great claims on our attention; but both promote a genuine vision quite unlike the spectacular climaxes pursued by Prinz and Jeannine. The book ends poised on the future, with Lady Amherst's old womb on the brink of an as yet unconfirmed pregnancy. Barth's respect for the real stops him short of the consummations so many of the characters desperately wait for. At the beginning of *LETTERS*, Lady Amherst, like Todd Andrews, had been shuffling toward the grave, a relic of a played-out humanism. Lonely and uneasy, she could only reflect on spoiled possibilities: "I am . . . what I am (rather, what I find to my own dismay I am become; I was not always so)" (4). She sees herself as an artist without an audience: "I have much to tell, no one to tell it to" (59).

This is just the kind of self-consciousness at which Barth's reviewers grimaced. But Lady Amherst's subjectivity is her point of origin, not her destination. In the course of realizing her ambitions to become a writer, she learns to cope with transformations and, eventually, to celebrate them. Nowhere is *LETTERS* more the "old-time epistolary novel" than in its suggestion that writing (an instrument of self-torture for some recent critics) and breeding (the deadliest of sins for some late 1960s polemicists) can point the way to self-definition and self-fulfillment. Beginning as an acknowledged ironist, Germaine abandons that mode of mastery for a more searching account of her motives and ambitions, culminating in the recognition that "what alarms me is *me* . . . my playing, at such cost to my self-image, peace of mind, and professional activity, my lover's stupid game . . . I love him! (It excites me to write it.)" (346–47). Writing, with its loving depiction of process and development, is just the reverse of the frozen stiffness of "self-image" and "professional activity." Writing is a living medium, able as no other to register the multiple shifts of an evolving sensibility. The visual image is like Jane Mack (whose memory, we recall, is "photographic" [60]), alluring but frozen. "I read and bleed" (252), says Lady Amherst, merging the ocean of story with the rhythms of living. She began her story in decline, being seduced because it was "too tiresome . . . not to"; she ends in confident serenity, taking her place in a story much bigger than her own.

At the end of the book, the old womb and the old-fashioned story are both rammed with life. A similar arc of feeling is traced in the career of Todd Andrews. At the beginning Todd gave a guileful funeral eulogy on behalf of Harrison Mack, a punning, wry monologue that few of his audience could understand. Yet submerged in his wryness was a despair. His first epistle heaped up corpses: "Under the stage of my drifting dreams," he tells us, appeared the "black faced" features of his father, a minstrel at his son's dance of death. "We fetch one body to the boneyard; a hearseful of ghosts hitches home with us" (12). Since Todd is a connoisseur of paradoxes, it is typical that out of such moribundity he should strike a new zeal for life. He loves fiction, and in his hands narrative becomes a way of exposing and celebrating the wriggling contradictions of everyday life. Todd explains his ethical code uncomfortably. He is a humanist with a tragic view of history, he explains, as his reader turns the pages nervously, a little nonplussed by these embarrassedly offered generalizations. But when he fleshes out his philosophy into narration, the whole scheme becomes vitalized. Picture if you will, he asks, a "Bourgeois-Liberal *TVH* fishing tackle in one hand, picnic basket in the other (in which are two corned beef sandwiches, two Molson's Ales, a bullhorn, a portable Freon airhorn, and a voice-operated tape-recorder); the sweat of fear in his palms and of July in his armpits; the smile of Sweet Reasonableness nervously lighting his countenance" (89). Writing can accommodate contradiction in a way visual images cannot. How, for instance, could a visual image capture the wholesale anomaly of Todd's "smile of Sweet Reasonableness" as he nervously crosses the Choptank River Bridge? Writing reconciles rational aspiration to anxious reality as Todd, the most unlikely of heroes in a book swarming with candidates for the job, shuffles off to his ideological showdown.

Todd's narrative insists on the inevitable contradiction between aspiration and reality. No sooner has he reaffirmed the complete significance of all things than he makes a firm decision to commit suicide. This decision, in turn, provokes still further contradictions: his suicide had been projected because of his meager life as a bachelor; but as a would-be suicide, he is pursued by a seemingly endless chain of tasks and duties that perpetually delay his departure. By the time Todd's suicide is arranged and on the brink of being carried out, its significance has changed utterly. Brought on by unsatisfying fascinations with the timeless (because frozen) Jane Mack and her glittering (but quiveringly self-absorbed) daughter, Todd's suicide has become a sacrifice. As he waits for the explosion in the Tower of Truth, Todd hopes that his sacrifice will revive the Tragic View of History, that stoical awareness of life's contradictions that so many of the book's characters have devoted their own careers to annihilating. It is hope, significantly enough, that all Barth's "writers" end with; it is hope, equally significantly, that his image makers are too impatient to entertain.

But Barth's most unlikely coup among his correspondents is Jake Horner. As a mythotherapist, the Jake of *The End of the Road* had been convinced that the self and language were arbitrary deities in an absurd world. Yet as a correspondent in *LETTERS*, Horner's destiny becomes enmeshed in the lives of other people, in whom he gingerly begins to take some interest. In the Jake Horner correspondence, Barth completes the circle of reciprocity his writers have described. For Jake's story too begins locked in the "I" and finally wheels out into a hesitant, troubled "we" in a final letter, addressed, significantly, to Todd Andrews, Barth's troubled custodian of common values.

Although Barth has not encouraged the procedure, it might be helpful to investigate Horner's past. In *The End of the Road*, Horner equated articulation with violence.

> Articulation! There, by Joe, was *my* absolute, if I could be said to have one. . . . To turn experience into speech—that is to classify, to categorize, to conceptualize, to grammarize, to syntactify it— is always a betrayal of experience, a falsification of it; but only so betrayed can it be dealt with at all, and only in so dealing with it did I ever feel a man, alive and kicking. It is therefore that, when I had cause to think about it all, I responded to this precise falsification, this adroit careful myth-making, with all the upsetting exhilaration of any artist at his work. When my mythoplastic razors were sharply honed, it was unparalleled sport to lay about with them, to have at reality. (119)

In *The End of the Road*, writing too is articulation, a mastery that reduces reality to the helplessness of the prostrate patient waiting to be shaved before the next mythoplastic operation. Writing is Horner's test of his manhood, not his fulfillment of it; the more writing swerves away from reality, the more it distorts it, then the greater the achievement of the writer. (Horner's two ad hoc verbs *grammarize* and *syntactify* are twin peaks on his rising scale of artifice.)

Such icy clarity is behind Horner at the beginning of *LETTERS*, where his world has virtually been severed into two incompatible opposites. In the first, Horner hides comfortably in the spatial and temporal vortices of global history. By piling up a catalog of significant dates, he avoids the fact that his own significance is defined by one tragic situation. He has retreated into what he calls anniversary history from a fear of confronting his own, where the memory of Joe Morgan's threatening Colt 45 makes him quiver with fear. To escape his own past, Jake has immersed himself in serial memory. When Jake does "lapse into writing," his efforts are ways of rinsing his hands pure of involvement: "There is nothing amiss in the stirrings of their bereft and sluggish blood, they take pleasure in the tonic of decorous fornication. And generally they experience less guilt and enjoy more remobilization with you than with a partner coeval to their late lamenteds" (100). Horner still daubs his adjectives over his victims like a painter—and one painting from a very great height. He begins, in other words, with an outsider's view of mankind, which only begins to crumble when he starts to "rewrite history." For history engages him with human beings in a way that mythotherapy cannot. Even repetitions become fraught with anxiety and anxiety makes Jake a wiser man. "It is impossible to be at ease in the Progress and Advice Room" (478), he says, repeating his words from *The End of the Road*. "But it is not easy elsewhere, either," he adds, with the kind of saturnine wryness that we expect of Todd Andrews. Once again prose does what it can do incontestably well, register the nervous flutter of the mind on the edge of new experiences while clinging fearfully to old ones.

All the novel's "writers" move from a desire for death to a reengagement with life. Jake, who is no exception, begins his narrative with the desire to end it. "If only roads *did* end," he laments. "Who wants to replay *that* play, rewalk that road" (279). But his involvement with the formidable Marsha Blank propels him out of self-confinement and into commitment. His last letter is addressed to Todd, not Jacob Horner. He no longer wields words like razors, but is willing to concede their resistance to mythotherapy. "Writing It All Down is difficult. . . . It is many years since I Wrote anything to anyone except myself" (739). And he goes on to allude to astronaut Neil Armstrong, offering perhaps a writerly reminder that heroism is not so much technological as moral: "I Do Not Expect the road of our New Life to be free of detours, forks, impasses, potholes, rocks. God alone knows where, past Wicomico and (maybe) Marshyhope, it will lead; nor is it my Intention to Record (ever again) our Passage down it. But with tomorrow's (admittedly tremulous) first step, it will begin" (745).

One small step for man, a giant one for Jacob Horner. The godly artistry of the book finally fills even this vacuum as Horner begins to write out his future ("it will begin") and then to unwrite it (he is admittedly tremulous). Where the image makers have marched toward an illusory vision, the writers have moved toward hesitant, complex futures. In a postindustrial world no longer fixed in moral and spatial boundaries, a world of potholes and astronauts, it is only writing that has the capacity to register the tentative affirmations and unsettled resolutions of lives poised between decisions and revisions. It is a fine irony that a book so occupied with images should have as its most lasting image that of the writer, nervously scripting a future less lethal but just as unnerving as the apocalyptic futures decreed by the book's more ambitious image makers. History does repeat itself—the cases of Lady Amherst, Todd Andrews, and Jacob Horner prove this—but the repetitions can be orchestrated into a larger design for survival. For behind this cast of characters is the figure of J. B., the artist who communicates with all of them, orchestrates their various voices in a choric design, and checks the move toward self-election by promoting a pattern of mutuality. The book's last paradox is its shift to the small scale, the area where Barth secures his aim to tell "the whole story." If

Todd, Germaine, and Jake all push toward a common end, so too does their creator, whose preference for interlocking mutualities over privileged subjectivities creates in *LETTERS* "not a story in Henry James's sense," but "a narrative . . . in Scheherezade's" (53). The book that began with a common end in view closes tentatively poised on a common future. Barth's career, which began with one voice being talked out of suicide by two other voices has now, in the manner of Captains Adam and Osborn, matched voice to voice in a comically various multiple narrative. Barth, who began as a percussionist, has manufactured his own orchestra at last.

Conclusion

One of the most damaging charges made against postwar literature has been that it is, in manner and procedure, against itself. That
is, postwar authors have turned in upon themselves, preferring an
epic self-examination to the exhaustive investigation of the individual
and society undertaken in the great fiction of the nineteenth and early
twentieth centuries.

One of the main purposes of this book has been to modify this
charge. Contemporary fiction is solipsistic, often maddeningly so; I
have not tried to deny this. But I have also tried to show how the *deus
artifex topos* offers the contemporary artist a vantage point from which
to survey his internal and external universe. Of course, that elevation
can be demonic as well as benign; the artist-god has the potential of
becoming a destroyer as well as a creator. There is always the danger
that the two poles of his vision—the subjective and objective, so to
speak—will collide. And when this occurs, a special kind of artist-
god may emerge, one propelled by the fierce intensity that he wields
as compensation for his incapacity to change external reality.

It is just this dualistic thrust in modern versions of the *topos*—
the godly artist's capacity for destruction and creation—that stimu-
lates each of the authors that this book has discussed. In the fiction of
Nathanael West these two faces coexist in a state of uneasy tension.
The Dream Life of Balso Snell is written by an author shocked at the
inevitable tendency of the world he has created to become a public
spectacle; in *Miss Lonelyhearts*, the hero can dream of redeeming the
world—of making the meter reader lie down with the advertising
man—only for as long as he can keep his dreams separate from reality. The case of Lem Pitkin, who becomes West's one successful godly
artist (he even has a public holiday called on his behalf) only at the
cost of martyrdom and reconstruction, proves how right Miss Lonelyhearts and Balso Snell were about technological reality. In West's last
book the godly artist dissolves into society at large. There, in an
illusion-saturated California, where everyman has become his own

godly artist, the ubiquity of artists replaces the authority of art; and the results are frighteningly apocalyptic.

West's apocalyptic conclusions are premises for both John Hawkes and John Barth. Hawkes's solution to the solipsism of postindustrial society is to stand West on his head. Where West focuses on the victim, Hawkes focuses on the victimizer, the man who insists on his right to make his illusions our illusions. Hawkes's fiction betrays the baneful consequences of such assertiveness; his heroes repeatedly claim that they are making a world; the plots of his novels show them to be destroying one. The limiting instance of this pattern comes in *Travesty*, as Hawkes's protagonist, his private world destroyed by betrayal, the larger world exhausted by attrition, turns his attention to the sole remaining reality—his audience.

The image of the artist-god as solitary destroyer is one that even the twentieth-century authors who have criticized it most keenly— Thomas Mann, James Joyce, Albert Camus, John Hawkes—have found difficult to refashion. The artist-god as solitary destroyer has proven a potent image for John Barth too. From his first novel, where Todd Andrews attempts to blow up his townspeople on board Capt. Adam's floating opera, to *LETTERS*, where Todd's main brief seems to be to defuse the destructive potential of others, the idea of apocalypse has haunted Barth. And frequently Barth's annihilators are men who thought they invented the world—godly artists of a solitary and self-devouring kind, like Jake Horner or Jerome Bray, or the self-hating, world-scorning narrator of "Night-Sea Journey" who peoples the ocean with his own self-image.

But Barth has, in several novels, managed to divert this apocalypse through the good offices of his "twinned" deity. Barth has repeatedly voiced his desire to tell "the whole story," to create a comic universe so full and varied as to enable him to join Shakespeare, Cervantes, and God, the comic godly artists of the past. Todd Andrews, who imagined a story like a floating opera, dependent on the participation of other people for its continued life, sketched the blueprint for such a narrative. But it was not until *LETTERS*, where Barth presented a story in which absolutist drove out absolutist, that he managed to create in structure the kind of multiplicity he had always promulgated as his intention, but only intermittently achieved. Such an achievement appears to need the past behind it to make it thrive; when Barth confines himself to the present, as he does in *Sabbatical*, he is no longer a godly maker. The immense weight of professional know-how and amateur enthusiasm that he brings aboard his fictional craft in this novel makes it a treatise on the art of sinking in fiction.

The postwar godly maker always sails between the Scylla of sol-ipsism and the Charybdis of inclusiveness. The one route leads to apocalypse, the other to a mistaken sense that, with enough tackle, the craft of fiction will somehow sail itself. The *topos* continues to fas-cinate contemporary authors; but it has so far failed to find its Ameri-can Rabelais.

Notes

All page references to the works of Nathanael West, John Hawkes, and John Barth are to the following editions:

The Complete Works of Nathanael West, ed. Alan Ross (New York: Farrar, Straus, and Cudahy, 1957).

John Hawkes, *The Cannibal* (New York: New Directions, 1962); *Second Skin* (New York: New Directions, 1964); *The Blood Oranges* (New York: New Directions, 1972); *Travesty* (New York: New Directions, 1977); *The Passion Artist* (New York: Harper Colophon Books, 1981).

John Barth, *The End of the Road* (New York: Bantam Books, 1969); *Lost in the Funhouse* (New York: Bantam Books, 1969); *The Floating Opera* (New York: Bantam Books, 1972); *LETTERS* (New York: G. P. Putnam's Sons, 1979); *Sabbatical* (London: Panther Books, 1984).

Introduction

1. Edmund Wilson, *Axel's Castle* (Glasgow: Collins, 1961), p. 27.

2. Frank Kermode, *Puzzles and Epiphanies* (New York: Chillmark Press, 1962), p. 56.

3. Frank Kermode, *Romantic Image* (London: Fontana Books, 1971), p. 13.

4. Randall Jarrell, *Poetry and the Age* (New York: Vintage Books, 1953), pp. 13–14.

5. Jerome C. Christensen, *Coleridge's Blessed Machine of Language* (Ithaca: Cornell University Press, 1981), see esp. pp. 118–85.

6. Denis Donoghue, *Imagination* (Glasgow: Glasgow University Press, 1974), pp. 21–22.

7. Christensen, *Machine of Language*, p. 163.

8. Frederic Jameson, *Fables of Aggression: Wyndham Lewis, the Modernist as Fascist* (Berkeley: University of California Press, 1979), p. 81.

9. Wilson, *Axel's Castle*, p. 16.

10. Letter to John Galsworthy, 11 Nov. 1901, *Joseph Conrad: Life and Letters*, ed. G. Jean Aubry (New York: Doubleday Page, 1927), I, 301–2.

11. Letter to Louise Colet, 21–22 Aug. 1853, *The Letters of Gustave Flaubert, 1830–1857*, ed. Francis Steegmuller (Cambridge, Mass.: The Belknap Press of the Harvard University Press, 1980), p. 197.

12. Carol Hryciw, *John Hawkes: An Annotated Bibliography* (Metuchen, N. J.: Scarecrow Press, 1977), p. 6.

13. Norman Mailer, *Cannibals and Christians* (New York: Dell, 1966), p. 214.

14. John Barth, "My Two Muses," *Johns Hopkins Magazine* 12 (1961), 9–13.

15. Ronald Sukenick, "The New Tradition in Fiction," in *Surfiction*, ed. Raymond Federman (Chicago: Swallow Press, 1981), p. 35.

16. Carl Becker, "Everyman His Own Historian," *American Historical Review* 37 (1932), 221–36. See also *New Liberties for Old* (New Haven: Yale University Press, 1941).

17. Letter to Evert A. Duykinck, 14 Dec. 1849, *The Letters of Herman Melville*, ed. Merrell R. Davis and William H. Gilman (New Haven: Yale University Press, 1960), p. 96.

18. Warner Berthoff, *A Literature without Qualities* (Berkeley: University of California Press, 1979); Gerald Graff, *Literature against Itself* (Chicago: University of Chicago Press, 1979).

19. Edward Said, *The World, The Text, and The Critic* (Cambridge, Mass.: Harvard University Press, 1983), pp. 46–47.

20. Frank Kermode, *The Art of Telling* (Cambridge, Mass.: Harvard University Press, 1983), see esp. Prologue, pp. 8–23.

21. Harold Bloom, *Kaballah and Criticism* (New York: Seabury Press, 1975), p. 52.

22. Frank Kermode, *The Classic* (Cambridge, Mass.: Harvard University Press, 1983), p. 138.

Chapter 1: *"Deus Artifex*: Transformation of a *Topos"*

1. Arthur O. Lovejoy, *The Great Chain of Being* (Cambridge, Mass.: Harvard University Press, 1936), p. 82.

2. *New English Bible* (Cambridge and Oxford: Cambridge and Oxford University Presses, 1970), Genesis 1, 1–31.

3. Robert Davidson, *The Cambridge Bible Commentary: Genesis 1–11* (Cambridge: Cambridge University Press, 1973), pp. 14–15.

4. F. M. Cornford, *Plato's Cosmology* (London: Routledge and Kegan Paul, 1937), p. 35.

5. W. H. Auden, "The Novelist," *Collected Poems*, ed. Edward Mendelson (London: Faber and Faber, 1976), p. 147.

6. E. R. Curtius, *European Literature and the Latin Middle Ages* (New York: Pantheon Books, 1953), p. 70.

7. Ernst Kris and Otto Kurz, *Legend, Myth, and Magic in the Image of the Artist* (New Haven: Yale University Press, 1979), pp. 38–60; Gabriel Josipovici, *The World and the Book* (Stanford: Stanford University Press, 1971). These supplement and expand the basic account offered by Curtius, *Latin Middle Ages*, pp. 544–46. See also Milton C. Nahm, *The Artist as Creator* (Baltimore: Johns Hopkins University Press, 1956).

8. Curtius, *Latin Middle Ages*, p. 544.

9. Jacob Burckhardt, *The Civilization of the Renaissance in Italy*, trans. S. G. C. Middlemore (New York: Harper Torchbooks, 1958), I, 243.

10. Alvin B. Kernan, *The Playwright as Magician* (New Haven: Yale University Press, 1979), p. 2.

11. See E. H. Wilkins, *Studies in the Life and Works of Petrarch* (Boston, Mass.: Medieval Academy of America, 1955), pp. 300–313, for a full translation of this speech.

12. Morris Bishop, ed., *Letters from Petrarch* (Bloomington: Indiana University Press, 1966), p. 198.

13. C. A. Patrides, ed., "'A Crown of Praise': The Poetry of Herbert," in *The English Poems of George Herbert* (London: Dent, 1974), p. 15.

14. Alan H. Gilbert, *Literary Criticism from Plato to Dryden* (New York: American Book Company, 1940), p. 506.

15. Quoted in M. H. Abrams, *The Mirror and the Lamp* (New York: Oxford University Press, 1953), p. 273.

16. Erwin Panofsky, *Idea* (Columbia: University of South Carolina Press, 1968), pp. 123–24.

17. Sir Philip Sidney, *A Defence of Poetry* (London: Oxford University Press, 1966), pp. 23–24.

18. Martin C. Battestin, *The Providence of Wit* (Oxford: The Clarendon Press, 1974), p. 4.

19. John Upton, *Critical Observations on Shakespeare* (London, 1748), pp. 134–35. See Battestin, *Providence of Wit*, p. 297.

20. Maximilian E. Novak, *Realism, Myth, and History in Defoe's Fiction* (Lincoln: University of Nebraska Press, 1983), p. 11.

21. Thomas Burnet, *The Sacred Theory of the Earth* (London: Centaur Press, 1965), pp. 13–15.

22. Ralph Cudworth, *The True Intellectual System of the Universe* (Stuttgart-Bad Constatt: Freidrich Frommann Verlag, 1964), I, 879–80.

23. Barbara Hardy, *The Appropriate Form* (London: The Athlone Press, 1971), p. 61.

24. Daniel Defoe, *Robinson Crusoe* (New York: Houghton Mifflin, 1927), II, 203, 41.

25. Battestin, *Providence of Wit*, p. 141.

26. Henry Fielding, *Tom Jones*, ed. Martin Battestin (Oxford: The Clarendon Press, 1974), II, 524–25.

27. Jonathan Swift, *A Tale of a Tub*, vol. 1 of *The Prose Works of Jonathan Swift*, ed. Herbert Davis (Oxford: Basil Blackwell, 1939), p. 81.

28. Letter to Thomas Poole, 23 Mar. 1801, *Collected Letters of Samuel Taylor Coleridge*, ed. Earl Leslie Griggs, II (Oxford: Clarendon Press, 1966), 709.

29. Samuel Taylor Coleridge, *Biographia Literaria*, ed. J. Shawcross (Oxford: The Clarendon Press, 1907), I, 202.

30. Friedrich Schlegel, *Dialogues on Poetry and Literary Aphorisms*, trans. Ernst Behler and Roman Struc (University Park: Pennsylvania State University Press, 1969), p. 126.

31. José Ortega y Gasset, *The Dehumanization of Art* (Garden City, N. Y.: Doubleday Anchor Books, 1956), p. 21.

32. Samuel Taylor Coleridge, *Poetical Works* (Oxford: The University Press, 1969), p. 296.

33. M. H. Abrams, "Coleridge, Baudelaire, and Modernist Poetics," in *New Perspectives in German Literary Criticism*, ed. Richard E. Amacher and Victor Lange (Princeton, N. J.: Princeton University Press, 1979), pp. 150–81.

34. *Baudelaire: Prose and Poetry*, trans. Arthur Symons (New York: Albert and Charles Boni, 1926), p. 275.

35. P. E. Charvet, ed., *Selected Writings on Art and Artists* (Harmondsworth: Penguin Books, 1972), p. 421.

36. Symons, *Baudelaire*, p. 80.

37. W. J. Harvey, *Character and the Novel* (London: Chatto and Windus, 1965), p. 32.

38. Steven Marcus, *Dickens: From Pickwick to Dombey* (London: Chatto and Windus, 1965), p. 217.

39. Henry James, "The Lesson of Balzac," in *The House of Fiction*, ed. Leon Edel (London: Rupert Hart-Davis, 1957), p. 85.

40. Marthe Robert, *Roman des origines et origines du roman* (Paris: Grusset, 1975), p. 254; quoted in Robert Alter, *Partial Magic* (Berkeley: University of California Press, 1975), p. 100.

41. E. M. Forster, *Aspects of the Novel* (London: Edwin Arnold, 1974), p. 65.

42. Cited in Harvey, *Character and the Novel*, p. 138.

43. Letter to Mademoiselle Leroyer de Chantepie, Mar. 18 1857, *The Letters of Gustave Flaubert, 1830–57*, ed. Francis Steegmuller (Cambridge, Mass.: The Belknap Press of the Harvard University Press, 1980), p. 230.

44. Letter to Louise Colet, 7 Oct. 1852, *Correspondance, Volume II 1851–58*, ed. Jean Bruneau (Paris: Gallimard, 1980), p. 168.

45. Letter to Louise Colet, 4 Sept. 1852, *Letters of Flaubert*, p. 169.

46. Gustave Flaubert, *Bouvard and Pécuchet* (New York: New Directions, 1971), pp. 347–48.

47. Thomas Hardy, *Tess of the D'Urbervilles* (London: Macmillan, 1974), p. 449.

48. Warner Berthoff, *The Example of Melville* (New York: W. W. Norton, 1972); see esp. pp. 41ff.

49. Herman Melville, *Pierre, or The Ambiguities* (New York: Signet Library, 1964), p. 295.

50. C. W. Bush, "This Stupendous Fabric: The Metaphysics of Order in Melville's *Pierre* and Nathanael West's *Miss Lonelyhearts*," *Journal of American Studies* 1 (1967), 269–74.

51. Mark Twain, *The Mysterious Stranger Manuscripts*, ed. William M. Gibson (Berkeley: University of California Press, 1970), p. 16.

52. Letter to John Galsworthy, 11 Nov. 1901, *Joseph Conrad: Life and Letters*, ed. G. Jean-Aubry (New York: Doubleday Page, 1927), I, 301–2.

53. Joseph Conrad, *The Secret Agent* (Harmondsworth: Penguin Books, 1973), p. 58.

54. Alfred Kubin, *The Other Side* (Harmondsworth: Penguin Books, 1973), p. 58.

55. George Orwell, *1984* (Harmondsworth: Penguin Books, 1969), pp. 35–36.

56. T. S. Eliot, "*Ulysses*, Order, and Myth," *The Dial* 75 (1923), 480–83; reprinted in *Selected Prose of T. S. Eliot*, ed. Frank Kermode (London: Faber and Faber, 1975), p. 177.

57. James Joyce, *A Portrait of the Artist as a Young Man* (London: Heinemann Educational Books, 1966), p. 199.

58. James Joyce, *Ulysses* (London: The Bodley Head, 1960), p. 249.

59. Thomas Mann, *Genesis of a Novel* (London: Secker and Warburg, 1961), p. 28.

60. I am indebted to two essays by J. P. Stern on this topic: "The Dear Purchase," *German Quarterly* 41 (1968), 317–36, and "From Family Album to Literary History," *New Literary History* 7 (1975), 115–33.

61. Thomas Mann, *Dr. Faustus* (Harmondsworth: Penguin Books, 1973), p. 381.

62. Jean-Paul Sartre, *Situations* (Greenwich, Conn.: Fawcett Publications, 1966), pp. 55–62.

63. Francis Jeanson, "Albert Camus ou L'âme revoltée," *Les Temps Modernes* 7 (1952), 2070–90.

64. Albert Camus, *The Fall* (Harmondsworth: Penguin Books, 1971), p. 19.

Chapter 2: "The Art of Significant Disorder: The Fiction of Nathanael West"

1. Jay Martin, *Nathanael West: The Art of His Life* (New York: Straus and Giroux, 1970), p. 335.

2. Maria Ujházy, "The Satire of Nathanael West," *Studies in English and American* (Budapest), 4 (1978), 35–62.

3. Warwick Wadlington, *The Confidence Game in American Literature* (Princeton, N. J.: Princeton University Press, 1975), p. 290.

4. Edmund Wilson, "The Boys in the Back Room," in *Classics and Commercials* (London: W. H. Allen, 1950), pp. 19–56.

5. R. P. Blackmur, *The Lion and the Honeycomb* (London: Methuen, 1956), pp. 43–50.

6. Max Schulz, *Radical Sophistication: Studies in Contemporary Jewish-American Novelists* (Columbus: Ohio State University Press, 1969), pp. 36–55.

7. James F. Light, *Nathanael West: An Interpretative Study* (Evanston, Ill.: Northwestern University Press, 1969).

8. Victor Comerchero, *Nathanael West: The Ironic Prophet* (Syracuse, N. Y.: Syracuse University Press, 1964); Stanley Edgar Hyman, *Nathanael West* (Minneapolis: University of Minnesota Press, 1962); Harold Bloom, *The Breaking of the Vessels* (Chicago: University of Chicago Press, 1982), pp. 21–25.

9. W. H. Auden, "West's Disease," in *The Dyer's Hand* (New York: Random House, 1962), pp. 238–45.

10. Leslie A. Fiedler, *Waiting for the End* (New York: Stein and Day, 1964), p. 49.

11. Jonathan Raban, "A Surfeit of Commodities: The Novels of Nathanael West," in *The American Novel in the Nineteen-Twenties*, ed. M. Bradbury and D. J. Palmer (London: Edwin Arnold, 1971), pp. 215–31.

12. Alan Ross, ed. *The Complete Works of Nathanael West*, p. xii; Randall Reid, *The Fiction of Nathanael West: No Redeemer, No Promised Land* (Chicago: University of Chicago Press, 1967).

13. Martin, *Nathanael West*, p. 127.

14. *Ibid.*, p. 73

15. George Mowry, *The Urban Nation* (London: Macmillan, 1967), p. 21.

16. William Leuchtenberg, *The Perils of Prosperity* (Chicago: University of Chicago Press, 1958), pp. 178–203.

17. A good discussion of these issues appears in Charles Baxter's "Nathanael West: Dead Letters and the Martyred Novelist," *West Coast Review* 9 (1974), 3–11; Wadlington's discussion in *The Confidence Game in American Literature* is also highly informative.

18. Martin, *Nathanael West*, pp. 246–7.

19. T. R. Steiner, "West's Lemuel and the American Dream," in *Nathanael West: The Cheaters and the Cheated*, ed. David Madden (Deloud, Fla.: Everett and Edwards, 1973), p. 160.

20. Martin, *Nathanael West*, pp. 334–35.

21. Donald I. Torchiana, "*The Day of the Locust* and the Painter's Eye," in Madden, ed., *Nathanael West*, pp. 249–82.

Chapter 3: "Nathanael West: Godly Maker in a Commercial World"

1. R. P. Blackmur, *The Lion and the Honeycomb* (London: Methuen, 1956), p. 63.

2. Malcolm Bradbury, "Style of Life, Style of Art and the American Novelist in the Nineteen Twenties," in *The American Novel in the Nineteen-Twenties*, ed. M. Bradbury and D. J. Palmer (London: Edwin Arnold, 1971), p. 11.

3. Frank Kermode, *The Art of Telling* (Cambridge, Mass.: Harvard University Press, 1983), pp. 9–10.

4. Hugh Kenner, "Notes Towards an Anatomy of 'Modernism,'" in *A Starchamber Quiry: A James Joyce Centennial Volume, 1882–1982*, ed. E. L. Epstein (London: Methuen, 1982), p. 4; see also pp. 3–42.

5. Michael Spindler, *American Literature and Social Change* (Bloomington: Indiana University Press, 1983), pp. 123ff.

6. Gore Vidal, "American Plastic," in *Matters of Fact and Fiction* (New York: Random House, 1977), pp. 99–126 and passim.

7. John Dos Passos, "The Writer as Technician," in *American Writers' Congress*, ed. Henry Hart (New York: International Publishers, 1935), p. 82.

8. Gertrude Stein, *The Geographical History of America* (New York: Random House, 1936), p. 29.

9. Ezra Pound, *How to Read* (London: Desmond Harmsworth, 1931), p. 21.

10. T. S. Eliot, "The Perfect Critic," in *The Sacred Wood* (New York: Harper and Row, 1960), p. 13.

11. Newton Arvin, *American Pantheon* (New York: Delacorte Press, 1966), p. xvi.

12. Ezra Pound, *ABC of Reading* (New York: New Directions, 1960), p. 75.

13. *Ibid.*, pp. 77–78.

14. F. R. Leavis, *How to Teach Reading* (Cambridge: Fraser, 1932), p. 3.

15. T. S. Eliot, *Selected Essays* (London: Faber and Faber, 1951), p. 114.

16. Gertrude Stein, *The Making of Americans* (London: Peter Owen, 1968), p. 34.

17. Gertrude Stein, *Four in America* (Freeport, N. Y.: Books for Libraries, 1947), pp. v–vi.

18. E. H. Gombrich, "The Preference for the Primitive," a lecture delivered at the Los Angeles County Museum of Art, 1981.

19. Stein, *Geographical History*, p. 29.

20. *Ibid.*, p. 181.

21. Thornton Wilder, *The Angel That Troubled the Waters, and Other Plays* (New York: Longmans Green, 1928), p. vii.

22. *Ibid.*, p. 5.

23. *Ibid.*, p. v.

24. Ernest Hemingway, *Death in the Afternoon* (New York: Charles Scribner's Sons, 1932), p. 2.

25. Leslie Fiedler, *Love and Death in the American Novel* (London: Paladin, 1970), pp. 295–96.

26. Jay Martin, *Nathanael West: The Art of His Life* (New York: Straus and Giroux, 1970), p. 336.

27. Malcolm Cowley, *Exile's Return* (New York: Viking Press, 1951), p. 27.

28. Frederick J. Ringel, ed., *America as Americans See It* (New York: Harcourt, Brace, 1932), pp. 20–30.

29. Henry Ford, *Moving Forward* (London: William Heinemann, 1931), p. 136.

30. *Ibid.*, p. 33.

31. Donald McCoy, *Coming of Age: The United States during the 1920s and 1930s* (Harmondsworth: Penguin Books, 1973), p. 115.

32. George Mowry, *The Urban Nation* (London: Macmillan, 1967), p. 11.

33. *Ibid.*, p. 14.

34. See also Edward A. Filene, *Successful Living in This Machine Age* (New York: Simon and Schuster, 1931).

35. See Spindler, *American Literature and Social Change*, pp. 102ff., for a fuller account of this shift; many of the authorities cited within this chapter provide "eyewitness" accounts.

36. Stuart Chase, "The Heart of Human Industry," in *America*, ed. Ringel, p. 20.

37. Leon Litwack, ed., *The American Labor Movement* (Englewood Cliffs, N.J.: Prentice Hall, 1962), pp. 5–6.

38. Frederick Allen, *Only Yesterday* (New York: Perennial Library, 1964), p. 140.

39. James Joyce, *Ulysses* (London: The Bodley Head, 1960), p. 278.

40. Allen, *Only Yesterday*, p. 141.

41. Jim Potter, *The American Economy between The Wars* (London: Macmillan, 1974), esp. pp. 46–50.

42. George Mowry, ed., *The Twenties: Fords, Flappers and Fanatics* (Englewood Cliffs, N.J.: Prentice Hall, 1963), p. 15.

43. Clifton Fadiman, "What Does America Read?" in *America*, ed. Ringel, p. 74.

44. *Ibid.*, p. 75.

45. Stuart Ewen, *Captains of Consciousness* (New York: McGraw-Hill, 1976), pp. 131–84.

46. Allen, *Only Yesterday*, p. 144.

47. Mowry, *Fords, Flappers and Fanatics*, p. 25.

48. *Ibid.*, pp. 4–5.

49. *Ibid.*, p. 11.

50. Quoted many times; see, for example, Elizabeth Stevenson, *Babbits and Bohemians* (New York: Macmillan, 1962), p. 48.

51. Arthur Knight, *The Liveliest Art* (New York: New American Library 1957), p. 249.

52. Ford, *Moving Forward*, p. 310.

Chapter 4: "The *Deus Artifex Topos* since 1945: Everyman His Own Godly Artist"

1. See E. H. Gombrich, *Art and Illusion* (New York: Pantheon Books, 1960), pp. 61–62.

2. Jean-Paul Sartre, *Literary and Philosophical Essays* (New York: Collier Books, 1962), p. 41.

3. Warner Berthoff, *A Literature without Qualities* (Berkeley: University of California Press, 1979), pp. 1–14; Gerald Graff, *Literature against Itself* (Chicago: University of Chicago Press, 1979), pp. 1–29.

4. Alan Wilde, *Horizons of Assent* (Baltimore: Johns Hopkins University Press, 1981).

5. Irving Howe, *The Decline of the New* (New York: Harcourt, Brace and World, 1970), pp. 3–33, 190–207.

6. Leslie Fiedler, "Cross that Border—Close that Gap," in *American Literature since 1900*, ed. Marcus Cunliffe (London: Barrie and Jenkins, 1976), pp. 344–66.

7. Frank Kermode, *Continuities* (London: Routledge and Kegan Paul, 1968), pp. 1–32.

8. Berthoff, *Literature without Qualities*, p. 32.

9. Werner Heisenberg, "The Representation of Nature in Contemporary Physics," *Daedalus* 87 (1958), 95–108.

10. Colin Clark, *Conditions of Economic Progress* (London: Macmillan, 1940), p. 7.

11. Nelson N. Foote and Paul K. Hatt, "Social Mobility and Economic Advancement," *American Economic Review* 43 (1953), 364–78.

12. Quoted in Donald N. Michael, "Cybernation: The Silent Conquest," in *The Corporation Take-Over*, ed. Andrew Hacker (New York: Anchor Books, 1965), pp. 192–93.

13. Richard Sennett, *The Fall of Public Man* (New York: Alfred A. Knopf, 1977), p. 328.

14. Hacker, *Corporation Take-Over*, p. 194.

15. Sennett, *Public Man*, pp. 327–33; C. Wright Mills, *The Sociological Imagination* (Harmondsworth: Penguin Books, 1971), pp. 113–32.

16. James Burnham, *The Managerial Revolution* (New York: John Day Co., 1941), p. 80.

17. Elton Mayo, *The Social Problems of an Industrial Civilization* (Cambridge, Mass.: Harvard University Press, 1945), p. 85.

18. H. M. McLuhan, *The Mechanical Bride* (New York: Vanguard Press, 1951), p. 126.

19. Robert Reich, "The Next American Frontier," *Atlantic Monthly* (Mar. 1983), 43–58; (Apr. 1983), 96–108.

20. Hacker, "Politics and the Corporation," in *Corporation Take-Over*, pp. 246–47.

21. Joseph Heller, *Something Happened* (London: Jonathan Cape, 1974), p. 44.

22. Hans-Magnus Enzensberger, *The Consciousness Industry* (New York: Seabury Press, 1974).

23. Tony Schwartz, *The Second God* (New York: Random House, 1981).

24. Marshall McLuhan, *Understanding Media* (New York: McGraw-Hill, 1965), p. x.

25. John Barth, *Lost in the Funhouse* (New York: Bantam Books, 1969), p. 123.

26. Charles Newman, "The Uses and Abuses of Death: A Little Ramble through the Remnants of Literary Culture," *Triquarterly* 26 (1973), 3–41.

27. See David Morrell, *John Barth: An Introduction* (University Park: Pennsylvania State University Press, 1976), p. 15; see also p. 48.

28. Dedication to J. D. Salinger, *Raise High the Roof-Beams, Carpenters and Seymour, An Introduction* (Boston: Little Brown and Co., 1963).

29. Sennett, *Public Man*, pp. 283–87.

30. Daniel Bell, *The Coming of Post-Industrial Society* (London: Heinemann, 1974), p. 480.

31. John Gardner, *On Moral Fiction* (New York: Basic Books, 1978).

32. Vladimir Nabokov, *Strong Opinions* (New York: McGraw-Hill, 1973), p. 32.

33. Vladimir Nabokov, *Nikolai Gogol* (New York: New Directions, 1944), pp. 40–41.

34. Vladimir Nabokov, *Bend Sinister* (New York: McGraw-Hill, 1974), p. xii.

35. Vladimir Nabokov, *Despair*, rev. ed. (New York: Capricorn Books, 1970), p. 9.

36. Nabokov, *Strong Opinions*, p. 11

37. Vladimir Nabokov, *Speak Memory* (New York: Pyramid Books, 1968), p. 17.

38. Vladimir Nabokov, *Invitation to a Beheading* (London: Weidenfeld and Nicolson, 1960), p. 82.

39. William Gass, *Fiction and the Figures of Life* (New York: Vintage Books, 1972), p. 12.

40. Gardner's remark is found in *Anything Can Happen: Interviews with Contemporary American Novelists*, ed. Tom LeClair and Larry McCaffery (Urbana: University of Illinois Press, 1983), p. 30.

41. William Gass, *In the Heart of the Heart of the Country* (New York: Perennial Library, 1969), p. 81.

42. Susan Sontag, *The Benefactor* (New York: Farrar, Straus and Co., 1963), p. 89.

43. Günter Grass, "On Writers as Court Jesters and on Non-Existent Courts," in *Günter Grass Speaks Out!* (New York: Harcourt, Brace and World, 1969), p. 47.

44. Günter Grass, *Local Anaesthetic* (Greenwich, Conn.: Fawcett Crest, 1971), p. 117.

45. Stanley Elkin, *The Living End* (New York: Warner Books, 1980), p. 137.

46. Stanley Elkin, *George Mills* (New York: E. P. Dutton, 1982), p. 15.

47. Heide Ziegler and Christopher Bigsby, eds., *The Radical Imagination and the Liberal Tradition* (London: Junction Books, 1982), p. 102.

48. Robert Coover, *The Universal Baseball Association, Inc. J. Henry Waugh, Prop.* (New York: New American Library, 1971), p. 36.

49. Gabriel García Márquez, *One Hundred Years of Solitude* (New York: Avon Books, 1971), p. 11.

Chapter 5: "John Hawkes's God: The Realist *Malgré Lui*"

1. Alan Trachtenberg, "Barth and Hawkes: Two Fabulists," *Critique* 6 (1963), 4–18.

2. John Enck, "John Hawkes: An Interview," *Wisconsin Studies in Contemporary Literature* 6 (1965), 141–55; *Anything Can Happen: Interviews with Contemporary American Novelists*, ed. Tom LeClair and Larry McCaffery (Urbana: University of Illinois Press, 1983), pp. 10–19.

3. Enck, "An Interview," p. 149.

4. John Kuehl, *John Hawkes and the Craft of Conflict* (New Brunswick, N. J.: Rutgers University Press, 1975), pp. 181–82.

5. Robert Scholes, "A Conversation on *The Blood Oranges* between John Hawkes and Robert Scholes," *Novel* 5 (1972), 197–207.

6. Nancy Levine, "An Interview with John Hawkes," in *A John Hawkes Symposium*, ed. Anthony C. Santore and Michael Pocalyko (New York: New Directions, 1977), p. 93.

7. Paul Rosenzweig, "Aesthetics and the Psychology of Control in John Hawkes's Triad," *Novel* 15 (1982), 146–62.

8. Carol Hryciw, *John Hawkes: An Annotated Bibliography* (Metuchen, N. J.: The Scarecrow Press, 1977), p. 6.

9. Tony Tanner, *City of Words* (New York: Harper and Row, 1971), p. 218.

10. Earl Rovit, "The Fiction of John Hawkes: An Introductory View," *Modern Fiction Studies* 10 (1964), 150–62.

11. Roger Sale, *On Not Being Good Enough* (New York: Oxford University Press, 1979), pp. 30–32.

12. John Hawkes, "Flannery O'Connor's Devil," *Sewanee Review* 76 (1962), 400–401.

13. Albert Guerard, Introduction to John Hawkes's *The Cannibal* (New York: New Directions, 1962), p. xix.

14. Paul Emmett and Richard Vine, "A Conversation with John Hawkes," *Chicago Review* 28 (1976), 163.

15. Thomas LeClair, "The Unreliability of Innocence: John Hawkes' *Second Skin*," *Journal of Narrative Technique* 3 (1973), 32–39.

Chapter 6: " 'Something Like a War Memorial': John Hawkes's *Travesty*"

1. Tony Tanner, "John Hawkes: No Instructions How to Read," *New York Times Book Review*, 28 Mar. 1976, pp. 23–24.

2. Heide Zeigler and Christopher Bigsby, eds., *The Radical Imagination and the Liberal Tradition* (London: Junction Books, 1982), p. 181.

3. Donald J. Greiner, *Comic Terror: The Novels of John Hawkes* (Memphis: Memphis State University Press, 1978), pp. 263–75.

4. Paul Emmett, "The Reader's Voyage through *Travesty*," *Chicago Review* 28 (1976), 172–87.

5. Ziegler and Bigsby, *Liberal Tradition*, p. 170.

6. Charles Baxter, "In the Suicide Seat: Reading John Hawkes's *Travesty*," *Georgia Review* 34 (1980), 871–85.

7. Letter to Arsene Houssaye, 18 Feb. 1866, *Correspondence*, ed. Claude Pichois (Paris: Gallimard, 1973), II, 610.

8. *Chicago Tribune*, 28 Mar. 1976, p. 7.2.

9. As quoted in Herbert R. Lottman, *Albert Camus* (New York: Doubleday, 1979), p. 670.

10. H. M. McLuhan, *The Mechanical Bride* (New York: Vanguard Press, 1951), p. 101.

11. *Anything Can Happen: Interviews with Contemporary American Novelists*, ed. Tom LeClair and Larry McCaffery (Urbana: University of Illinois Press, 1983), p. 18.

12. Henry W. Sams, "Swift's Satire of the Second Person," *English Literary History* 26 (1959), 36–44.

13. Paul Rosenzweig, "Aesthetics and the Psychology of Control in John Hawkes's Triad," *Novel* 15 (1982), 146–62.

14. Brenda Wineapple, "The Travesty of Literalism: Two Novels by John Hawkes," *Journal of Narrative Technique* 12 (1982), 130–37.

15. Emmett, "The Reader's Voyage," p. 178.

16. Theodor Adorno, *The Philosophy of Modern Music* (New York: Seabury Press, 1973), pp. 9ff.

17. John Ruskin, *Sesame and Lilies*, in *The Works of John Ruskin*, vol. 18, ed. E. T. Cook and Alexander Wedderburn (London: George Allen, 1905), pp. 1–187. Note that Ruskin's second lecture, "Lilies: of Queen's Gardens," ends with a fox and grapes parable.

18. Richard Chase, *The American Novel and Its Tradition* (New York: Doubleday Anchor, 1957), p. 106.

Chapter 7: "The Nihilist *Deus Artifex*: The Short Fiction of John Barth"

1. John Barth, "My Two Muses," *Johns Hopkins Magazine* 12 (1961), 9–13.

2. John Barth, "The Literature of Replenishment," *Atlantic Monthly* (Jan. 1980), 65–71.

3. Jerome Klinkowitz, "John Barth Reconsidered," *Partisan Review* 49 (1982), 407–11.

4. John S. Barth, "Lilith and the Lion," *Hopkins Review* 4 (1950), 49–53.

5. Leslie Fiedler, "John Barth: An Eccentric Genius," *New Leader* (Feb. 1961), 22–24.

6. John M. Bradbury, "Absurd Insurrection: The Barth-Percy Affair," *South Atlantic Quarterly* 68 (1969), 319–29.

7. Barth, "Literature of Replenishment," p. 71.

8. John Barth, "The Literature of Exhaustion," *Atlantic Monthly* (Aug. 1967), 229–34; reprinted in *Surfiction*, ed. Raymond Federman (Chicago: Swallow Press, 1981), p. 20.

9. John J. Enck, "John Barth: An Interview," *Wisconsin Studies in Contemporary Literature* 6 (1965), 3–14.

10. Barth, "Literature of Exhaustion," p. 27.

11. Richard Noland, "John Barth and the Novel of Comic Nihilism," *Wisconsin Studies in Contemporary Literature* 7 (1966), 239–57.

12. Campbell Tatham, "John Barth and the Aesthetics of Artifice," *Contemporary Literature* 12 (1971), 60–73; Beverly Gross, "The Anti-Novels of John Barth," *Chicago Review* 20 (1968), 95–109.

13. Thomas LeClair, "John Barth's *The Floating Opera*: Death and the Craft of Fiction," *Texas Studies in Language and Literature* 14 (1973), 711–30.

14. Henry Adams, *The Education of Henry Adams* (New York: Time Inc., 1964), 2: 293.

15. My argument has been aided immeasurably by the following two monographs: James M. Cox, *Mark Twain: The Fate of Humor* (Princeton, N. J.: Princeton University Press, 1968); Robert Alter, *Partial Magic* (Berkeley: University of California Press, 1975), esp. pp. 218–45.

16. Guy Davenport, "Like Nothing Nameable," *New York Times Book Review*, 20 Oct. 1968, p. 4; R. V. Cassils, "The Artist as Art," *Washington Post Book World*, 15 Sept. 1968, p. 16; Walter Harding, "Fiction," *Library Journal*, 15 Sept. 1968, p. 3153.

17. Tony Tanner, "No Exit," *Partisan Review* 36 (1964), 294–99.

18. Edgar H. Knapp, "Found in the Barthhouse: The Novelist as Savior," *Modern Fiction Studies* 14 (1969), 446–51.

19. Michael Hinden, "*Lost in the Funhouse*: Barth's Use of the Recent Past," *Twentieth-Century Literature* 19 (1973), 107–18.

20. Beverly Gray Bienstock, "Lingering on the Autognostic Verge: John Barth's *Lost in the Funhouse*," *Modern Fiction Studies* 19 (1973), 69–78.

21. Linda Westervelt, "Teller, Tale, Told: Relationships in John Barth's Latest Fiction," *Journal of Narrative Technique* 8 (1978), 42–55.

22. Carol Shloss and Khachig Totolyan, "The Siren in the Funhouse: Barth's Courting of the Reader," *Journal of Narrative Technique* 11 (1981), 64–74.

23. Linda Westervelt, in her previously cited article, has made many interesting parallels between McLuhan and Barth. The American publication details for McLuhan are as follows: *The Gutenberg Galaxy* (New York: McGraw-Hill, 1965); *Understanding Media* (New York: McGraw Hill, 1965); *The Medium Is the Massage* (New York: Bantam Books, 1967); and, with Quentin Fiore, *War and Peace in the Global Village* (New York: Bantam Books, 1968).

24. H. H. Stuckenschmidt, *Arnold Schoenberg: His Life, World and Work* (London: John Calder, 1977), p. 546.

Chapter 8: "The Global *Deus Artifex*: John Barth's *The Sot-Weed Factor* and *LETTERS*"

1. David Morrell, *John Barth: An Introduction* (University Park: Pennsylvania State University Press, 1976), p. 28.

2. Earl Rovit, "The Novel as Parody: John Barth," *Critique* 6 (1963), 77–85.

3. John Enck, "John Barth: An Interview," *Wisconsin Studies in Contemporary Literature* 6 (1965), 8.

4. Ebenezer Cooke, "The Sot-Weed Factor" (Annapolis: 1731), reprinted in Ronald Gottesman et al., *The Norton Anthology of American Literature* (New York: W. W. Norton, 1979), 1: 175.

5. Joseph Epstein, "Too Much Even of Kreplach," *Hudson Review* 33 (1980), 97.

6. Philip Stevick, "Letters from Incongruent Worlds," *Nation*, 13 Oct. 1979, p. 341.

7. Ian Watt, "Serious Reflections on *The Rise of the Novel*," *Novel* 1 (1968), 205–18, is indispensable here.

8. David Lodge, "Barth's Folly," *Times Literary Supplement*, 30 May 1980, pp. 607–8.

9. Josephine Hendin, "*LETTERS*: A Novel by John Barth," *New Republic* 181 (1 Dec. 1979), 32, 34.

10. Peter Prescott, "An Excess of Epistles," *Newsweek*, 1 Oct. 1979, p. 32.

11. Hendin, "*LETTERS*," p. 32

12. George Steiner, "Dead Letters," *New Yorker*, 31 Dec. 1979, p. 60.

13. *Ibid*.

14. Lodge, "Barth's Folly," p. 61.

15. Prescott, "Excess of Epistles," p. 32.

16. Max F. Schulz, "Barth, *LETTERS*, and the Great Tradition," *Genre* 14 (1981), 95–115.

17. Gerald Graff, "Under Our Belt and off Our Back: Barth's *LETTERS* and Postmodern Fiction," *Triquarterly* 52 (1981), 150–63.

18. George P. Reilly, "An Interview with John Barth," *Contemporary Literature* 22 (1981), 1–23; Heide Zeigler, "An Interview with John Barth," *Granta* 1 (1980), 169–77.

19. John Barth, "Tales within Tales within Tales," *Antaeus* 43 (1981), 45–63.

20. Karl Marx, *The Eighteenth Brumaire of Louis Napoleon* (New York: International Publishers, 1963), pp. 18–19.

21. Alan H. Gilbert, *Literary Criticism from Plato to Dryden* (New York: American Book Co., 1940), p. 505.

Index

Note on the Author

Jan Gorak is a member of the department of English at the University of the Witwatersrand, Johannesburg. After taking an undergraduate degree at the University of Warwick, he did postgraduate work in Britain and the United States. He is currently writing an extended history of the godly artist.